THE KENT STATE COVERUP

THE
KENT STATE
COVERUP

by Joseph Kelner

and James Munves

HARPER & ROW, PUBLISHERS

NEW YORK

Cambridge
Hagerstown
Philadelphia
San Francisco

1817

London
Mexico City
São Paulo
Sydney

To Robert Kelner, who worried and slaved in this great cause, and to those whose support meant so much: Libbie, Gail and Dr. Kenneth Kelner.

J.K.

Grateful acknowledgment is made for permission to reprint:

Lyrics from "Street Fighting Man." © 1968 Abkco Music, Inc. All Rights Reserved. Reprinted by Permission.

Excerpt from "Guard Wrong at Kent: Del Corso" reprinted from the September 29, 1975 issue of *The Plain Dealer.* Reprinted by permission.

Lyrics from "Ohio" written by Neil Young. © 1970 Cotillion Music Inc. and Broken Arrow Music. All rights reserved. Used by permission.

FIRST EDITION

Designer: Sidney Feinberg

Library of Congress Cataloging in Publication Data

Kelner, Joseph.

  The Kent State coverup.

  Includes index.

  1. Ohio. State University, Kent—Riot, May 4, 1970. I. Munves, James, joint author. II. Title.

LD4191.O72K44 1980   378.771'37   77-11813

ISBN 0-06-012282-X

---

80 81 82 83 84 10 9 8 7 6 5 4 3 2 1

Tin soldiers and Nixon comin'
We're finally on our own
This summer right here they're comin'
Four dead in Ohio

Gotta get down to it
Soldiers are gunnin' us down,
What if you knew her
And found her dead on the ground?
How can you run when you know?
Four dead in Ohio,
Four dead in Ohio. . . .

from "Ohio,"
Crosby, Stills and Nash, July, 1970

"He has affected to render the Military independent of and superior to the Civil Power . . . quartering large Bodies of Armed Troops among us . . . protecting them, by a mock Trial, from Punishment for any Murders which they should commit on the Inhabitants of these States."

from the Declaration of Independence,
Thomas Jefferson, July 4, 1776

"Kent State . . . marked a turning point for Nixon. . . . [The] beginning of his downhill slide toward Watergate."

from *The Ends of Power,*
H. R. Haldeman and Joseph Dimona

Contents

Illustrations

MAPS

Acknowledgments

—

The authors acknowledge with thanks the generous assistance provided by the Reverend John Adams, Arthur Krause and Peter Davies; and by Ramsey Clark, David Engdahl, Nelson Karl, Galen Keller, Steven Keller, Robert Kelner, Professor Jerry Lewis, Fred Mandel, Bernard Mazel, Sanford J. Rosen, Steven Sindell, Benson Wolman, and all the Kent State shooting victims and their families, whose painful memories were regretfully invoked. A special word of thanks is due our editor, Ted Solotaroff, who labored manfully to clarify a complex narrative.

THE KENT STATE COVERUP

Chronology

APRIL 8–MAY 5, 1970

April 8–10		Student disturbances in Cleveland, 952 national guardsmen called out
April 16, 17		Student disturbances in Oxford, Ohio, 561 national guardsmen called out
April 18, 19		Student disturbances in Sandusky, 96 national guardsmen called out
April 29		Governor Rhodes issues proclamation calling out Ohio National Guard in aid of civil authorities to northeastern Ohio because of wildcat strike of Teamsters; 3,257 guardsmen called out
		Student disturbances at Ohio State University in Columbus; 2,861 guardsmen called to campus
April 30		President Nixon announces invasion of Cambodia
May 1	noon	Constitution burial ceremony, Commons, Kent State University
	5:30 P.M.	President White leaves Kent State for Mason City, Iowa
	8:00 P.M.	Disturbances in downtown Kent begin; $10,000 damage, 60 persons arrested
	midnight	Kent Mayor Satrom calls office of Governor Rhodes
May 2	12:30 A.M.	Mayor Satrom declares state of civil emergency
		Mayor Satrom announces curfew effective 8:00 P.M. in city and 1:00 A.M. on Kent State campus
		Headline in *Kent Record-Courier:* NIXON HITS BUMS WHO BLOW UP COLLEGE CAMPUSES
	5:30 P.M.	Mayor Satrom requests National Guard
	7:30 P.M.	Crowd gathers at ROTC Building, Kent State campus
	8:30 P.M.	ROTC Building begins to smolder
	9:05 P.M.	Kent firemen arrive at ROTC Building
	9:30 P.M.	Ohio National Guard arrives in Kent; 1,196 men
May 3	10:00 A.M.	Governor Rhodes arrives in Kent by helicopter
	11:00 A.M.	Governor Rhodes gives press conference in firehouse, denounces students, and vows to use all force necessary to keep campus open

	11:45 A.M.	President White arrives at Kent airport, meets Governor Rhodes
	4:00 P.M.	Kent State University, instructed by Ohio National Guard, issues letter prohibiting "all forms of outdoor demonstrations and rallys [sic]—peaceful or otherwise . . ."
	9:30 P.M.	Students sit down on Main Street at intersection with Lincoln Street
	11:00 P.M.	Students on Main Street dispersed by guardsmen
May 4	10:30 A.M.	Meeting at Kent firehouse, presided over by General Canterbury
	11:20 A.M.	Meeting ends
	11:40 A.M.	Students and guardsmen confront each other on Commons
	11:50 A.M.	Riot Act read to students
	12:24 P.M.	67 shots fired at students; 4 killed, 9 wounded
May 5		Governor Rhodes issues proclamation stating that martial law existed since April 29

Cast of Characters

I. THE PLAINTIFFS

Alan Canfora, Barberton, Ohio	Wounded in wrist
John Robert Cleary,[1] Scotia, N.Y.	Wounded in chest
Thomas Mark Grace,[2] Syracuse, N.Y.	Wounded in foot
Mrs. Arthur Holstein, Plainview, N.Y.	
Mother of	
Jeffrey Glenn Miller, Junior,* dcd.	Died instantaneously from head wound
Dean Kahler,[3] E. Canton, Ohio	Wounded in back
Mr. and Mrs. Arthur Krause, Pittsburgh, Pa.	
Parents of	
Allison Krause, dcd.	Died in ambulance from chest wound
Joseph Lewis, Jr.,[4] Massillon, Ohio	Wounded in abdomen, leg
Donald Scott MacKenzie, Summit Sta., Pa.*	Wounded in neck
James Dennis Russell, Teaneck, N.J.	Wounded in forehead, thigh
Mr. and Mrs. Martin Scheuer, Youngstown, Pa.	
Parents of	
Sandra Scheuer, dcd.	Died in ambulance from neck wound
Mr. and Mrs. Louis Schroeder, Lorain, Ohio	
Parents of	
William Schroeder,* dcd.	Died in hospital from chest wound
Robert Stamps,[5] S. Euclid, Ohio	Wounded in buttock
Douglas Wrentmore, Northfield, Ohio	Wounded in leg

*Transferred from another school. 1. Suit by Robert Cleary, his father and next friend. 2. Suit by Thomas V. Grace, his father and next friend. 3. Suit by Elaine Kahler, his mother. 4. Suit by Elizabeth Lewis, his mother and next friend. 5. Joined in suit by father, Floyd Stamps.

II. THE DEFENDANTS

JAMES A. RHODES, governor of Ohio, 1963–1971, 1975–
ROBERT WHITE, president of Kent State University, 1963–1971
SYLVESTER DEL CORSO, adjutant general, Ohio National Guard, 1968–1971
ROBERT H. CANTERBURY, assistant adjutant general, ONG, 1968–1971
CHARLES E. FASSINGER, lieutenant colonel, 107th Armored Cavalry, ONG
HARRY D. JONES, major, 145th Infantry Regiment, ONG

MEMBERS OF TROOP G, 107TH ARMORED CAVALRY, ONG

RAYMOND J. SRP, captain
ALEXANDER D. STEVENSON, lieutenant
MYRON PRYOR, first sergeant
*DENNIS BRECKENRIDGE, sergeant
OKEY R. FLESHER, sergeant
†JAMES McGEE, spec. 4
†BARRY MORRIS, sergeant
†WILLIAM E. PERKINS, spec. 4
†JAMES E. PIERCE, spec. 4
†LAWRENCE SHAFER, sergeant
LLOYD W. THOMAS, JR., spec. 4
†RALPH W. ZOLLER, spec. 4

MEMBERS OF COMPANY A, 145TH INFANTRY REGIMENT, ONG

JOHN E. MARTIN, captain
HOWARD R. FALLON, lieutenant
DWIGHT G. CLINE, lieutenant
RODNEY R. BIDDLE, pfc
*JAMES K. BROWN, sergeant
*WILLIAM CASE, pfc
*JAMES W. FARRIS, pfc
*ROBERT HATFIELD, pfc
WILLIAM F. E. HERSCHLER, sergeant
*LONNIE HINTON, pfc
ROBERT D. JAMES, spec. 4
*ROGER MAAS, pfc
†MATTHEW McMANUS, sergeant
*RUDY MORRIS, pfc
LAWRENCE MOWRER, pfc
*RONNIE MYERS, pfc
*PAUL NAUJOKS, pfc
*PHILLIP RABER, pfc
RUSSELL E. REPP, JR., spec. 4
*JOSEPH SCHOLL, pfc
*RICHARD SHADE, pfc

†Leon H. Smith, spec. 4
*Richard B. J. Snyder, pfc
*Paul Zimmerman, pfc

Members of Company C, 145th Infantry Regiment, ONG

James R. Snyder, captain
Richard K. Love, sergeant

III. THE LAWYERS

For the Plaintiffs

    Joseph Kelner, New York, N.Y.   chief trial counsel
    Clyde Ellis, Columbus, Ohio
    David Engdahl, Denver, Colorado
    Michael Geltner, Columbus, Ohio
    Nelson G. Karl, Cleveland, Ohio
    Robert Kelner, New York, N.Y.
    Fred H. Mandel, Cleveland, Ohio
    Steven Sindell, Cleveland, Ohio
Paralegals
    Galen Keller, Columbus, Ohio
    Steven Keller, Columbus, Ohio

For Governor Rhodes

    R. Brooke Alloway, Columbus, Ohio

For President White

    Robert Blakemore, Akron, Ohio

For the National Guardsmen

    Charles E. Brown, Columbus, Ohio ⎫
    Burt Fulton, Cleveland, Ohio   ⎬ chief trial counsel
    John Clark, Columbus, Ohio
    William Johnston, Columbus, Ohio
    Robert H. Olson, Columbus, Ohio
    Richard A. Waltz, Columbus, Ohio

---

*The charges against the defendant were dismissed by the plaintiffs in the course of the trial.
†The defendant was indicted by the federal grand jury, March 29, 1974, and acquitted by Judge Battisti, November 8, 1974.

Prologue

—

On Tuesday, July 22, 1975, in the federal courthouse in Cleveland, Ohio, Sylvester Del Corso, former adjutant general of the Ohio National Guard, was sworn as a witness in the Kent State civil trial.

It was the first time that the man who had been in command of the Ohio Guard was to be publicly called to account for the killing of four students and the wounding of nine others on the Kent State campus on May 4, 1970.

As chief counsel for the victims, I, Joseph Kelner, had at my disposal all of the records and documents of every investigation ever made into the shootings. I knew that Del Corso had given his opinion that the guardsmen should not have opened fire at the students, and I felt that his statements could overwhelm the defense.

Individual guardsmen who had testified up to now had maintained that they had fired at onrushing students out of fear for their lives. This was the only way the shootings could be justified. How then could we possibly lose our case if the jury heard the Ohio Guard's highest officer say that the men should not have pulled the triggers? All I had to do was ask Del Corso for his opinion.

It was hot in the modernistic, low-ceilinged courtroom. The air-conditioning wasn't working well, and Burt Fulton, Del Corso's defense counsel, was nervously squirming in his chair, worrying about the thrust of my questions.

"Is it a fact, sir," I asked, "that you did testify before the federal grand jury, the state grand jury, and have been interviewed by the FBI and others? Is that right, sir?"

"Yes." Del Corso was a short man with rugged features who carried himself like the football middle-lineman he once had been.

"And you have had access to photographs and have had access to various official documents and investigative reports concerning this incident, is that right, the shooting incident?"

"Yes," Del Corso answered, "limited access to some of the photographs."

"And you have spoken, I dare say, to General Canterbury many, many times concerning the events that occurred, is that right, sir?" (General Robert Canterbury, assistant adjutant general of the Ohio National Guard, was the highest-ranking Guard officer on the Kent State campus on May 4, 1970.)

"Yes."

"Now, sir, did General Canterbury tell you that the closest student to the Guard at the time of the shooting was 20 yards?"

"I recall that something, the closest student to him, I think, is what he said. I don't recall, I recall something about 20 yards."

"Is it a fact that stones had been thrown at various times that day, based upon your knowledge and statements to you by General Canterbury and other sources of information?"

Fulton got up. "I am going to object to this testimony, and I would like to approach the bench, because I have an idea where we are heading." He then told the judge that he would object to my asking the general any question on justification for the shooting based on his testimony before the federal grand jury.

Judge Don J. Young refused to look at the federal grand jury testimony I brought to the bench and cut off this line of questioning.

His ruling was devastating to our case. It was contrary to the federal rules of evidence, and it resulted in the suppression of vital testimony.

No member of the jury, no one in that courtroom besides the attorneys, was to know until September 29, six weeks after the trial had ended, what had been suppressed. On that day, a banner headline on the front page of the *Cleveland Plain Dealer* proclaimed, GUARD WRONG AT KENT: DEL CORSO.

Sylvester Del Corso, adjutant general when the Ohio National Guard shot and killed four students at Kent State University in 1970, repeatedly told a Federal grand jury that the Guardsmen were unjustified in their actions, The *Plain Dealer* has learned.

The *Plain Dealer* has been shown a copy of Del Corso's secret testimony to a Federal grand jury in Cleveland. In that testimony given last year, Del Corso stated sixteen times that the Guardsmen were not justified in shooting, or even aiming at an anti-war rally on campus.

The *Plain Dealer* quoted Del Corso as having told the grand jury, with regard to the shootings, "I say it was unjustifiable, because as I see it, I can't see how it can be justified. And to me, overall, like I say, I can't see any justification in it. I can't for the life of me find any real justification for the shooting there. . . ."

Since May 1970, one governmental agency after another had managed to suppress evidence and shield those responsible for the shootings in a monumental coverup. The same process continued in the Cleveland courtroom. How had I gotten into this predicament? Why was I spending a hot summer battling in a hostile courtroom far from home?

Part One

THE LONG ROAD
TO THE CLEVELAND
COURTHOUSE

Jeffrey Glenn Miller. *(Valley Daily News)*

Allison Krause. *(UPI)*

Sandra Scheuer. *(UPI)*

1

I Get Involved

━━━

It all began a couple of days after the shootings, when I received a call at my New York law office from Elaine Miller in Queens. Mrs. Miller, a high school principal's secretary, was the mother of Jeffrey Glenn Miller. A photograph of her son's dead body, beneath the tortured face of the long-haired girl with outstretched arms, had been flashed around the world to become the symbol of the Kent State tragedy.

Jeff Miller had transferred to Kent State in January 1970, just four months before he was killed. He was a gregarious young man who, until abruptly growing six inches, had been a four-foot-eleven, accident-prone runt, always struggling to keep up with his peers. The summer of 1969 had been tumultuous for Jeff, with his parents divorcing and his idolized older brother moving to New Jersey. He had gone to Woodstock and suddenly adopted the youth culture of the late 1960s, wearing a fringed jacket, beads, and headband and spending long hours in his room practicing on the drums.

His mother saw him off to Kent State at the end of the winter break, just before his twentieth birthday at the end of March. On the morning of May 4 he telephoned to ask his mother whether she minded if he were to attend a campus rally scheduled for noon.

That afternoon, as she drove home from school, Elaine heard news of the Kent shootings on her car radio. She telephoned Jeff to urge him to come home. The call was answered by a young man named Bruce.

"Let me speak to Jeff," Elaine said.

"Who is it?" Bruce asked.
"His mother."
"He's dead."

I was used to talking to people who are tearful, angry, and bewildered; but listening to Elaine Miller was unusually upsetting. She had been receiving telephone calls from strangers who said that her son deserved what he got and letters to the effect that Jeff was a depraved hippie Communist and that all such people should be shot or chased out of the country. She had overheard people in the school office where she worked, in Hicksville, Long Island, say that what had happened to her son was her fault. The high school Jeff had attended in Plainview had refused in any way to mark his death. Mrs. Miller told me that she wasn't interested in money. But she was proposing a civil suit in order to get the case into a court to show that Jeff was innocent and that whoever had shot him was wrong. She wanted the world to know that her son had been murdered, and she wanted the murderers held accountable.

My first reaction was that a criminal prosecution of the guardsmen by the State of Ohio rather than a civil suit offered the best means of clearing her son's name. Such a prosecution was, of course, beyond our power, but I wanted to believe that if national guardsmen had violated any law in shooting the students, those responsible would be brought up on criminal charges. That very week, Vice President Spiro Agnew had stated on the David Frost television show that if the guardsmen had not deliberately murdered four students, they were at least guilty of manslaughter. Next to a criminal conviction, even a successful civil suit would be a poor second, besides being costly and interminable.

In the following weeks, as more details were revealed, I became convinced that the shootings were unjustified, and I agreed to take on Mrs. Miller's case. When a Mississippi doctor's letter to his son, expressing the usual antistudent sentiments, was published on the op-ed page of the *New York Times,* I was prompted to write a reply, which appeared in the same space.

> For every lunatic dynamiter, there are a thousand serious-minded young people who really give a damn about American ideals and dreams. . . . Young Americans are a proud and sturdy lot who are not going to disappear. They are keenly aware of the current scene. . . . They think we can do better to put our values in order. They have the natural impatience of youth against decades of indolence and inertia which have permitted America to deteriorate. Why the violent protests when we marched into Cambodia without Congressional authority? To them this was an extension of Vietnam's horror, a compounding of the original felony. . . . The

complaint of our youth is not against the Constitution but that its spirit is being ignored and circumvented by hypocrisy.

I continued to represent Mrs. Miller, but most of the legal work was being handled by Ohio lawyers representing the other victims. I never expected that, five years later, I would be called to Ohio as chief trial counsel for all thirteen victims of the Kent State shootings, who had entered a cluster of civil suits against the governor of Ohio, James Rhodes; the former president of the university, Robert White; the former adjutant general of the Ohio National Guard, Sylvester Del Corso; and numerous other guardsmen, ranging from a general to the sergeants and privates who had pulled the triggers.

I hadn't asked for this responsibility. Ramsey Clark, former U.S. attorney general, was slated for the assignment; I was to have been just one of seven or eight lawyers working with him. But only a few weeks before the trial, he found that circumstances compelled him to withdraw, and the other lawyers on our team asked me to take his place.

I am not a so-called civil rights lawyer, a political lawyer, or a "Movement" lawyer. I have a reputation as a trial lawyer, but that is something different. My experience included criminal and civil cases of all kinds: cases in which children had been maimed by careless or unneeded surgery, cases in which housewives had been slaughtered by defective auto steering columns. I had litigated countless defective-product liability cases, malpractice cases, shooting cases, assaults, airplane crash cases, cases arising from explosions and other disasters. I have faced countless complex legal challenges, and I love a good fight.

I knew that in the courtroom in Cleveland our task would be to bring past events to life. As a trial lawyer, that is my specialty. Damage cases are exercises in historic re-creation. Truth is elusive; it enters the courtroom secondhand, through the memories and words of witnesses whose recollections may or may not be accurate and through certain "records" of events: tire marks, fingerprints, torn clothing, photos, documents, injuries, and various other fragments of life. The challenge is always to convince the jury that one's version of the truth is more probable than that of one's opponent.

This often requires the mastery of complex details: the intricate maze of relationships between certain nerves and muscles and the brain; the workings of electronic devices; the characteristics of guns. In tragic accidents there are, in addition, the critical factors of time, space, and distance. *Where* a person was at a particular instant, the exact *sequence* of events (did A happen before B or B before A?), and the *directions* in which participants or witnesses were moving are the essential material out of which cases are built. My task always is to present facts and clarify them in the jury's mind against the attempts of opposing counsel, usually representing insurance companies or big corporations, to prove that positions, times, and distances or causation factors were different from those my witnesses had asserted, or to confuse the jury with irrelevant details. Such elements would be the very fiber of the Kent State case.

I arrived in Cleveland with my wife, Libbie Kelner, and my son, Bob Kelner, who was a lawyer in my firm, on Thursday, May 15, 1975. The trial was slated to begin the following Monday.

I knew we had a rough road ahead of us. In the five years that had passed since the shootings, not a single person had been punished—despite the fact that four students had been killed and nine others wounded in broad daylight, before hundreds of witnesses, the events documented by photographs; despite the fact that President Nixon's Scranton Commission had termed the shootings "unnecessary, unwarranted and inexcusable"; and despite the fact that every other impartial group that had looked into the incident, including the *Akron Beacon Journal* reporters who had assembled a Pulitzer prize-winning supplement on Kent State, had declared the shootings unjustifiable.

It was obvious that powerful pressures had been exerted all along to keep justice at bay.

The Ohio National Guard itself had taken no disciplinary action. Instead of court-martials and dismissals there were promotions. At the lowest level, the officers on the scene produced no real accounting of expended bullets or assigned weapons. At the higher levels, several days after the shootings, a CBS reporter overheard General Canterbury telling someone that guard chaplain John Simons, who felt the shootings unjustified, had to be "shut up." The Portage County coroner called for a grand jury to determine whether the deaths by military bullets were "accidental or homicidal," but the local prosecutor, Ronald Kane, hesitated and, after ten weeks, made the convening of the county grand jury contingent on receiving at least $75,000 in extra funds from the state to finance the investigation. On August 3, a week after Kane's request and three months after the shootings, Governor Rhodes superseded Kane by appointing a special grand jury whose emphasis was on investigating not the shootings but the "illegal and criminal acts . . . associated with campus unrest" that led to them.

This special grand jury, instructed by special prosecutors who were political allies of the governor and who were selective with the evidence (the jurors never saw the Justice Department summary of the FBI reports), indicted not guardsmen but twenty-four students and nonstudents and one professor and issued a report condemning students and the university administration. (The report was later expunged by order of Federal Judge William K. Thomas.)

No member of the Ohio National Guard was indicted by the State of Ohio for the shootings at Kent State.

At the federal level, Nixon initially promised fast action by the Justice Department, which sent more than a hundred FBI agents to Kent, and on June 13 established a special presidential commission (the Scranton Commission) to investigate.

Although the civil rights division of the Justice Department soon ascertained, through study of the FBI reports, that several guardsmen were liable for prosecution under section 18:242 of the federal Civil Rights Act, no federal grand jury was convened for three and a half years, until after the Watergate investigation had begun and control of the Justice Department had passed to Attorney General Elliot Richardson. Previously, under Attorney General John Mitchell, the Nixon Justice Department had merely offered to cooperate with Ohio authorities, informing them that it thought some guardsmen were liable under Ohio criminal law, instead of acting on its own.

The Scranton Commission, although given broad subpoena powers, curtailed its investigation of the Kent State shootings and did not take the testimony of any enlisted guardsman, so as not to interfere with the ongoing state and federal investigations. (Guard officers Raymond Srp and Alexander Stevenson prevailed on the U.S. District Court to vacate Scranton Commission subpoenas on the basis that their testimony would prejudice the special state grand jury investigation.)

The Justice Department declared that the guardsmen had not been threatened and that "there was reason to believe the claims of self-defense were fabricated"; Ohio Attorney General Paul Brown declared that the shootings would result in prosecutions; U.S. Attorney General Mitchell declared several times that his department would act if Ohio did not, but in November 1970 President Nixon secretly ordered Mitchell not to summon a federal grand jury. Indeed, the investigations and commissions seemed to cancel each other out. Guardsmen refused to testify before the Scranton Commission for fear of injuring themselves before the state grand jury, which in fact was investigating not them but the Kent students and faculty; the Scranton Commission made no use of its broad subpoena powers because of a mistaken belief that federal action was imminent.

Nothing was done until the federal grand jury convened in Cleveland on December 18, 1973. After it had indicted eight guardsmen, the judge, Frank Battisti, dismissed the charges before the case went to the jury on the grounds that the government had not shown that the defendants had shot students with an intent to deprive them of specific civil rights.

Now, in the summer of 1975, we would be seeking a judgment for damages against (among others) a sitting governor for causing wrongful deaths, assault and battery, and violations of civil rights. This action was unprecedented in American jurisprudence.

After settling ourselves in a comfortable furnished apartment that was a few minutes' walk from the courthouse, Bob and I walked up the street to another apartment complex, where Mike Geltner and Clyde Ellis, two lawyers for the American Civil Liberties Union, had all the discovery documents and testimony.

I was shocked. Until I saw it, I had had no idea of the magnitude of documentation. Looking at the dozens of cartons, I knew I could not hope to familiarize myself with the material before the trial began. It would have to be done on a continuous, day-to-day basis throughout the trial. I was heartened by the assurances of two young paralegals, Steven Keller and Galen Keller (not related despite their identical surnames), that they had read and classified all of it.

"Do you mean to say you know all of this material?" I asked.

"Try us," Galen suggested.

I looked down at a list of witnesses in my hand. "What did Captain Srp do on the hill?" I asked as a random question.

Galen reached into a box and handed me a folder. "That has his Ohio Highway Patrol statement, his FBI statement, his state grand jury testimony, and the deposition Clyde Ellis took. You'll find he told the FBI he saw no danger on the hill, that there was no reason for his men to shoot. You'll also see that he fudged this in his depositions."

I was impressed. I was to keep her sitting next to me at the counsel table throughout the trial, depending on her infallibility in retrieving facts when needed. She proved invaluable.

The two aides then pointed to a big pile of documents on the floor. This was the testimony presented to the federal grand jury that had indicted the eight guardsmen in 1974 (those were the charges that were dismissed by the judge before the case went to the jury). There had been a lot of delay in obtaining this material, and they had only just started to go through it. All in all there were sixty cartons of information: the most documented homicides in American history.

This particular shooting down of unarmed people by men in uniform, cloaked in the authority of the law, was not a unique event. Other killings by so-called law-enforcement officials had occurred in Orangeburg, South Carolina, in February 1968, when twenty-seven black college students were wounded and three killed by uniformed troopers of the South Carolina Law Enforcement Division. Another had taken place in Chicago in December 1969, when thirteen uniformed policemen broke into an apartment and killed Fred Hampton and Mark Clark and wounded three other Black Panthers. And ten days after Kent State, there were fourteen black victims (two dead) at Jackson State College in Mississippi.

No one had been punished for any of these homicides. Indeed, it was usually the surviving victims who were indicted. The perpetrators seemed to be immune from the criminal law, and thus far not a single civil suit had prevailed. The problem is a reluctance of citizens serving on juries to believe that highway patrolmen, police, or national guardsmen are capable of evil; they don't want to know that the man to whom they entrust a lethal weapon in their defense is capable of employing it against *them*. That's why our suit was so important. A victory would serve notice on trigger-happy lawmen everywhere that they could be liable for large sums for damages.

2

The Shooting Victims

The first of the clients I talked to in Cleveland was Arthur Krause. I met Arthur with Peter Davies, who had been closely associated with him almost from the time Krause's daughter Allison had been killed.

Krause, a big, dynamic, fearless man, was the only one of the victims' parents who had immediately appreciated the magnitude of the problem they would face in trying to obtain justice for their children. In the beginning, when he called for congressional hearings and federal intervention, the other parents of the dead had thought him mad. They had joined him only as bitter experience taught them what he already knew.

Krause, an executive with a large Pittsburgh-based corporation, had only one ally to begin with, and that was Peter Davies, an insurance agent from Staten Island who had no personal stake in the tragedy. Davies, a British immigrant and private citizen, had been appalled by the shootings and, on his own, had spent months poring over photographs and other clues to the events of May 4. Krause's second ally was the Reverend John Adams of the United Methodist Church, who, a year after the shootings, published a report of Peter's findings in order to prod the Justice Department into convening a federal grand jury. This report was the genesis of Peter's interesting book, *The Truth About Kent State.**

Even sitting at a table, Arthur towered over me, his eyes gleaming behind

*Peter Davies, *The Truth About Kent State: Challenge for the American Conscience* (New York: Farrar, Straus & Giroux, 1973).

his glasses with an intimidating fervor. He had been colossally angry ever since the moment, five years before, when his brother Jack had telephoned him from Cleveland with the news that Allison had been shot. He was angry at the university that had sent a check for the unused portion of Allison's tuition without any acknowledgment of concern, at President Nixon, at Vice President Agnew, at Governor Rhodes and the guardsmen, at those who had written to newspapers expressing their pleasure at what the guardsmen had done, and especially at those who had telephoned in the weeks after the shooting to inform him that if he'd done his duty as a parent his daughter would not have been shot—and those who had written him that Allison was a "hippie" or a "cheap slut" or a potential killer herself. Krause's nightmare drive that Monday afternoon from Pittsburgh to Ravenna, the sight of his daughter's greenish face on the hospital slab, the surliness of the police at the hospital doorway, the uniformed guardsmen on the roof of the hospital, the armed men and tanks surrounding the courthouse—none of this had dimmed in his memory.

Arthur Krause had become a gadfly, on familiar terms with newspapermen, senators, editors, clergymen, and film producers. He appeared on radio and television talk shows and wrote letters to editors. He had engaged a young Cleveland lawyer, Steven Sindell, to institute a civil suit, and he had obtained contributions for the legal struggle. He was also to provide us with a talented fund raiser, Bernard Mazel, and to assist him in raising more than $300,000 for our legal expenses. (The guardsmen's defense was paid for by the State of Ohio, which had laid out almost half a million dollars by the time we entered the courtroom.)

The objective of Krause's volcanic activity was to obtain justice: the vindication of his daughter Allison and the punishment of those who had caused her death. "Have we come to such a state in this country," Krause had asked television newsmen shortly after the shootings "that a young girl has to be shot because she disagrees with the actions of her government?"

The fact that a federal grand jury had finally investigated the shootings was a result of his, Davies' and Adams' unceasing efforts.

Allison Krause was a tall, attractive brunette of nineteen who had enrolled at Kent State as an honors student and, finding the university insufficiently demanding, had made plans to attend the State University of New York at Buffalo in the fall of 1970.

Shortly after arriving at Kent State she met Barry Levine, a slender, poetic young man from Valley Stream, Long Island, and they became inseparable. A conscientious student with an inquiring mind, highly regarded by her

Arthur Krause and Sarah Scheuer look on while Joseph Kelner faces reporters at the conclusion of the 1975 civil trial. Seated left of Kelner are Elaine Holstein, mother of Jeff Miller, Joe Lewis, Jr., Dean Kahler and, standing behind Dean, his mother. *(UPI)*

instructors, Allison took part in the Vietnam peace mobilization movement. In March 1970 she moved into a single dormitory room where she lived with a brown and gray cat named Yossarian. On Sunday night, May 3, she was badly frightened when she and Barry were chased by guardsmen from the practice field to the nearby Tri-Towers dormitory complex. At Tri-Towers she found the building barred to nonresidents by faculty members. With the guardsmen closing in and helicopters overhead, she became hysterical. When finally admitted, she spent a near sleepless night in the crowded building, fearful of crossing the campus back to her room.

On Monday she met Barry at the rally. She wore blue jeans, a gray T-shirt with the legend "Kennedy," an old army jacket, and sneakers. In the bright noon, her fears of the previous night dissipated, and she taunted the guardsmen after she was chased from the Victory Bell, yelling at them from the Pagoda before running down to the parking lot.

She and Barry were relieved when the guardsmen left the practice field. Then shots rang out. They quickly got down behind a car.

Barry thought they were safe until Allison murmured that she'd been hit.

Talking with Krause and Davies, I learned that Peter regarded the shootings as a kind of murder mystery that I must solve in the courtroom, in the manner of Perry Mason, by cracking Sergeant Myron Pryor, whom he regarded as the potential "John Dean" of Kent State. He believed that Pryor could be forced to reveal a conspiracy to kill and maim the students.

I got a different point of view when I talked to Steven Sindell. He thought that Michael Delaney, a guardsman who had attended a secret meeting on Sunday morning, May 3, at which Governor Rhodes had stressed the need to prevent student demonstrations, would prove to be our most important witness.

Saturday morning I met with all the surviving victims and their families in a meeting room in my apartment building. All the lawyers were there: for the ACLU, Nelson Karl, Mike Geltner, Clyde Ellis, and their paralegal assistants, Galen Keller and Steven Keller. (The ACLU's only clients were Mr. and Mrs. Martin Scheuer, parents of the dead Sandra Scheuer.) The other lawyers were Steven Sindell and Fred Mandel from Cleveland, and David Engdahl, a young law professor from Colorado. With my son Robert and me, the clients had a sizable staff to marshal and present the evidence. Most of our lawyers were short on experience but long on hope and determination.

Reverend John Adams was also present, a big, soft-spoken man with a shock of graying hair and the fierce look of an eagle protecting its young. He went easily among the clients, enveloping their hands in his huge ones, commanding respect and trust. He had brought them together and would shepherd them through the ordeal. Adams, director of his church's Department of Law, Justice and Community Relations, had long been concerned with the indiscriminate employment of firearms by law-enforcement people throughout the country; he had seen National Guard troops in action in the summer of 1967 in Newark and Detroit. Sixty-six civilians had been killed in those two cities, including small children.

I was introduced to each of the surviving victims, nine young men, and to a number of middle-aged couples, including the parents of the dead.

The living, by class in 1970, were:

Freshmen: Dean Kahler, Joseph Lewis, Jr., John Cleary. (These three were probably the most seriously wounded. Coincidence? The naiveté of freshmen?)

Sophomores: Thomas Mark Grace, Douglas Wrentmore, Robert Stamps. Junior: Alan Canfora.

Seniors: Donald Scott MacKenzie, James Russell.

The parents of the dead were Arthur and Doris Krause of Pittsburgh, Pennsylvania, parents of Allison; Elaine Holstein ,(formerly Elaine Miller) of Queens, New York, mother of Jeff Miller; Martin and Sarah Scheuer of Youngstown, Ohio, parents of Sandra; and Louis and Florence Schroeder of Lorain, Ohio, parents of William.

The parents of the survivors who had been minors *(legal infants)* in 1970 were there as plaintiffs themselves. Among them were Elaine and John Kahler, of East Canton, Ohio; Joseph and Betty Lewis of Massillon, Ohio; Thomas and Collette Grace of Syracuse, New York; and Floyd and Charlotte Stamps of South Euclid, Ohio. Other parents had come to lend their moral support to their sons. They included Doug Wrentmore's mother, Jan, from Northfield, Ohio, and Albert and Ann Canfora from Barberton, Ohio.

Of the dead, Krause, Scheuer, and Miller were Jewish; Schroeder was Protestant. Of the wounded, Grace, Canfora, and Lewis are Roman Catholics; the rest are Protestants except Stamps, whose mother is Jewish. I felt they were no gang of Weathermen or revolutionaries, but typical Middle Americans with roots in conservative family traditions.

I told them that to overcome the prejudices of the community, represented by the jury, would require a great deal of self-control. We had to keep our eye on the objective, which was to win the case and bring those guilty of shooting unarmed people to accountability. Some strange destiny, I said, had placed in our hands the obligation to uphold the vital freedoms of speech and assembly.

The appearance of the plaintiffs would, of course, weigh heavily with the jury. I was favorably impressed with all of them. The parents were solid-

Florence and Louis Schroeder at a memorial service on the anniversary of their son William's death. On the right is Reverend John Adams of the United Methodist Church. *(UPI)*

It took the death of their daughter and years of disappointment to bring Sarah and Martin Scheuer (standing rear, center) into the ranks of active protestors. Here they challenge the authorities over the extension of the KSU gym onto Blanket Hill. *(UPI)*

looking citizens, and the young men were attractive, earnest, and alert. I suggested, however, that those with hair below their ears do some trimming, and that they wear suits, dress shirts, and neckties in the courtroom. There were some protests, but I explained that we must reckon with the prejudices of the jury. By the law of averages, I said, we were bound to get a middle-aged jury with less education than they had had. My son Bob, a member of their generation, was a big help in the discussion even though his hair was shorter than that of most of the plaintiffs. The one holdout was Alan Canfora. He refused to sever his pony tail, but he agreed to pin it up and to cover his own hair with a wig.

I urged all the plaintiffs to attend the trial as much as possible. Otherwise the jurors might resent having to sit through long hours of testimony in behalf of persons not interested enough to share their ordeal.

I also explained that jurors think of themselves as sleuths and keep watching the conduct and appearance of parties to the lawsuit even when they are not on the witness stand. In effect, the plaintiffs would be on camera at all times and should act accordingly. I warned everyone to keep cool and to avoid outbursts in the courtroom.

Several of the victims, understandably, had been embittered and alienated, not so much by the shootings as by the abuse and indifference they had received afterward. Three—Tom Grace, Alan Canfora, and Robbie Stamps— had been radicalized, and they and Jerry Lewis, a Kent State sociology professor who was helping us, kept insisting that there was no way we could win our case.

"You don't know the people around here," Robbie Stamps told me. "They hate us. They *wanted* us shot. To them, the minute we get into that courtroom, it will be *us* who are on trial, not the guardsmen."

I explained that prejudice was nothing new and that our system of justice was designed to overcome it.

"This isn't an accident case where someone has been run over by a car," Robbie said. "We've been run over by the governor and the whole state of Ohio. Any jury we get is going to think of themselves as protecting Ohio against a bunch of Communist hippies."

"Robbie," I said, "you've got to give the system a chance. We have laws that are the same for governors and hippies alike."

"Look what happened to Nixon."

"He had to resign," I said.

"He's not in jail."

"No," I admitted, "but Mitchell is. Just don't jump to conclusions. I've won plenty of tough cases. We have rules of evidence; the truth can't be kept out of a courtroom. The system does work."

"Not in Ohio," Robbie said.

"Wait and see," I advised. I could understand his cynicism, yet I thought I could prove him wrong. One of the main benefits of this trial, I decided, would be to restore young people's faith in their country.

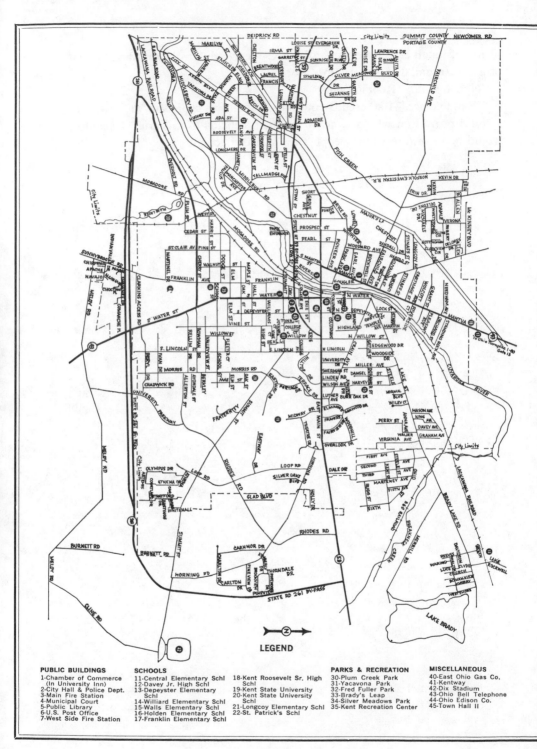

LEGEND

PUBLIC BUILDINGS
1-Chamber of Commerce (In University Inn)
2-City Hall & Police Dept.
3-Main Fire Station
4-Municipal Court
5-Public Library
6-U.S. Post Office
7-West Side Fire Station

SCHOOLS
11-Central Elementary Schl
12-Davey Jr. High Schl
13-Depeyster Elementary Schl
14-Williard Elementary Schl
15-Walls Elementary Schl
16-Holden Elementary Schl
17-Franklin Elementary Schl
18-Kent Roosevelt Sr. High Schl
19-Kent State University Schl
20-Kent State University Schl
21-Longcoy Elementary Schl
22-St. Patrick's Schl

PARKS & RECREATION
30-Plum Creek Park
31-Yacavona Park
32-Fred Fuller Park
33-Brady's Leap
34-Silver Meadows Park
35-Kent Recreation Center

MISCELLANEOUS
40-East Ohio Gas Co.
41-Kentway
42-Dix Stadium
43-Ohio Bell Telephone
44-Ohio Edison Co.
45-Town Hall II

Kent, Ohio. (*Kent, Ohio, Telephone Book*)

3

Kent, Ohio, U.S.A.

▬

Steven Sindell, the young lawyer retained by many of the victims, is a short man with a fair complexion, high cheekbones, and thinning jet-black hair, whose spectacles give him a studious, gnomelike appearance. He had been out of law school only three years when Arthur Krause first came to his office.

After lunch, Sindell offered to drive us to the Kent State campus so that Bob and I could see firsthand the Commons, Taylor Hall, the Pagoda, the practice field, and the other places that figured in the events of May 4.

Northeastern Ohio, where Kent is located about 32 miles south of Cleveland, is one of the most heavily industrialized regions of the planet, a landscape marked by huge towers, great long rusting sheds, convoluted pipes, belching chimneys, long black sierras of coal, railroad yards, and storage tanks. It is a place of fickle weather, of precipitous changes in temperature, where clouds, drizzle, and sunshine follow each other in rapid succession. Ravenna and Kent can count on no more than sixty days of sun a year.

The original Yankee settlers, mostly of English or Dutch stock, were augmented by southerners who came up across the Ohio River. Later, as industrialization took hold, waves of immigrants arrived from Germany, Hungary, Poland, Italy, and other parts of southern and eastern Europe, and still later, great numbers of Appalachian whites moved up from West Virginia to be followed, last of all, by blacks from the rural south. The area around Kent has a considerable admixture of former West Virginians. Ravenna, six miles east of Kent and the seat of Portage County, is full of former hillfolk; Akron has been termed the "second largest city in West Virginia." Portage County can be better understood when one remembers this Appalachian heritage with its aroma of "white lightning," its distrust of strangers, and its habitual use of rifles for everything from coon hunting to avenging insults.

Kent, formerly a mill town that drew power from two falls in the Cuyahoga River, became a railroad center in the Civil War era. Today it is a community of tree-shaded lanes, some light industry, and a notable concentration of bars; it is dominated by the Kent State University campus of 800 acres (about the size of New York's Central Park).

Among the ingredients in the cauldron in which the events of May 4 were brewed are the climate of Kent, the people of the area, and the size of the university in proportion to the community (Kent population, 30,000; university population, 20,000). The town-versus-gown problem, which had worsened everywhere in the 1960s as the clothing, hair, and habits of the young came to differ markedly from those of their elders, was exacerbated to a high degree in Kent, and to some extent by the political activism of the student body. (Stephen Ogilvie, first president of the SDS, was a Kent State dropout.)

Mothers guided their children to the other side of the street when approached by students who resembled extras from western movies. Their hostility reached into the local courts, where a student arrested for a misdemeanor was given a choice between a month in jail or cutting his hair and signing a pledge not to join any organization dedicated to the overthrow of Ohio or the United States. Nor was the students' respect for the law enhanced by Ohio's narcotics statutes, which provided from 2 to 15 years in jail and up to a $10,000 fine for the mere possession of marijuana, and 20 to 40 years for selling it.

Taylor Hall, the home of the architecture and journalism departments of the university, sits atop a hill in the center of the campus. With its line of columns extending three stories from ground to roof, it is unlike any other structure at Kent State. The hill slopes downward to the northeast, to the boiler of the campus heating plant, leveling off into a field suitable for softball or throwing frisbees. There are trees on the rise near Taylor, and near them, in a brick housing, is a one-foot brass bell that is traditionally rung when the Kent State team wins a football game or to call students to a meeting or demonstration. This field, near and below the brass Victory Bell, is known as the Commons; centrally situated, it bears periodic streams of traffic as students cross on their way to and from classes, dormitories, cafeterias, and athletic activities. It is the open-air town hall of the campus.

The southwest prospect of Taylor Hall overlooks a steeper slope, Blanket Hill, that in 1970 descended in one direction (southwest) to the gymnasium and in the other (southeast) toward a football practice field and a parking lot that fronts on a dormitory, Prentice Hall. It was in this parking lot area that

Aerial view of center of KSU campus, scene of events of May 4. *(Akron Beacon Journal)*

1. Commons
2. Site of burned ROTC Building
3. Victory Bell
4. Taylor Hall
5. Pagoda
6. Blanket Hill
7. Prentice Hall
8. Prentice Hall parking lot
9. Practice field
10. Road to gymnasium
11. Modern sculpture
12. Johnson Hall
13. Lake Hall
14. Fence
15. Gymnasium

Jeff Miller, Bill Schroeder, Allison Krause, and Sandra Scheuer were slain. Today a small monument marks their passing. About fifty feet from one corner of Taylor Hall, between it and the gym, and at the very crest of the hill, stands a kind of concrete "folly," a small rectangular, roofed structure built in April 1970 by a group of architecture students. Nicknamed the Pagoda, it was to become famous as the point where the guardsmen turned and fired at the students.

There was something incongruous about a monument to two dead young women and two dead young men beside a dormitory; about bullets, hatred, and death on this American college campus. Death? Why here? Why not on other campuses? It gave me the shivers.

None of us was in a very good mood going back to Cleveland. The country-side looked endlessly graceless and mindless. A station wagon sped past us, and Libbie gasped. A young man in the wagon had lowered his trousers and was confronting us with the twin spheres of his hairy buttocks.

Welcome to Ohio!

4

Obstacles and Roadblocks

—

The first question in the Kent State civil cases was whom to sue. We knew we could operate on two levels, suing in the Ohio courts under Ohio law and in federal court under federal law, and that we could bring our state suits into federal court to be tried simultaneously with the federal suits. The state cases would be tort actions of the kind I handle all the time—suits for damages as a result of negligence, assault and battery, and wrongful death.

Assault and battery and wrongful death, however, are not federal causes of action. What *is* a federal offense is an injury to a person's civil rights, if perpetrated by someone acting "under color of law," that is, by a person who is a law-enforcement official of some kind, such as a policeman, a sheriff, or a national guardsman. Our federal suits, therefore, were brought under the federal Civil Rights Act, for deprivation of the plaintiffs' rights to due process (instead of summary punishment from the barrel of a gun), and to peaceably assemble on their campus.

With regard to the state case, we had to decide whether to sue the State of Ohio or individuals. (This problem did not come up in the federal case because the Eleventh Amendment bars suits in federal court by individuals against states.) My first instinct was to sue Ohio, on the theory that it is easier to get a jury to vote an award against an entity than against individuals. We found, however, that Ohio was one of the few states that did not permit suits against itself.

The question then became simply, which individuals would we sue?

In 1970, when we were beginning the suits, all the lawyers—Sindell, Gelt-

Judge Edwin Jones of the Ohio Court of Common Pleas, Ravenna, made the special state grand jury report public. *(UPI)*

Federal Judge William K. Thomas of Cleveland ordered the special state grand jury report destroyed. *(UPI)*

Federal Judge Frank Battisti of Cleveland dismissed the government's charges against the eight indicted guardsmen. *(UPI)*

Federal Judge Don J. Young of Toledo. *(UPI)*

ner, and I—reached the same conclusions. We entered suits *(Krause* v. *Rhodes, Scheuer* v. *Rhodes,* and *Miller* v. *Rhodes)* under federal and Ohio laws against Governor Rhodes, Adjutant General Del Corso, General Canterbury, numerous other guardsmen, and Kent State President White.

There was a long, rocky road between our filing the suits in the summer of 1970 and bringing the cases to trial in the spring of 1975. The suits were thrown out by the Federal District Court and by the Circuit Court of Appeals on the grounds that a suit against the governor was a suit against the state, and it took a United States Supreme Court decision in the spring of 1974 to give us the right to trial.

The opposition was fierce—much of it, I believe, because we insisted on naming Governor Rhodes among the defendants. A lot of judges seemed to think there was something subversive in suing a governor for damages resulting from an executive decision.

Geltner and Sindell argued our case before the Supreme Court in December 1973. The Court handed down a unanimous opinion, remanding our case to the Federal District Court in Cleveland for trial. One reason for the astonishing unanimity was that the Court at that time was confronted with another issue of executive malfeasance involving President Nixon's White House tapes. It was not a propitious time for any executive to claim immunity for his actions.

I knew that many members of our legal team had hoped that William K. Thomas, who was regarded as the brightest and most fair-minded of the federal judges in the Northern District of Ohio, would be called to preside over our trial. Among other things, Thomas was the judge who had expunged the biased report of the state grand jury. That was not to be, however; Chief Judge Frank Battisti had had to go outside Cleveland for a judge because the local district judges had heavy workloads, and the lot had fallen to Judge Don J. Young. All I knew about him was that he came from Toledo and was a nephew of Fred Mandel's friend, Senator Stephen Young. I asked Mandel, a member of our team who had practiced law in Cleveland for many years and had served as a U.S. attorney, what he thought of Young.

"I think he is a good judge," Mandel told me. "At the pre-trial conferences he certainly appeared fair. I would say that he has almost consistently ruled in our favor."

Mandel's favorable views about Judge Young were supported by the other Ohio lawyers. They believed that he had a liberal image in civil rights matters. A few days before I arrived in Cleveland, a feature article in the *Cleveland Plain Dealer* had detailed Judge Young's background. He was a graduate of Western Reserve University in Cleveland who had entered the bar in 1934 and practiced in his native Toledo; he had become a state judge in 1952. Thirteen years later he had attained the federal bench under the sponsorship of his uncle, the popular liberal Senator Stephen Young. He would be sixty-five years old on July 13.

Mandel told me that Judge Young had granted almost everything we asked for during the many months of pre-trial maneuvering, including examination of the federal grand jury minutes, and he had proposed a twelve-person jury, with nine votes required for a verdict, rather than a six-person jury, whose verdict had to be unanimous. As fanatics were more likely to be found on the guardsmen's side than on ours, we reasoned, the three-fourths requirement was definitely in our favor. "And the judge has stuck to that," Mandel said, "in spite of defense efforts to get him to change his mind."

Mandel also thought that the judge's agreeing that both parties could, at the beginning of the trial, read into the record an account of the events of May 1–3 was helpful to us. Such a stipulation of facts would prevent the defense's repeatedly bringing up the downtown trashing and the burning of the ROTC Building in the days preceding the shooting and would keep the trial on the main issue, the events of May 4.

"I think he's going to be a fair judge and a good judge," Fred Mandel said. This was all-important because of the great power of federal judges. They can convey their opinions to juries and sway them into verdicts. And jury verdicts are extremely hard to reverse.

Mandel anticipated that the defense would try to show that the guardsmen had not fired the first shot. Even though the Ohio Guard had admitted that it had no evidence of a sniper, Mandel said, there were people who believed, or wanted to believe, that the shooting had been triggered by someone else. He cited a story that had appeared in the *Plain Dealer* a couple of months earlier in which Colonel Peltier, the former inspector general who had investigated the shootings for the Guard, had been quoted as saying that there had been a sniper.

"They have two approaches to this," Mandel said. "One, they can try to show that a photographer, Terry Norman, fired his pistol just before the shooting. Two, they can try to show that Scott MacKenzie was hit by a nonmilitary bullet. There was a doctor at the Akron hospital with MacKenzie who claimed at the time that the wound was too small to have been produced either by .30 caliber M-1 ball ammunition or by a .45."

"Could Norman have shot MacKenzie?" I asked.

"I don't believe they were anywhere near each other," Mandel said.

"What about Norman?" I asked.

"There may be a problem. There is considerable testimony that he did not brandish his pistol until several minutes *after* the shootings. In any case, Norman denies firing, and the two people who checked his pistol, a campus detective, Tom Kelly, and Harold Rice, a campus policeman, will testify it didn't fire. On the other side of the coin, there is some television news film that shows a black man with a briefcase chasing Norman back to the Guard lines and yelling, 'Stop that man! He fired four shots!' Something like that."

"What was a photographer doing with a gun anyway?" I asked.

"According to Sergeant Delaney, who was the Guard press officer, he issued Norman a press pass when told that he worked for the FBI."

"Did he?" I asked.

"The Bureau denies it, for whatever that's worth. We have other testimony, though, that he was taking pictures for the campus police."

My last thoughts as I went to bed Sunday night were of the jury I would be picking the following morning. I knew that our adversaries had available an expensive "jury cooker" study that had been prepared for the 1974 criminal trial. Like most studies, this one simply confirmed what anyone with any common sense would know, for example, that college-educated people under twenty-four years of age, or Jews, or blacks, or women would be inclined to vote against the guardsmen. From the defense point of view, the perfect juror would be a middle-aged member of the Veterans of Foreign Wars and the National Rifle Association who had been a Vietnam hawk.

I did not favor investing our limited funds in any scheme to pre-analyze jurors, most of whom, I knew, would be prejudiced against our clients. We had commissioned one study to see whether there would be any advantage in holding the trial in Judge Young's home territory, Toledo, and we had learned that in both Toledo and Cleveland about 75 percent of the population believed the shootings were justified.

I also realized that we were handicapped by the fact that Governor Rhodes had been reelected in 1974. This meant that by the law of averages a majority of the jurors, all of whom would be Ohioans from the sixteen-county area around Cleveland, had just voted for the chief defendant in the case. Then, too, I felt it would be naive to assume that our opponents had not investigated the political affiliations of every prospective juror on the jury list. Nevertheless, I was willing to take my chances with whatever jurors we got, provided that the presiding judge let us have a fair trial.

5

Picking the Jury

It was a pleasant walk from our apartment to the federal courthouse. We strolled west, toward the central green of the city, where a statue in a verdant grove memorializes Cleveland's famous socialist mayor, Tom Johnson. Central Cleveland has an airy graciousness that one associates with seaboard New England cities. It is indeed a seaport; Lake Erie could be seen glittering to the north as we crossed street intersections. The federal courthouse and customs house, just to the east of the green, is an imposing Romanesque building.

I have climbed the steps to many courthouses in my day, and I always feel the same exhilaration that I feel when I step out onto a tennis court to warm up for a good doubles match.

Courtroom 202, on the western end of the second floor of the courthouse, was rectangular and functional, with a twelve-foot-high ceiling composed of fiber panels in which fluorescent lights were embedded. The ceiling and the walls above the oak wainscoting were a pale, characterless yellow. The room had a subterranean feeling, despite the fact that it was twenty feet above ground. The decor was about as inspiring as that of a motel waiting room.

The courtroom was full when I entered it at nine o'clock on Monday morning and sat down with the other lawyers at our table. The front rows of seats were occupied by the plaintiffs. Dean Kahler, in his wheelchair, sat at the end, in the outer aisle. The rows behind the plaintiffs were occupied by potential jurors and, in the rear, representatives of the press, radio, and television. Outside, in the corridor, were a great many people who had been unable to gain admittance.

Everyone's attention was focused on the persons sitting in two rows of chairs set up against the wall that ran along the right side of the courtroom from the far end, near the door to the judge's chambers, to the first row of seats. These were the forty-four defendants. It was the first time that most of the plaintiffs had a good look at the men who had shot them, or ordered them shot, or created the conditions that allowed them to be shot.

Dean Kahler, Tom Grace, and the others remembered them as monstrous-looking creatures in goggle-eyed gas masks, mushroom-shaped helmets, and wrinkled green fatigues. Now they found themselves looking at a collection of ordinary human beings in sports shirts and jackets, many with their hair over their ears, some wearing eyeglasses. It was as though a play had ended and the performers had removed their masks ("It was all fooling, boys . . . only a game."). In their midst, in a special high-backed leather chair like the one the judge used, sat Governor Rhodes. All his pleas of immunity, sovereign and executive, had failed. He had not escaped having to sit in this courtroom with his adjutant general and officers and enlisted men of the Ohio National Guard —salesmen, truck drivers, masons, mechanics.

The American flag hung limp on its staff. The door in the rear wall opened and, as the bailiff made his announcement and everyone stood, United States District Judge Don J. Young climbed the short stairway to his desk. The judge was a thin man of medium height with a high bony forehead, dark gray hair neatly parted and brushed back, and pinched features.

Except for Engdahl, the law professor from Colorado who had replaced Sindell as Krause's lawyer, our legal staff had been favorably impressed with the judge. Engdahl had thought Young was all right until two weeks before, when the judge had chastised Arthur Krause for violating his order forbidding participants to discuss the case publicly. It wasn't the accusation itself so much as the manner in which the judge had expressed himself that had alarmed Engdahl.

What had happened was that on May 3, the eve of the fifth anniversary of the shootings, Arthur Krause had taken part in a candlelight vigil on campus at the spot where Allison was shot down. He had told a television newsman that the students who had been killed and wounded at Kent State were to be thanked for the fact that American troops had left Southeast Asia and that the nation was finally at peace.

The judge reprimanded Krause for speaking at a *so-called* memorial rally on the campus of Kent State University" and for having signed a letter that was sent out to raise funds for the trial. Krause and Engdahl thought that the judge's remarks impugned the motives of those who had gathered to commemorate the shootings and revealed a bias against the victims.

Sunday morning, May 3, 1970. Governor James A. Rhodes (second from left) and Adjutant General Del Corso (right, in dark suit) inspect the remains of rifles, their wooden stocks consumed in the burning of the ROTC Building. *(UPI)*

Seven of the guardsmen indicted in the federal government's criminal case. From left to right: Leon Smith, Barry Morris, Matthew McManus, James McGee, Lawrence Shafer, Ralph Zoller and James Pierce. *(UPI)*

Now the judge sat with his long, pale fingers resting against his upper lip. "Are counsel ready to proceed?" he asked in a thin, reedy voice.

"Yes, Your Honor," I said.

"Yes, Your Honor. We have certain motions to make at this time." The speaker, standing at the other table, had a light complexion and the square, regular features of a man considerably younger than was implied by his crew-cut gray hair. He wore aviator's glasses with gold-filled temples and had a swaggering way about him, an air of boyish earnestness. This was Burt Fulton, lead counsel for the guardsmen. He and Charles Brown, who shared his duties, were familiar types to me. Brown was a tall man whose features were not unlike those of an oversized Clark Gable, including the mustache. Charlie Brown, as everyone called him, was what used to be known as a "snappy dresser," given to wearing white suits and matching shoes. He expressed himself in a loud, rasping voice with gestures of his large, bearlike hands and shoulders, walked in a flat-footed fashion, and somehow always looked rumpled after his first few minutes in court. Both Fulton and Brown were veterans in defending negligence and malpractice cases, often for insurance companies. I faced men of their stamp almost every time I entered a courtroom. Fulton and Brown were assisted by two young lawyers, William Johnston and Robert Olsen, from Brown's law firm, and by Richard Waltz, on leave from the office of the Ohio attorney general.

Fulton made motions for the judge to dismiss the complaints and call off the trial, and requested that the court order a unanimous jury verdict instead of the 9–3 arrangement.

These motions and requests had been made and denied previously, and they were denied again in the courtroom.

Now came the voir dire, the examination of the jury panel. Seventy prospective jurors were seated in the middle rows of the courtroom. The judge began by directing the plaintiffs and their lawyers to stand, turn 360 degrees, and identify themselves so that the jurors could see whether they knew any of us.

Dean Kahler, seated paralyzed in his wheelchair, was excused from standing. After Dean came Joseph John Lewis, Jr. and his mother, Elizabeth Lewis, who, because he had been a minor in 1970, had joined her son in the complaint. Last of all stood Robert Stamps and his father, Floyd.

"Those are the parties plaintiff to this action, ladies and gentlemen," Judge Young said, "and I am now going to give you the names and ask the parties defendant to stand. Since these people are on this side of the courtroom, they won't have to turn around. If they will just stand long enough for the prospective jurors to get a good look at them.

"The first person listed is Governor James A. Rhodes. Your Excellency. . . ."

There were some quick intakes of breath. Fred Mandel was frowning. Arthur Krause was glaring at the judge. Joseph Sindell, seated next to his son Steve, looked pale. Martin Scheuer's face was contorted. I was shocked. Fred Mandel, who as a local U.S. attorney had served in this same courtroom, whispered that it was an expression he had never dreamed of hearing in an American courtroom.

"Your Excellency" and a special leather chair. In treating one of the defendants with such regal deference, the judge, at the very beginning of the trial, was violating an elementary principle of justice, that all are equal before the law. I was stunned by this blunt show of favoritism.

Governor Rhodes' attorney, R. Brooke Alloway, was a chestnut-haired, older, and heavier version of actor Lloyd Nolan. The former Kent State University president, Robert White, was represented by Robert Blakemore, a portly, soft-spoken gentleman with straight yellow hair.

Lawyers shape a jury by a process of elimination called challenging. There are two types of challenges: *for cause* and *peremptory*. Challenges for cause are unlimited in number. They are used to excuse jurors who are admittedly biased against either side or who have relationships with the parties to the lawsuit or their lawyers. Peremptory challenges are used to eliminate jurors considered by counsel to be undesirable for such reasons as a likely favoritism toward the other parties or lawyers, or attitudes indicating likely prejudice, or associations or activities indicative of sympathy to the other side.

Burt Fulton would use a peremptory challenge to get rid of a long-haired young man who lived in a commune. Similarly, I would use a peremptory challenge to unseat a housewife who had lost two sons in Vietnam. Judge Young had given each side twenty peremptory challenges.

I began the examination by introducing myself, telling the jurors that I came from New York City. Before long, one of my opponents interrupted my questioning to fire a sarcastic objection, adding the hooker, "Is that the way they do it in New York?" I had expected this; it happens every time I try a case away from New York City. My stock rejoinder at such times is to ask the jurors, "Can you decide this case only on the evidence, or will you decide it on the basis of where I came from or where my client comes from?"

I watched the jurors carefully, searching for fleeting expressions that would betray what their words concealed. Certain prejudices, I knew, could not be uprooted. Any juror would probably resent any hint that we were attacking the governor's office or the state. I had to keep making it clear that the defendants on trial were individuals, not institutions. I also had to measure each juror's toleration of political dissent. There was no evading the fact that the students had been protesting on May 4. Unless the juror understood the constitutional right of peaceful assembly and protest, he or she would automatically blame the victims for their fates.

Several incidents occurred which betrayed the strong feelings lurking among many of the prospective jurors. One juror, when asked if he could be impartial, rose in the jury box, looked at Governor Rhodes, and in a loud, emotional voice said, "No, I can't be impartial. I am prejudiced in favor of this great governor who has done everything a good governor should do." Even more significant than this statement was the murmur of approval that was heard in the courtroom.

The pattern of challenges that we expected our opponents to follow was not long in coming. The defense consistently challenged the young and the college-educated. Curiously, there were almost no blacks or Jews on the panel. After a *Plain Dealer* article pointed out this imbalance, two black veniremen were seated.

During lunch hours and morning and afternoon recesses, we would retire to a room at the rear of the court to assess the various jurors. Almost everyone was pleased with the two black jurors, Albert Hunt, a retired liquor salesman, and Bobbie Joe Collins, a forty-five-year-old machinist. The consensus was that blacks would be sympathetic with victims of oppression, particularly with anyone who had been shot by the National Guard (an organization that almost totally excluded blacks and that had shot a number of blacks in the ghetto riots of the late 1960s). A few of the plaintiffs, however, feared that any black who got on the jury panel was likely to be a compliant Uncle Tom. The Schroeders were worried about Albert Hunt's having been a Seagram's district salesman before he retired because Ohio's liquor stores are state operated, thereby forcing liquor salesmen to work with the political establishment. Florence Schroeder also feared that Bobbie Joe Collins would follow the lead of the older and more prosperous Hunt.

There was much discussion of the juror who had thus far been seated the longest, Stanley Davis, Jr., a middle-aged assistant engineer at the Firestone Rubber Company. Mr. Davis, who admitted knowing some national guardsmen, had a daughter who was a music student at Oberlin, a "liberal" midwestern college. We took the chance that his possible pro-Guard views had been tempered by the pro-student views of his daughter.

John Cleary, one of the nine who had been wounded, worried that too high a proportion of the jurors were middle class and members of his parents' generation and older. Robert Stamps felt the same way and told me that most of the panelists hailed from the red-neck areas of Cleveland.

"Now you see what you're up against," he said.

"What do you mean?" I asked.

"The judge is letting Fulton tell the jury you're an outsider from New York and you don't belong here."

"That's nothing," I said. "The jury will see through it."

"Not these people. They're just waiting to get us."

"You will hear them take their oaths to judge the cases on the evidence."

"Do you believe that, Joe, really?"

"Robbie," I said, "I'm going to prove it to you."

I was sorry to see that Robbie Stamps' views were confirmed by John Dunphy, one of the outstanding *Akron Beacon Journal* reporters whose coverage of Kent State had won a Pulitzer. Dunphy took me aside to tell me that we didn't have a chance of winning.

"Why not?" I asked.

"You'll never get an Ohio jury to vote against the guardsmen."

"I have faith in the jury system," I replied.

"You don't know Ohio," Dunphy said.

After Stanley Davis, Jr., the most discussed juror was Mrs. Martha E. Dotterer. Mrs. Dotterer, a plain-looking farmer's wife from Rittman, was a member of a fundamentalist religious sect that did not believe in lawsuits. My instincts warned me to keep her off the jury. However, during the lunch recess, John Adams said he respected the strength of her religious convictions and pointed out that she would be unlikely to bow to other jurors on the grounds of expediency. Later he checked with some of his friends in the clergy and was told that she would be likely to decide the case properly under the law and on the evidence.

That afternoon I got into a small personal exchange with the judge when Roland D. Wiles, a telephone company serviceman, admitted knowing the families of Russell Repp and another of the defendant guardsmen on his service route.

Judge Young questioned Wiles minutely about this, asking him whether, if the judgment went against Repp, he would "hesitate to sign the verdict because of your embarrassment of going to his parents' home on some other occasion afterwards."

"It would probably create a little problem," Wiles replied, "but I would still have to use my own conscience."

I had been told by members of our group that Wiles had nodded amicably to some of the defendants in the courtroom, but he denied knowing any of them when I questioned him. As it seemed likely that Wiles knew the defendants and their families better than he admitted, I went to the bench and requested that he be removed for cause. "He knows the [Repp] family," I said. "He comes into their home. There is no compulsion to keep seated a man with such obvious leanings."

"I don't know where he practices law," Fulton put in. "Perhaps in the Big City they do it that way, but merely because one is a serviceman and goes into someone's home does not mean he knows them. That is the weakest case I ever heard for dismissing a prospective juror for cause."

"This Court is not so naive," I told the judge, "that he doesn't know that the man living in the same community and knowing the family will have a friendly——"

The judge interrupted me. "I was brought up and practiced law in a very small town, and it was not unusual for the jurors to be acquainted with the parties to the litigation before them. We bumped into that all the time, and we didn't give it any thought unless the juror said it would embarrass him to find against a man he said he knew."

It was hard for me to believe this conversation. Fulton cast me as "Big City," while Judge Young talked about his "small town" experience. The judge's attitude meshed perfectly with the defense counsel's. I had to use a peremptory challenge to remove Wiles.

The questioning continued to be exhaustive, and it wasn't until near the end of the fourth day that the panel was finally complete.

The twelve jurors were: Stanley Davis, Jr., of Akron, the Firestone assistant engineer; Richard Williams of Cleveland, a balding, high-domed armature winder in his forties or early fifties; Mrs. Roberta Heckman of Avon, a fortyish service repair worker; the two blacks, Albert Hunt of Shaker Heights and Bobbie Joe Collins of Warrensville Heights; Mrs. Edith Jakaitis of Euclid, a fiftyish inspector for White Motor Corporation; Roland Miller of Wooster, a thirty-year-old shipping clerk for Rubbermaid who had long sideburns; Mrs. Martha Dotterer, the farm housewife with religious scruples; Mrs. Ellen Gaskella of Lorain, a pretty blond accountant who appeared to be in her late twenties; Mrs. Patricia Meyers of Parma Heights, an attractive savings bank teller in her thirties, who wore her hair below her shoulders in the manner of the younger generation; Mrs. Cecilia Klancar of Euclid, an earnest, solid-looking lady whose husband was a retired baker; and Stephen Pohorence of Brook Park, a long-haired, mustached machinist who bore a startling resemblance to Edgar Allan Poe.

The four alternates were Douglas J. Watts of Mogadore, a middle-aged Ford Motor Company foreman; Mary L. Blazina of Lorain, a machinist's wife, whose brother had graduated from Kent State in 1970; Blanche Layman of Cleveland, a retired office worker; and Richard E. Hunt of Middleburg

The jury (from left to right): Ellen Gaskella, unidentified man, Albert Hunt, Cecelia Klancar, Roberta Heckman, Martha Dolterer, Richard Williams, unidentified man, Patricia Meyers, Stephen Pohorence, Bobbie Joe Collins, two unidentified men. Missing from this picture are Stanley Davis, Jr., Roland Miller and Mary Blazina. *(UPI)*

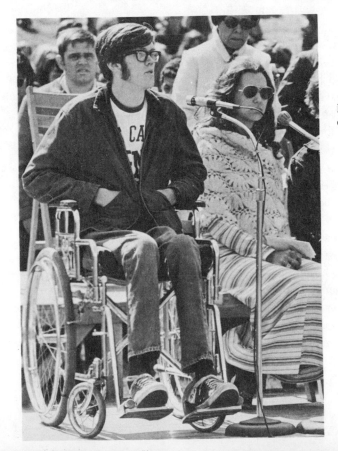

Dean Kahler at a memorial service, one year after he was shot. *(UPI)*

Heights, a young FAA traffic controller who had served in Vietnam.

This was essentially a blue-collar jury. Lacking any young, college-educated persons, it was hardly a cross section of the whole community. Despite the fact that almost a quarter of the population of the Cleveland area of jury age was in its twenties, only a single juror, Ellen Gaskella, was in the age group of the shooting victims. No juror came from any of the parts of Cleveland that Robert Stamps considered enlightened, and some—Mrs. Meyers, Mrs. Jakaitis, and Mrs. Klancar—came from places he regarded as downright frightening (Parma Heights and Euclid).

John and Elaine Kahler looked forward to the trial with mixed feelings. They knew that their son Dean would have to testify; they knew also that his appearance would renew the hate mail, the sideways glances, and the whispered remarks they had received five years ago.

The Kahlers lived in a white clapboard bungalow set at the corner of several acres of pleasant, green land along a rural side road in East Canton. Their three older children were now gone; they lived in the house with their youngest son, Allen, and a small white poodle. John Kahler, a white-haired, fine-featured gentleman, grew vegetables behind the barn and went every day to the Hercules Division of the White Motor Corporation plant. Elaine, a slightly plump lady with curly red hair, button-bright eyes, and a snub nose, worked as a checker in a K-Mart store a few miles from home.

In 1970 Dean Kahler was a young man with chestnut-colored hair, horn-rimmed glasses, and freckled features that duplicated his mother's. He was six feet two inches tall, weighed 160 pounds, could run a mile in five minutes and a hundred yards in ten seconds, and had played offensive tackle on his high school football team. His ambition was to major in physical education and to become an athletic coach.

May 1, 1970, was Dean's twentieth birthday. That Friday afternoon, after the K-Mart closed, Elaine drove to Kent to bring her son home for the weekend, his first visit since enrolling at the university five weeks before. At home Dean heard about the trashing downtown, the ROTC fire, and the coming of the Guard. He assumed, as the television commentators and newspapers all said, that some wild, radical students were the cause of the trouble.

His father drove him back to Kent State on Sunday afternoon. Dean was nervous about riding in cars because he'd been in an automobile accident five months before. The injury he received had left his jaw deformed; he still had difficulty chewing, and he had to cut his food into small pieces with a hunting knife that he carried everywhere. (This knife was later displayed among the student "weapons" seized in the dormitories a week after the shootings.)

Arriving at the university, Dean and his father were surprised to find jeeps, armored personnel carriers that looked like tanks, and national guardsmen everywhere. John Kahler was reminded of the army of occupation in Okinawa, where he had been stationed at the end of World War II. He warned his son to stay out of trouble.

At his dormitory, Wright Hall in Tri-Towers, Dean learned that his friends were among those who had been gassed and chased with bayonets the night before and that he could not even play softball because the Guard would disperse any gathering of four or more students.

That night Dean joined a group of students who marched to President White's house to ask him to explain what was happening. They were met by a line of guardsmen who lobbed tear gas at them. Dean's eyes smarted and he choked. He ran back to Tri-Towers and washed his face until the discomfort ceased. As he combed his hair, he considered whether or not to join some friends in a protest against the curfew, proclaimed since Saturday by the mayor of Kent, that confined them to the campus after 8:00 P.M.

Dean decided to join the march, which would be part of the protest against the war. As a participant in a demonstration, he would have something to tell his children, just as his father had told him about his part in World War II. He did not fear injury, for he had no intention of causing any damage; besides, he could run faster than any guardsman.

The group of students went to Main Street, which formed the northern boundary of the campus, and marched west toward the center of Kent. "One, two, three, four," they chanted, "We don't want your fucking war." At Lincoln Street, which formed the western boundary of the campus, they were stopped by Ohio highway patrolmen and sheriff's deputies whom they could see in a line, blocking their way downtown, and also to their right, between them and the restaurants, gas stations, and shops along the opposite side of Main Street. They sat down in the street, demanding that Mayor Satrom and President White come and explain what the Guard was doing on campus, the rules under which it was operating, and when it would leave.

At about half past ten a student with a bullhorn announced that the guardsmen would leave the front campus. Someone asked when Mayor Satrom was coming. "Satrom is on the way," the student announced, "and they are trying to get White."

Sit peacefully, the word went around, don't make trouble, we'll be all right. Satrom and White are coming.

A little while later the bullhorn was heard again. A gravelly voice rasped out that the students were violating an eleven P.M. curfew. While the students *in the street shouted their outrage at this sudden change in the rules (the campus curfew ordinarily went into effect at one A.M.), a line of guardsmen suddenly appeared from beneath the trees on the campus, their bayonets gleaming in the streetlights. Suddenly Dean saw that he and the others were surrounded. Canisters of tear gas began to land in their midst.*

Choking, barely able to see, Dean ran through the campus, scampering alongside a parking lot and beneath some trees. He could hear shouts and screams behind him and the roar of helicopter engines overhead. Powerful searchlights swept back and forth so that buildings, trees, and a chimney exploded into view.

Scores of students, young men and women, battered the glass doors of Tri-Towers, screaming to be admitted to the locked building. Their shouts were drowned out by a helicopter, their disorder frozen in a blaze of light. More tear gas dropped from the night sky. Guardsmen approached. A dorm councilor opened the door, and the crowd rushed inside.

When he got upstairs, Dean learned that his mother had been trying to reach him. It was after one in the morning when he got to the telephone.

"They lied to us, Mother," Dean said. "They lied to us."

Elaine asked him what he meant.

Dean told her he had been sitting with other students in the middle of Main Street, waiting for Mayor Satrom and President White. "They told us they were coming, and we waited. They said the Guard was leaving the front campus. They lied to us."

"Who lied?" Elaine Kahler asked.

"They did. They told us we were breaking the eleven o'clock curfew. But there is no eleven o'clock curfew. It's at one. And the Guard didn't leave the front campus. They gassed us and chased us."

"What did you do?"

"Nothing."

"You didn't do anything?"

"All we did was sit and wait for President White. They said he was coming."

"There must be a communication gap," Elaine Kahler said. She couldn't believe that her son had been lied to.

Dean couldn't sleep. Helicopters bleated, searchlights flitted feverishly across his window, acrid whiffs of tear gas floated into the room. His mind was in turmoil. Why did these people have to lie? Whom could one trust?

He was awakened at nine by a phone call. His minister, Gordon Blucher, had been asked by his mother to find out what was troubling him.

That morning Dean had an appointment in the administration building to discuss his dropping zoology. He got up too late to keep it and, after ten, left for his English class. It was such a rare, beautiful blue day that he could hardly credit the nightmare of a few hours before. He was determined to attend the rally that was scheduled for noon.

After class Dean took his books back to Wright Hall, then left for the Commons. It was half past eleven. Somewhere a voice on a loudspeaker warned people to stay away from the rally. "All outdoor demonstrations and gatherings are banned by order of the governor. The National Guard has the power of arrest."

As Dean trudged across a grassy field in the sun, Captain Raymond Srp of Troop G and First Sergeant Myron Pryor were discussing plans to feed their men. (Troop G and portions of Companies A and C had been summoned a half hour earlier to the cordoned off area where the burned ROTC Building had stood.) In Bowman Hall, Professor Robert Dyal's American philosophy class had put aside its assignment to talk about what it meant to have armed men on campus. And in Professor Thomas Lough's political science class, Robbie Stamps was asserting that Governor Rhodes was taking a tough stance in order to beat Robert Taft in the contest for the Republican nomination for the U.S. Senate in the next day's primary election. Professor Lough dismissed the class early to attend the rally.

Dean Kahler reached the Commons at about 11:45, a few minutes before the 11:50 class break. He found a couple of hundred students milling around the slope beneath the budding trees, while the brass bell clanged insistently beneath the blue sky. At the far end of the field were jeeps, guardsmen in green uniforms, and students thronging the pathways on their way to lunch. Between Dean and the guardsmen, from left to right, blew a pleasant breeze.

More students were crossing the Commons now. Bruce Phillips, on his way from an accounting class to his room at Johnson Hall, stopped on the sidewalk to see what was happening. Some students paused by the Victory Bell, others passed on. Two students waved black flags, one bearing the green letters K-E-N-T. A voice blared from a loudspeaker down by the burned out building. Students laughed and jeered. Dean could not hear the announcement.

A jeep drove slowly across the Commons toward the students and the trees. "This assembly is unlawful. This crowd must disperse immediately. This is an order." More laughter, more jeering, more waving of black flags. Some students were giving the men in the jeep the finger.

The jeep turned in front of the students. Dean could see two guardsmen in steel helmets in back, rifles between their knees, and in front, a campus policeman with a bullhorn. "Disperse. Go back to your dormitories. This assembly is unlawful." The jeep wheeled around and came back, then headed toward some students, who gave way. As the jeep retreated, a rock struck one of its rear tires.

Raised fists, jeers, catcalls, and chants followed the jeep to the far end of the field.

Several guardsmen moved out in front of the others and stopped. There were popping sounds, and smoke spouted from several places on the turf. Now there was running and coughing, people holding handkerchiefs over their faces, someone hurling a gray, smoke-spewing canister back toward the Guard troops. Everyone was moving away from the bell. (The tear gas drove Bruce Phillips into Johnson Hall. With his girlfriend Pat Frank and her roommate Joy Hubbard, he went up on the roof to see what would happen next.)

Dean was part of a group hurrying up the hill between Johnson and Taylor halls. Looking back over his shoulder, he could see a broad line of men in green uniforms strolling purposefully in his direction, their rifles at port arms.

Dean ran past the Pagoda and waited long enough to see the guardsmen, strange and anonymous in their gas masks, emerge beyond the corner of Taylor Hall. Then he ran down to the tennis courts below the football practice field, a lanky, red-headed, fresh-looking kid with a snub nose and horn-rimmed glasses. He threw stones at no one in particular and at no one who was close enough to be hit.

Leaving the practice field, the guardsmen formed up and climbed the hill. Dean shouted at their retreating figures. The confrontation was over. The guardsmen had marched, but the students were still on the campus.

Dean turned away and decided to return to Wright Hall. He walked along the grass at the edge of the practice field, his right side toward the guardsmen who now were just reaching the crest of Blanket Hill. He heard sharp sounds, and shouts, and from the corner of his eye saw students jumping onto the grass. He jumped down too, and put his hands on top of his head. Then all of a sudden he got hit on his left side, under the armpit, and his back felt as though it had been touched by a live wire. He couldn't feel his legs. Lying there, he remembered a zoology experiment in which a frog's leg jumped when the nerve was touched by electricity.

6

Blueprints for a Trial

In the evenings of that week of jury selection the other lawyers and I reviewed the evidence, read depositions, and discussed the order in which witnesses would be called.

The heart of our federal civil rights case, as distinct from our case under state law, was excessive force, which boils down to the principle that no one has a right to shoot a person for calling a name or throwing a stone. We would also argue that the Guard had provoked the students by breaking up a peaceful assembly.

Excessive force violated the due process clause of the Fifth Amendment because it was summary punishment: guardsmen had acted as prosecutors, judges, jury, and executioners. The act of breaking up the peaceful assembly violated the First Amendment.

We were claiming that the defendants were responsible for these constitutional violations in various ways: Governor Rhodes for invoking martial law, ordering assemblies dispersed, and arousing the guardsmen with a reckless speech; General Del Corso for drafting improper riot control instructions and inadequately training his men; General Canterbury for dispersing the noon assembly and improperly leading the men in the field; he and the other officers for failing to control the men under their command; and the guardsmen for failing to follow the designated steps in crowd control procedure and recklessly employing excessive force.

Some of these claims were matters of law to be decided by the judge; others were matters of fact to be decided by the jury. The principal legal question was

Rhodes' invocation of martial law in the proclamation he issued on the day after the shooting (and which, we felt, was implicit in his previous actions). This act was illegal because martial law can exist only when the civil courts are unable to function. Judge Young, however, had refused during the pre-trial period to rule on this matter. Thus he would be handing it on to the jury as a question of fact: whether or not Rhodes, as his legal adviser John McElroy claimed, was telling the truth when he said that in the May 5 proclamation he had cited the martial law statute by mistake.

We also had to consider the defense strategy.

With regard to the dispersal of the rally, the defense would claim that an Ohio riot statute authorized the breaking up of "violent and tumultuous assemblies that presented a clear and present danger to persons or property." To counter this we would have to show that the assembly had been peaceful before the students were told to disperse. Another defense approach would be to get the judge to instruct the jury (when it came time at the end of the trial to interpret the law for them) that the behavior of the students on May 1, 2, and 3 could justify the dispersal of even a peaceful assembly on May 4. To accomplish this, the defense would have to show that the rally had been banned by the university, for the only exception to the Supreme Court's long-standing abhorrence of the prohibition of assemblies was when it was done by a university in the interest of maintaining normal classroom operations. There was evidence, however, that the Kent State assemblies had been banned by the governor and the Guard.

On the main civil rights issue of excessive force, the guardsmen had just one line of defense: that the men who pulled the triggers had been in genuine fear for their lives and their safety.

We also anticipated that Fulton and Brown would throw up a defense of contributory negligence. Contributory negligence is careless conduct on the part of a victim that helps to cause an accident—for example, the throwing of stones at a guardsman, who then shoots because he is afraid of being stoned. Contributory negligence would not enter into the federal civil rights suit because our clients could not claim under the law that their civil rights were impaired by the defendants' negligence. Contributory negligence could, however, be a defense against the claims we were making under state law (assault and battery and wrongful death). In these claims we *were* charging negligence; therefore, with respect to these claims, the defense could rightfully offer proof of stoning and other provocative acts committed by students. The jurors would not be expected to understand that this defense applied only to the state part of the case and was irrelevant to our claims under federal law. It would be the responsibility of the judge, at the conclusion of the trial, to make this clear.

In any event, little contributory negligence could be demonstrated on the part of the plaintiffs. Canfora and Kahler admitted to having thrown small stones. That was it. No doubt the defense would try to make something of Canfora's waving a black flag and perhaps Jeff Miller's and Joe Lewis' giving the Guard the finger, but none of this behavior could honestly be found to be contributory to anything more violent than a scolding or, for the stone throwing, a jailing.

We recognized, however, that the disturbances of the three preceding days could not be ignored. After all, they explained why the Guard was in Kent and why there was antagonism between the students and the Guard (see Table 1).

At the same time, we were worried that paying too much attention to those events could be prejudicial to our case. We knew that the defense would be constantly trying to divert the jury from the real issues of the case and trying to play on any latent hostility on the part of jurors toward young people and dissidents. For this reason we had readily accepted Judge Young's suggestion, made during the pre-trial period, that plaintiffs and defendants agree on a description of the events of May 1–3 that could then simply be read to the jury.

Once these stipulations were out of the way, we would concentrate on the governor's visit to Kent on May 3 and the events of May 4.

Our plan was to open our case with a description of the events of May 4, calling on witnesses who were not party to the suits (mostly former Kent students and faculty), the plaintiffs, and guardsmen. We could have omitted the guardsmen, leaving them to be called by the defense when they presented their side of the case, but we decided it would be better strategy to call them in presenting our case. We could use them to confirm that the noon rally had been peaceful (their depositions were almost unanimous in stating that no rocks had been thrown before the assembly was ordered to disperse); and, with the photographs we had, we anticipated no trouble in discrediting their claims of firing in self-defense. Once all these witnesses had testified, we would bring up the matter of Ohio National Guard regulations and put Adjutant General Del Corso on the stand. Then we would turn to Governor Rhodes and his intemperate Sunday pronouncements, which, fortunately, had been recorded on tape.

After that would come the witnesses to the Monday morning meeting, at which General Canterbury decided to disperse the noon rally even before seeing what it would be like. These witnesses would include defendant Robert White, former president of the university, who we believed had failed to protect the students from the invasion of his campus.

TABLE 1: Activities of Plaintiffs, May 1–4, 1970

Plaintiff	May 1 Friday	May 2 Saturday	May 3 Sunday	May 4 Monday	Distance from Guard when shot
Canfora		C		VB, PL, S	200'
Cleary		C		C	100'
Grace		C		VB, PL	200'
Kahler			PW, MS	VB, PL, S	330'
Krause	DK	C		VB, PL	343'
Lewis		C		C	60'
MacKenzie		C	PW, MS		750'
Miller		C	MS	VB, PL	265'
Russell	DK		MS		360'
Scheuer		C			390'
Schroeder	DK			C	382'
Stamps		C			550'
Wrentmore		C		C	350'

C: On the Commons (on May 2, at time of assault on ROTC Building; on May 4, at noon)
DK: In downtown Kent during the evening
PW: On the march to President White's house
MS: In the Main Street sitdown
VB: Near the Victory Bell
PL: In the Prentice Hall parking lot
S: Threw a stone in the direction of guardsmen on the practice field

We had a lot of powerful evidence in our arsenal:

1. Still photographs showing that the guardsmen were neither surrounded nor menaced before they fired their weapons.

2. A motion picture film of Blanket Hill and the guardsmen, covering several minutes up to the time of the shooting; analyzed by the Justice Department, it shows only a few students moving toward the Guard, none of them closer to the troops than eighty-five feet.

3. A tape recording of the entire thirteen-second sequence of shots, together with an analysis prepared for the Justice Department that showed that the first three shots had been fired from military M-1 rifles situated between Taylor Hall and the Pagoda. This analysis would counter defense efforts to show that the first shot had come from a sniper.

4. A tape recording of Governor Rhodes' statement at the May 3 press conference advocating the use of all necessary force: "We are going to eradicate the problem. We are not going to treat the symptoms. . . . These people just move from one campus to another and terrorize the community. They are worse than the brownshirts and Communist element and also the night riders and the vigilantes. They are the worst type of people that we harbor in America. . . . There's no sanctuary for these people."

5. Testimony by a former guardsman, Michael Delaney, that before the press conference he had heard Rhodes at a private meeting tell Guard officers and other law-enforcement people that he wanted all assemblies at Kent banned.

6. Testimony by two university administrators that Rhodes told them he was taking over and they should "stay out of it."

7. The Matson-Frisina letter, a circular letter issued on the afternoon of Sunday, May 3, stating that the "Governor, through the National Guard, has assumed legal control of the campus and city of Kent." The letter was signed by a vice president of the university, Robert Matson, and the president of the student body, Frank Frisina.

8. Testimony by Matson and a Guard officer that the letter was based on information from the National Guard.

9. Two proclamations signed by Governor Rhodes on April 29 and May 5, 1970. The May 5 proclamation states that the Guard was called out on April 29 under a martial law statute that places the Guard directly under Rhodes' command.

10. Testimony of former president White and other university administrators that at a meeting in downtown Kent on Monday morning, May 4, before the noon rally was held, General Canterbury made the decision to disperse it.

11. Excerpts from two crowd control manuals: army field manual 19–15 and annex F to PLAN 2 of the Ohio National Guard, showing that, contrary to U.S. Army regulations, the Ohio National Guard authorized shooting at rioters.

12. Testimony of two National Guard officers, Major General Dana Stewart and Lieutenant Charles J. Barnette, that Ohio guardsmen on crowd control duty habitually loaded weapons without a specific command.

It was a logical plan; we would portray the events with photographs and move step by step from the witnesses of and participants in the shootings to Del Corso and Rhodes.

The noon rally had been dispersed by three Guard units: Troop G of the 107th Cavalry and Companies A and C of the 145th Infantry Regiment. Except for two men who strayed, Company C was not involved in the practice field events or the shootings. Following the initial dispersal of the group at the Victory Bell, Company C had marched to a position between Taylor and Prentice halls to prevent students from returning to the Commons by that route. Meanwhile, Troop G and Company A had pursued the students over Blanket Hill, down to the practice field, and back up again.

We decided that there was a significant difference in the respective behaviors

Michael Delaney, the former National Guard sergeant who testified about the closed Sunday morning meeting at the Kent firehouse. *(UPI)*

Peter Davies devoted himself to obtaining justice for the Kent State victims. *(James Munves)*

Galen Keller, the paralegal with the infallible memory, holds her youngest child. *(James Munves)*

of Troop G and Company A. Most of the shooting had been done by Troop G, which was made up almost entirely of blue-collar workers in their late twenties or early thirties from around Ravenna. Company A was composed of generally better-educated younger men from the Wooster area and was representative of the newer recruits, many of whom had joined the Guard to escape the draft. (After the fall of 1969, when the draft lottery replaced student deferments, guardsmen were more secure from the draft than students were.) Several members of Company A had brothers or sisters attending Kent State; one was the son of a professor. With very few exceptions, these men, so far as we knew, had fired their rifles in the air or at the ground after Troop G had started shooting. Afterward a number of them had expressed remorse, and one was later discharged as a conscientious objector.

Thirty-two of the defendant guardsmen were enlisted men. Almost all of them had admitted firing their weapons, but only six had admitted firing at students. Two of the others, Leon Smith and Matthew McManus, had fired shotguns under circumstances indicating that one had hit plaintiff Jim Russell. (These were the eight guardsmen who were indicted in 1974.) Of the other twenty-four, nineteen had admitted firing and five were suspected of firing. Some may have been lying.

Nine defendant officers had been on the campus that day. None of them admitted firing, but Captain Raymond Srp of Troop G told the FBI that one of the platoon leaders, Lieutenant Alexander Stevenson, had fired an M-1. The FBI also had ballistic evidence that the .45 signed out to Lieutenant Howard Fallon of Company A was fired on Blanket Hill.

Those who admitted shooting at students were former guardsmen James Pierce, William Perkins, Lawrence Shafer, Ralph Zoller, James McGee, and Barry Morris. They had admitted firing a total of between seventeen and twenty-one shots, six from Morris' .45 and the rest from M-1s. However, photographs showed at least nine members of Troop G leveling rifles at students in the Prentice Hall parking lot. The FBI counted thirty-two holes in cars and still others in the metal sculpture, trees, and buildings in the cone of fire. (One bullet entered the wall of an apartment a mile away.) When to these are added the thirteen wounds suffered by students, the total number of shots fired in their direction must have been at least double the admitted maximum of twenty-one. Sixty-seven shots were counted on the tape. Some, but not all of these were fired by guardsmen who claimed to have fired into the air or at the ground. There was no way of telling how many of the seventy-two guardsmen who had been on Blanket Hill had lied in denying that they had fired, but five of them were strongly suspected of having done so on the basis of photographs, eyewitness testimony, or the testimony of other guardsmen.

We knew that some guardsmen would be lying, and we hoped they might give themselves away by their demeanor on the stand. We thought that, under careful grilling, some might break and implicate others. During the criminal trial, McManus, one of the two who had fired a shotgun, had sounded off against the governor and General Canterbury.

Many stories had changed in the five years since 1970, and witnesses might claim faulty memories. Our job would be to convince the jury that it was not the guardsmen's memories but their veracity that was defective. Our witnesses, the photos, and our other evidence would have to do the job.

We strongly suspected that the guardsmen's stories of being surrounded and forced to shoot to defend their lives had been invented before they knew about all the photographs. This was suggested a few months after the shootings, in the summary that the Justice Department prepared on the basis of the FBI investigation.

As the coming Monday would be Memorial Day, we had a long weekend before us. On Tuesday the jury would have a guided tour of the Kent State campus, so our opening statements (described by Judge Young as the picture on the cover of the jigsaw puzzle box) would not come until Wednesday.

Libbie and I flew to New York, taking along the depositions of several guardsmen. Bob stayed behind, interviewing potential witnesses. I would spend Friday at my office, digging out from under the pile of work that needed my attention, and then devote the rest of the weekend to Kent State. Sunday night I would fly back to Cleveland. This was to be my routine for the next fifteen weeks.

Of all my experiences that first week in Cleveland, I was affected most by my meetings with the plaintiffs.

Sarah Scheuer remembered that she had taken her daughter Sandra a red blouse on the Saturday before the shooting.

Sarah, whose other, older daughter had just married and moved to Pittsburgh, had always found pretexts for visiting Sandra at Kent. One weekend she and her mother, who lived nearby, would take a cake; another weekend it would be a roast chicken. On Saturday, May 2, they took along some spring clothing.

Sandra was a friendly, motherly young woman whose ambition was to be a speech therapist. She was always helping others, carrying books for a classmate who had been injured in an automobile accident, cooking meals for any friend (Jeff Miller, among others) who happened to drop in on her cozy little off-campus apartment. She was the sort of cheery, stable person to whom others told their troubles, a person attuned more to the people she knew, and to what she could accomplish with her own hands and brain, than to the issues of the larger world outside her experience. She worried more about a child who stuttered than about the war in Vietnam.

On Monday afternoon, May 4, 1970, Sarah was outdoors in the sun, painting the house, stopping occasionally to peek through the window to see that a dachshund puppy Martin had given her that morning was all right.

The dachshund was an anniversary present; that day was the Scheuers' twenty-seventh wedding anniversary.

The telephone had been ringing for some time before Sarah heard it. It was Martin, calling to tell her there was trouble at Kent State. Sarah telephoned her daughter's apartment, and a roommate told her that Sandy had been hurt.

"Where is she?" Sarah asked.

"I don't know. I don't know, Mrs. Scheuer."

"What was she wearing?"

"The red blouse, you know? The one you brought Saturday."

Sarah tried to call the university, then the hospital in Ravenna. The lines were busy, but finally she reached the director of the hospital. He didn't know anything about a Sandra Scheuer.

"She was wearing a red blouse," Sarah said.

"Maybe you had better come," the hospital director told her.

By this time Martin was home and Sarah's mother, who had heard about the shooting on her television, had driven over. Martin, Sarah, and Sarah's mother drove to Ravenna at eighty miles an hour.

All that summer, whenever Sarah looked into the backyard, she thought she saw Sandy sunbathing.

They sold the house and moved to another part of Youngstown.

Yet even when a Youngstown city councilman said that 4,004 students should have been killed, they assumed that the State of Ohio would punish their daughter's murderers. It was only when they read the special state grand jury report that they began to doubt that justice would be done.

Someone, Sarah decided, had aimed at Sandy's red shirt. If Sandy hadn't been wearing the red shirt, if she hadn't taken it to her on Saturday, Sandy would still be with them.

Talking with the parents, I soon discovered that they had all become mistrustful of authority. Arthur Krause had been cynical from the first, but now even Louis Schroeder, a scoutmaster, and Jan Wrentmore, who had publicly supported Nixon's move into Cambodia, had become skeptics.

The nine young men who had been shot had adopted different modes of dealing with their experience. A few of them had become confirmed political radicals, frustrated, antagonistic, and bitter; others had striven to forgive the shooters or had enfolded themselves in mystical doctrines that reduced historical events to meaninglessness. As in Arthur Koestler's formulation, some had become commissars and some had become yogis. (In a study commissioned by the Defense Department, Professor Jerry Lewis concluded that excessive force created more revolutionaries than pacifists.)

Tom Grace dreamed of leveling a loaded M-1 from the top of Blanket Hill at Rhodes and the guardsmen milling unarmed below. Dean Kahler believed that the guardsmen, like himself, should purge their hearts of hatred. Doug Wrentmore, who believed in reincarnation, thought that the students and the guardsmen were linked in some ancient cycle of violence. MacKenzie was deep into yoga, Canfora into socialist reform. Stamps went to a psychiatrist. Russell and Lewis had become wanderers. Only one of them, John Cleary, was pursuing his career—as an architect—as though nothing had happened.

7

Opening Statements

▬

Our plan for the opening statements was that I would make the introduction and the wrap-up, and in between, five other members of our team would each take a specific topic. Sindell would talk about Rhodes and Del Corso. Nelson Karl, a Cleveland associate of the ACLU who sported mod suits and an impressive mustache, would describe the peaceful nature of the assembly at noon on May 4. Engdahl would cover its dispersal. Geltner would outline the Ohio National Guard's rules of engagement and the manner in which they differed dangerously from those of the Army. And Fred Mandel would present the case against President White.

The judge had allotted each side two hours. I would take about half an hour at the beginning and half an hour at the end; my five colleagues would divide the other hour between them.

Our discussions during the briefings focused on the fact that we were faced with a massive coverup by the Guard. It was clear that the officers on the scene had been sloppy in inspecting weapons and counting ammunition, and the Guard's higher echelons had only cursorily investigated the shooting incident. Furthermore, there were reports that they had tried to silence Chaplain John Simons' criticism of the Guard officers, and I shared the Justice Department's suspicion that the self-defense justification had been invented after the shooting. I also knew I would have to address myself to the disorders of the three days preceding May 4 and the rock throwing on May 4. Even if the events of May 1–3 were excluded from the trial by stipulation, they were bound to be mentioned in the defense opening, and it would be damaging if the defense convinced the jury that we condoned lawlessness.

In the first part of my opening statement, after reminding the jurors of their responsibility and of the historical importance of the case, I stressed my abhorrence of violence and lawlessness of all kinds, saying that the burning of the ROTC Building "should be condemned by every right-thinking person in the community and in the campus and in the nation. Not excusable, to be condemned, and everyone doing it should be and probably was arrested. That is not our concern here. A number of individuals participated in the burning, but that would not explain the shooting down of students on May 4, and we say that none of the people who are participants in this case did."

I was careful in my references to Governor Rhodes. After describing how he had inflamed the situation with his rhetoric on May 3, I said that we "care not whether every one of the jurors voted for Governor Rhodes, and everyone might have voted for him. We might say in abstract discussion that he may be a gentle and fine, capable governor, but we do say that Governor Rhodes acted in a manner which would . . . inflame those who wanted to abandon the legal rights of students to assemble peacefully . . . he did so improperly, illegally, carelessly, and unreasonably, giving a blank check to the guardsmen to use force without restraint and without controls."

I described the rock throwing after the noon demonstration was broken up as "something that we don't say we have to condone or should condone or forgive, but we do say that the first stone in effect was cast by an improper, illegal dispersal of a peaceable assembly which was the students' right on their campus . . . to protest what they thought our government was doing wrong . . . the heritage of everybody American."

I pointed out that the students did not know that the Guard's weapons were loaded and were never given any prior warning that they might be shot. I then traced on a map the path of the guardsmen, indicating where the injured students were standing in relation to them, at distances ranging from 60 to 750 feet—prima facie evidence that the guardsmen had not shot in self-defense.

It is perhaps the most absurd feature of this case that there could even have been serious discussion of self-defense against unarmed persons at those distances.

Steven Sindell went into the May 3 meeting of the governor and law-enforcement officials in detail, quoting remarks that, he said, the jury would hear for itself on tape. Nelson Karl described the Commons on May 4 as a center of campus traffic, a place surrounded by buildings and normally crossed by students on their way to and from classes. As classes broke at 11:50, he said, hundreds of students who had nothing to do with the rally had poured out of buildings; those attending the rally were peaceful and law-abiding.

David Engdahl added that even General Canterbury, the top officer of the National Guard on the scene, had testified that there was no rock throwing and no damage or threat to property before the assembly was ordered to disperse. Engdahl explained to the jury that it would have to decide who was in control of the campus on May 4; Governor Rhodes, President White, and General Canterbury were each pointing the finger at the other. He suggested that the guardsmen had acted in a violent and vindictive manner, stating that three of the victims, Allison Krause, Jeff Miller, and Alan Canfora, had been conspicuous in their taunting of the guardsmen.

Mike Geltner stated the military rules for dealing with civilian disturbances with a show of force rather than with the use of force. He described General Del Corso's lax policy of authorizing the routine loading of guns with live ammunition, showed the difference between Army and Ohio National Guard regulations, and went into the manner in which virtual martial law had been established on the campus.

Fred Mandel told the jury that after President White returned to Kent on May 3 and found the campus under Guard control, he neither interceded with the Guard on behalf of the students nor called the state attorney general to find out what his legal position was. "What we are saying," he concluded, "is that he . . . totally abdicated his responsibility."

In my wrap-up I referred to the photographs that would prove that the guardsmen's lives had not been threatened at the time of the shooting, and I talked about how we would try to separate the guilty from the innocent among the defendant guardsmen.

"You will find that some of these individuals said they had not shot, they said that they could account for the bullets they had originally . . . the number of unspent or unfired bullets may be pertinent. But we do know [that] those who had done some shooting . . . were taken to a separate place. We will inquire as to what was said to them, because, remarkably, the same day statements were made and signed, almost like parrots, one echoing the other, saying, 'I was in fear for my life, we were being rushed by students, I was afraid my life was in danger' . . . statements were signed, but remarkably, at the time, those who had taken photographs had not had time to develop and have them printed . . . The photographic proof . . . showed that many of the statements . . . to validate the shooting were false and not worthy to believe.

"We will show there was no onrush of students . . . We will cover every area to prove to you, by photographs and eyewitnesses, there was no surrounding, no imminent danger, no present danger, no reasonable claim of danger, no reasonable claim [of] self-defense . . . We say definitely it was a coverup.

"What we say is that this was an unprecedented improper killing of unarmed persons in this state and in this nation."

The main burden of the defense's opening was taken up by Charles Brown, the big, silver-haired lawyer from Columbus with the white shoes and the florid neckties, who made certain right at the beginning that the jury knew he was one of them, an "Ohio boy." There was nothing subtle about Charlie. Outside the courtroom he was friendly and jovial; in the courtroom his forte was sarcasm and frequent references to my being from New York. The pitch for local favoritism, tolerated by the judge, was to persist throughout the trial.

The issue, Brown said, was not constitutional freedom, it was terror and safety. It was whether, as he put it, "we live in a country of laws or a country of men. Whether or not lawlessness and terror prevail or whether American citizens have a right to enjoy their lives and their property in safety and in peace."

To dramatize his picture of the terror and lawlessness that had prevailed in Kent in May 1970, Brown—until he was stopped by objections—gave a history of college uprisings, beginning with the Berkeley free speech movement in 1964. Most of his opening was then devoted to a description of the first three days of May in Kent, days of "burning, looting, rioting, and terrorism," with Kent merchants threatened unless they put peace signs in the windows of their shops.

As much as we sought to distinguish the gatherings—the peaceful assembly of May 4 from the disturbances of May 1 and 2—Brown cleverly sought to confuse them. "Now you have heard the opening statement of plaintiffs' counsel," he said, "to the effect that the meeting on May 4 was allegedly peaceful and so forth. We are not there yet, we are at May 2, what happened on May 2 at the ROTC Armory with the peaceful students.

"Rocks were thrown, flares were thrown into the ROTC Building, many policemen were assaulted, firemen who came to put out the fire were physically abused."

He told how Governor Rhodes had arrived to survey the situation and how, later Sunday afternoon, Vice President Matson of the university had issued a letter stating that "demonstrations, rallies, and assemblies are prohibited."

"Now this, ladies and gentlemen, is not from the Ohio National Guard who plaintiffs' counsel indicate the evidence will show took over," Brown said. "This is from the Kent State University to the students." (Later we will see what this letter really said.)

Brown went on to describe further "rioting" that took place Sunday night in "the campus area at Lincoln and Main streets" and the scene at the Commons on May 4, "when the peaceful crowd threw an untold number of rocks at the jeep" that went out to read the riot act.

"What was the Guard doing? Saying, 'Please disperse. Go back to your dorms. This is an unlawful assembly.' The language that was used at that time . . . is . . . so vile I will not repeat it. But they were saying such things as 'Sieg heil,' reminiscent of World War II days."

Rocks were thrown, tear gas was used and the canisters thrown back, "somebody threw a parking meter off the top of one of the buildings at the Guard. . . . The evidence will show the FBI, Highway Patrol, and other people picked up rocks by the sacksful, and many of them were not indigenous to or were not found there on campus, they had been brought in." He told the jury that on the practice field seventy guardsmen had confronted thousands of students "completely lawless, disorderly, violent, throwing rocks, cursing, doing every vile thing imaginable. . . ."

As Troop G and Company A reached the top of the hill, he said, "the noise of the crowd reached a crescendo, yelling every epithet you can think of, hurling rocks at the Guard, 'Kill the pigs, kill.' This is what the evidence will show, ladies and gentlemen, this is not fiction.

"As they reached the top of the hill there was a sudden surge of the crowd toward the Guard.

"The evidence will show that many of the guardsmen were in fear of dying right then and there. Some of them were fearful that the crowd would take their guns away and bayonet them or shoot them . . . this is insurrection, this was rebellion, this was the antithesis of everything this country stands for.

"At this point, you will hear tapes of this, you will hear evidence as to this, there was the report of the sound of a weapon, which we identified by some witnesses as a weapon other than a National Guard weapon.

"The evidence will show that the National Guard had M-1 rifles, some shotguns, and a few .45 pistols. Immediately following the sound the Guard fired, there is no question. . . .

"The evidence will conclusively show that there was never an order to fire, there was never an order to fire. As soon as the firing commenced, General Canterbury, Major Jones, and others started yelling, 'Cease fire. Stop. Quit,' and they did.

"And I think the evidence will show that the firing lasted approximately thirteen seconds. Immediately after the firing, a civilian, a civilian. . . . whose name is Terry Norman, ran into the Guard lines for protection for fear he was going to be killed. And the evidence will show he did have a pistol on him.

"The evidence will show that at least one of the plaintiffs in this case was struck by a weapon other than a military weapon. Mr. MacKenzie, he had a bullet enter the back of his neck and come out his cheek . . . So there is evidence of at least one weapon that was shot other than a military weapon."

Brown asserted that the Ohio National Guard was trained according to U.S. Army standards, had had considerable riot control experience, and habitually loaded weapons in riot situations because "of the length of time it takes to put a clip into the weapon. . . .

"The evidence will clearly show," he concluded, "martial law did not exist at the time. . . . the mob was about to overtake and overcome the Guard. . . . nobody, nobody, including the Ohio National Guard, must wait until they are overrun and perhaps killed themselves before protecting themselves."

After that performance, Alloway's and Blakemore's statements sounded anticlimactic. Alloway, Rhodes' lawyer, after endorsing and approving in his low-key way everything that Brown had said, went on to explain that the governor had followed his usual proper legal procedures in calling the Guard to Kent. "When all the evidence is in," he concluded, "it will be clear to you that the only part Governor Rhodes had in this tragic situation was the performance of his constitutional duty."

Blakemore, representing President White, described how the university had mushroomed during the student boom of the 1950s and 1960s into a typical Middle American university, "not a hotbed of radicalism or of radical education. We expect the testimony to show that on the day in question less than 10 percent of the student body of Kent State University [was] . . . actually involved in the particular situation." He explained that although White was absent from the university from Friday afternoon to Sunday noon, he had been actively concerned about what was happening and, together with General Canterbury, wanted "to get the Ohio National Guard's troops off the campus because that is not the place for troops."

To show that President White had not been in control of events, Blakemore pointed out that all decisions, including the one to ban the noon rally, were taken off the campus, and that the Monday morning meeting at the Kent firehouse was chaired by General Canterbury. "We expect the evidence to show," he concluded, "that Robert White did not either by omission or act or by any act . . . in any way bring about any harm or . . . death [to] the students. . . ."

It seemed to me that Charlie Brown was trying to invoke the antagonism toward students that had surrounded the events of May 4. It was the voice of passion, failing to distinguish between one student and another, lumping them all into one insidious mob. (As early as May 24, 1970, the *Akron Beacon*

Journal had pointed out that many of the students at the May 4 rally had not even been on the campus during the weekend.)

More interesting than what Brown said was what he did *not* say. He had no word of explanation for why the guardsmen—firing at a supposedly danger-ous, surging crowd that threatened to seize their weapons—had hit no one closer than 60 feet away and had in fact inflicted death and injuries on persons more than 250 feet away and concentrated in one small area. Would the defendants try to prove that the guardsmen had fired point-blank at hundreds of students, only to miss all of them and hit those in the parking lot?

Part Two

AT LAST, OUR DAY IN COURT

Saturday, May 2. The ROTC Building burns while guardsmen of Troop G watch.
(Wide World)

Sunday, May 3. Student sitdown on Main Street. *(UPI)*

8

Friday and Saturday Nights

▬▬▬

Soon after the trial began we had an alarming session with Judge Young on
the subject of the stipulated facts for the period May 1–3. We had gone along
with the judge's proposal because we did not want the background of disturbances to dominate the trial, and we had conceded everything the defense had
stated about the trashing downtown on Friday and the burning of the ROTC
Building on Saturday, while asserting that none of the plaintiffs had participated in these outrages. At a bench conference that morning we had reminded the judge that, although for three weeks he had had the list of facts
to which both parties had agreed, he had not ruled on them. The judge had
promised to do so following the opening statements.

We expected the stipulations to be adopted after some discussion of the
wording. However, when Fulton and Brown argued against the whole idea of
stipulations, the judge heeded their objections and added some of his own.
Fulton said that if we wanted to introduce testimony concerning Governor
Rhodes' remarks of May 3, to show that they had inflamed the guardsmen,
he was entitled to bring in the events of May 1–3 to show that they too had
affected the guardsmen's thinking. Testimony on the Friday night trashing was
also needed, he argued, to show why the Guard had been summoned.

The judge observed that the mere reading of the facts as stipulated would
prevent the jurors from properly appreciating the events of May 1–3. "They
have got to go back five years and try to reconstruct in their own minds what
the people saw and heard at that time and how they felt about it."

Trying to penetrate the judge's thinking, I argued that if his concern was to insure that the jurors understood the guardsmen's frame of mind, the stipulations would serve the purpose. I pointed out that as the guardsmen had arrived in Kent at around 9 P.M. Saturday, what had happened on Friday night, and on Saturday before they came, had in effect been stipulated to them.

Alloway argued that the governor's May 3 press conference could not be understood without consideration of the events of the two preceding days. Steve Sindell countered with the argument that, with respect to May 1 and 2, the governor had also had no firsthand knowledge, only reports from others.

"Your Honor," Charlie Brown said, "if I may be very brutal about this, with all due respect, they are not doing this to shorten the trial, it is just for their own advantage. They want to preclude us from trying our case the way it should be presented, and I think it is improper."

The judge decided to open the trial to all testimony regarding the background events; in addition to the reasons the defense had given, he wanted to make the record complete, "so that anybody in the future that wants to take a look can see . . . what was the best that our system could do toward producing the truth."

He tempered this ruling with the remark that his decision was not final and that he would have several weeks to ponder the problem before the defense started presenting its case. Despite this expectation, however, his decision had immediate consequences.

We began to present our case on Wednesday afternoon. Our first objective was to show that excessive force had been used and then to move on to its causes. If there had been one cause, our task would have been simpler. If, for example, excessive force had resulted from Governor Rhodes' orders to disperse all gatherings and his endorsement of the "use whatever force is necessary" principle, he would have been the only defendant.

Unfortunately, we were unable to assign the blame to any one person. It seemed to us that several different decisions had led to the shootings. True, Rhodes had ordered the Guard to Kent and told them to break up rallies. But it was Del Corso's policy that had caused the guardsmen to be there with loaded weapons and had authorized the firing of them to disperse crowds.

(In a federal case initiated by Geltner on the issue of Ohio National Guard practices at Kent State, *Gilligan* v. *Morgan,* the Court of Appeals had asked the district court to decide:

> Was there and is there a pattern of weaponry training and orders in the Ohio National Guard which singly or together *require or make inevitable* the use of fatal force in suppressing civilian disorders when the total circumstances at the critical

time are such that non-lethal force would suffice to restore order and the use of lethal force is not reasonably necessary?)

The case had eventually been lost in the Supreme Court. But the Court had indicated in its positive ruling on our civil suit that this was a question a jury could be expected to answer.

Then there was General Canterbury, who had issued the order to disperse the noon rally before he saw it. Was he required to do so under his orders from Rhodes and Del Corso? Or was he acting on his own responsibility?

Then there were the other officers in the field. Had they controlled their men sufficiently? Had one of them issued an order to shoot?

There were also the enlisted men. Had they been ordered to shoot or had they fired of their own accord?

If we could get some witnesses to open up, we could be more definite in fixing blame. But until somebody talked, all we could do was to go after everyone who might have contributed to the shootings.

We had given a lot of thought to choosing our first witness. We wanted to give the jury an overall picture of the events of May 4, and we had agreed that a photographer who had been there from beginning to end, and whose eyewitness testimony would be supported by his photographs, would be best. We settled on a former student, Howard Ruffner, a bearded, muscular Air Force veteran who now worked for the public relations department of Ohio Bell Telephone. Ruffner's coverage was the most complete, and he would make a good impression on the jury. He had the quiet manner of a mature person who weighed his words carefully.

Ruffner was one of a number of Kent State students who had done a remarkable job of capturing the events of May 4 on film. There had been many photographers on the campus that day with far more experience, from the major networks and newspapers, but most of the significant on-the-spot photographs were taken by Ruffner, John Filo, John Darnell, Beverly Knowles, and other students. Ruffner had been standing in front of Taylor Hall, near John Cleary. When the shooting broke out, he dropped to the ground, trying to protect his cameras with his body. Later, when he viewed the prints made from his negatives, he was horrified to see that one guardsman had been aiming a rifle at him. So graphic were his photos that seasoned newspaper editors thought they had been faked.

Ruffner had taken ten photographs of the guardsmen moving from the practice field to the crest of Blanket Hill. Much of the case against the guardsmen was wrapped up in these photographs. We projected them on a large screen so that the jurors could see for themselves that no students were near the guardsmen at any time.

Ruffner described the Guard's progress up the hill minute by minute. "My observation would put no student in front of the Guard as they were going up," Ruffner said, "and I don't recall other than a few individual students maybe 150 feet behind them, 200 feet, maybe. . . . The students were still . . . spectators. I witnessed nothing being thrown in the air. I witnessed nothing in the air coming down in the area of the Guard."

Ruffner told how he had climbed the hill to a place between a metal sculpture and the Taylor Hall veranda and heard no announcements from the guardsmen as they reached the top of the hill. The students, he said, were 150 feet from the Pagoda, and some were chanting, " 'Pigs off campus' and the like." He said that he had no reason to believe that the guardsmen's weapons were loaded and that he was the closest student to them. "[I] paralleled their walk in. I don't recall anybody between me and the Guard as they began their final turn."

"How close were you, Mr. Ruffner?" Sindell asked.

"Between 80 and 100 feet from the Guard, to their right." He added that there were not enough students to his left, further from the Guard, to attract his attention.

"What if anything at this point in time did you observe the students doing?"

"The students to my right, the students behind me, there was no missiles coming over my head, there was nothing falling in front of me. Some vocal noises coming from the group, but that's about all, mostly watching."

"How much time elapsed from the time as depicted in the photograph, as you recall it, until the time when you heard a discharge of weapons?"

"Five to eight seconds at this point in time. The Guard reaches the crest of the hill, turns and fires, just a few steps."

Sindell projected a photograph taken by Ruffner as the shots rang out.

"What kind of sound did you hear . . . ?" he asked.

"I heard rifle fire. . . ."

"Where was the rifle fire coming from?"

"From the area between the Pagoda and Taylor Hall."

"Was it coming from any other area?"

"Not to my knowledge, no."

"At this point in time who was the closest student that you could observe?"

"Again, myself. No one between the Guard and myself."

"This would be what distance?"

"Eighty to ninety feet."

Burt Fulton now cross-examined Ruffner. I had heard from our lawyers that he was fast on his feet and had a temper. His style, I was soon to observe, was quite different from mine. I cultivated a poker face and a dispassionate manner. I never let a judge see that I am annoyed by an adverse ruling, and I never permit opposing counsel to tell by my expression that he has scored a telling blow. The last thing I want is to give the jury a clue to my emotions.

Not so Burt Fulton. He always looked miserable when testimony ran in a direction he did not like. He appeared to find it inconceivable that any adverse ruling could be correct or that any testimony that hurt his case could be true.

In line with their objective of making the plaintiffs guilty by association with the building burners and window smashers, the defense put in evidence sixty-nine additional photographs, forty-five of which had nothing to do with May 4. The twenty-four photographs taken on May 4 were of students rather than guardsmen, and they depicted some of the plaintiffs: Jeff Miller giving the guardsmen the finger, Allison Krause by the Pagoda, Alan Canfora waving a black flag. The famous John Filo photograph of the fourteen-year-old girl wailing over Jeff Miller's body was used to buttress Fulton's claim that outside agitators had been on the Kent campus!

The other forty-five photographs dealt with the burying of the Constitution; a Black United Students rally on May 1; the burning of the ROTC Building on May 2; damaged buildings on campus (the ROTC hulk, two damaged sheds, a smashed light pole, a broken fence); and scenes of the student Sunday night sitdown in Main Street.

When Fulton announced that he was going to have these photographs projected for the jury, I objected that they were irrelevant unless it would be shown that the plaintiffs in the case "actively participated in any of these acts."

We succeeded in keeping all but ten from being projected, but not in excluding them as evidence. Judge Young accepted Fulton's argument that the photographs dealt with "allegations of the plaintiffs that the Guard shouldn't have been on campus." Yet we had never argued that the Guard should not have been on the campus.

The defense's emphasis on testimony concerning the events of May 1, 2, and 3 was looming as a bigger and bigger problem. It appeared that they were going to bring in those disturbances every chance they got. Fulton did so with my next witness by a very roundabout route.

I put a journalism professor named Charles Brill on the stand to testify about the shootings he had witnessed in front of his office in Taylor Hall. Fulton, however, ignored this testimony and instead used the fact that Brill had driven his wife downtown on May 2 as a pretext to ask him to describe the damage that was still visible from the night before. We could not believe that Judge Young had anticipated this harping on the background disturbances when he decided against the stipulations. We therefore moved that such questions be excluded in the future.

When we met in the judge's chambers a few hours later for his ruling, he explained that the admission of testimony concerning events prior to May 4 represented two distinct matters. Following my suggestion that the events that had occurred before the Guard arrived on Saturday night were in a different category from those that occurred afterward, he said that the events that followed the Guard's arrival had to be admitted as bearing on their state of mind. On the other hand, he said, the events that preceded their arrival were relevant only to the governor's decision to call the Guard to Kent. Therefore they could be excluded, he said, if we agreed that the Guard had been "properly called to Kent."

Since we were willing to concede that the Guard should have been called, and questioned only whether the procedures the governor had used were "proper," the judge's stance was puzzling. I told the judge for at least the fifth time that we condemned the acts of violence of May 1 and 2, and I repeated that we did "not quarrel with the right of Governor Rhodes to call up the National Guard. . . . We did, however, question the . . . unlawful manner in which he called up the Guard. Specifically, my colleagues and I referred to the fact that he gave the National Guard broad, unlimited, and unlawful powers based upon the manner of the callup. . . . He did not proclaim martial law, he did that a day after the shootings." In his public speech on Sunday, I argued, he inflamed the guardsmen, totally abandoning his function as commander-in-chief and abdicating his responsibility. He had even claimed, I said, not to know that the guardsmen carried loaded weapons.

"We are conceding that the governor had a right to call up the National Guard," I said. How could I say it more plainly? I added that if the judge did not restrain the defendants' repeated presentation of the incidents prior to May 4, there would be an invasion of the right to a fair trial.

The judge, however, insisted on allowing all the testimony regarding the events prior to the arrival of the Guard. His message in effect was: *If you want to keep out the events that preceded the arrival of the Guard on Saturday night, drop your case against Governor Rhodes.*

We did not accept the judge's implicit offer. The price was too high. In our view, Rhodes was the principal defendant in the case, the commander-in-chief without whose incendiary pronouncements and other acts and omissions the shootings could not have happened.

9

It Speaks For Itself

During the next few weeks we put some of our best witnesses on the stand, continuing the line of testimony we had begun with Howard Ruffner. We called two other photographers, John Filo and John Darnell; a former student, Bill Montgomery; Dean Kahler, the most grievously wounded of the living victims; Joseph Lewis, another seriously injured student; and the man who shot him, Sergeant Lawrence Shafer.

John Darnell had used his last frame on Blanket Hill to take the famous *Life* magazine picture of Sergeant Myron Pryor leveling his pistol. When Nelson Karl wished to use the projector to show this and other of Darnell's photographs to the jury, Charlie Brown objected that it was unfair of us to highlight a few of the thousands of photographs. The objection was sustained.

I didn't pay much attention to the judge's ruling because I assumed that I would still be able to walk over to the jury box and show them any photographs that were in evidence. About an hour later, Governor Rhodes' lawyer, Brooke Alloway, showed John Darnell a photograph taken on the Commons before the dispersal and asked him if it included Sandra Scheuer. Since Alloway now could not use the projector either, the jury had no way of knowing what Sandra (if it was she) was doing. The suggestion that the photograph showed something of great significance was heightened by Alloway's request that Darnell, who had attended Youngstown High School with Sandra, encircle her face with a red marker.

On my redirect examination, I thought I'd clarify this matter for the jury by asking Darnell what Sandra was doing in the photograph.

"Just standing there," Darnell replied.

"Objection," Alloway said. "The photograph speaks for itself."

I ignored this at the time, but I was soon to learn that the policy of regarding inanimate objects as articulate, first enunciated by the governor's lawyer, was to prevent us from using one of our most powerful pieces of evidence, the Matson-Frisina letter that banned all demonstrations, "peaceful and otherwise." After Darnell admitted having read it in 1970, I offered it in evidence. The judge asked Fulton if he had any objection.

Neither Fulton nor Brown said anything.

"It will be received," Judge Young said.

At last I thought I would be able to show the jury that what the defense had been calling a university ban on rallies was really an unlawful ban by the governor. "May I read this portion of it at this time, Your Honor?"

"No," Judge Young said. "It will speak for itself. The jury will read it at the proper time."

I was stunned at this obstructive ruling. The jury had heard Fulton describe the letter as a university ban on rallies. Now, holding in my hand the letter stating that "the Governor, through the National Guard, has assumed legal control of the campus and the city of Kent," I was not allowed to correct the misinformation.

First articulate photographs, now articulate documents! In all my years of practice I had never run into such a barrier. I had never heard of a judge's preventing a jury from seeing photographs or hearing the contents of documents already received in evidence, until the end of a trial. In a long case this delay would prevent the jury from judging the relationship between events as they were narrated and the documents and photographs that were meant to confirm or contradict the testimony.

Since Judge Young also prohibited the showing of the photographs to the jury, I developed a poor substitute technique to handle the problem. While questioning witnesses about events depicted in the photos, I rested the photos on the witness box, facing them on an angle toward the jury. The most important photos were enlargements two feet high, and therefore visible, although not in clear detail, to the jury ten to twenty feet away.

The testimony of three early witnesses, Darnell, John Filo, and Harry Montgomery, all had a bearing, among other things, on the case against Sergeant Pryor—if not as a central figure, in Peter Davies' terms, at least as a shooter. Like Howard Ruffner, Filo had been in the line of fire, but about a hundred feet farther down the hill, near the end of Taylor Hall. He testified that he saw smoke and the recoil as Pryor fired his .45 "at random, at a rapid rate."

Another former Kent student, Ohio Bell Telephone lineman Harry William Montgomery, had had a clear view of Sergeant Pryor's actions on the hill. He was well qualified to describe what he had seen, as he was a wounded Marine veteran of Vietnam. On May 4, 1970, he had followed the guardsmen down the hill to the practice field and back up again; Filo's photos showed Montgomery in the foreground as the guardsmen marched up to the Pagoda. He was quoted in James Michener's book on Kent State as saying he believed that the guardsmen had been militarily foolish in marching down to the cul-de-sac in the practice field after having completed their mission of dispersing the crowd. More important, he had told the FBI that he had seen Sergeant Pryor tap several other guardsmen on the backside just before they had turned around and fired.

Montgomery had been standing on the grass about ten feet in front of the metal sculpture, holding his fiancée's hand. "I was standing there watching the Guard go up the hill," he said, "and I saw one man that was hanging behind was carrying a .45 pistol. . . . I saw him with his right hand tapping . . . the guardsmen. He was up there close to them, behind them. . . ."

"How many guardsmen did he tap?"

"Three, four, in there."

"Then what happened?"

"Then he turned, he was the first one to turn. He turned and he fired."

"With what?"

"A .45 pistol."

"What hand?"

"He had it in his left hand."

"What did the other men do?"

"Almost simultaneously, the men that were directly in front of him, seemingly he had communications with, turned and began firing."

"With what?"

"Their rifles."

"Where?"

"Down the hill toward the students."

"Who fired the first shot, if you can tell us, which person?"

"Like I said, the man with the .45 pistol fired the first shot."

"Did you hear the sound of the firearm when it was discharged?"

"There was one shot, and immediately there was a volley. And, yes, I saw the recoil of the pistol."

I tried to get Montgomery to testify that the Darnell photo showed the exposed barrel of Pryor's pistol, indicating either that the weapon was being fired or that it was in the position it assumed after all its rounds had been fired,

Monday, May 4, the students on the Commons, before being ordered to disperse.
(Valley Daily News)

A few minutes later, tear gas has been fired and the guardsmen have started their advance. In the center, leaving the Commons with a folder in his left hand, is William Schroeder. *(Valley Daily News)*

Driven from the Commons, students reassemble between Taylor and Johnson halls. *(Howard E. Ruffner)*

Guardsmen, having dispersed the students between Taylor and Johnson halls, approach the Pagoda. The tall girl under the Pagoda is Allison Krause. *(Howard E. Ruffner)*

The practice field: Alan Canfora taunts kneeling guardsmen with his flag.
(Valley Daily News)

The guardsmen ascend Blanket Hill. *(UPI)*

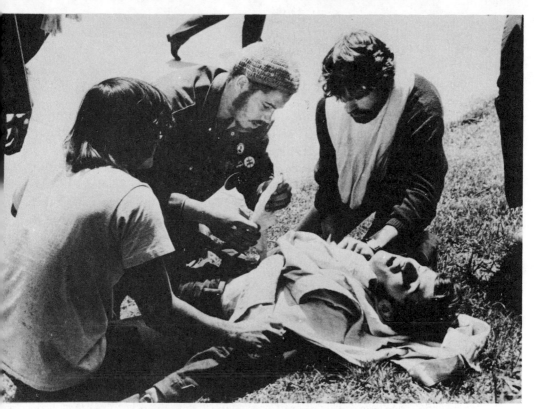

John Cleary, shot in the chest while advancing the film in his camera. *(UPI)*

Scott MacKenzie was more than 700 feet from the guardsmen when shot. *(UPI)*

but the judge once again cut me off on the grounds that the picture spoke for itself.

"I have repeatedly told counsel I will not let people testify about what they think the photographs show," he told me. "The jury can look at the photographs and the jury will determine what the photographs show."

This became policy for the remainder of the trial. The jury was in the same position with regard to the photographs as the gamblers in the Damon Runyon story were with respect to the dice that Big Julie rolled in his hat, calling the results without showing the dice to anyone. The jury saw photographs being handed to witnesses and had no way of telling what the details of the photographs showed. It was true, as Judge Young said, that they would get to see all the photographs at the end of the trial and would be able to examine them in the jury room. But how could they then judge the significance of hundreds of photographs after hearing weeks of testimony during which they were not even permitted to take notes?

Since the photographs supported our version of what had occurred before and during the shootings on May 4 and not the defense version, this policy seriously hurt our case.

The Dean Kahler who rolled his wheelchair up beside the witness stand on Wednesday afternoon, June 4, 1975, bore little resemblance to the young man who had been gunned down on the Kent campus five years before. He wore a long General Custer mustache, shaggy hair, and an air of dark, brooding intensity. For four years, ever since returning to Kent State in the spring of 1971, he had been struggling to complete his education. He had changed his goals several times, from political science to history to sociology, searching for explanations of what had happened to him on the campus of his college.

He had followed the jury selection process with great interest. When the jurors were finally seated and he had studied their faces, it came to him that they would never understand him or any of the plaintiffs. They weren't seeking answers; they looked like the guardsmen and their wives. He had suddenly felt physically ill and had to leave the courtroom.

The defense strategy with Dean was to counteract any sympathy that his appearance in a wheelchair and his demeanor might arouse in the jury. The defense introduced photographs showing Dean sitting down in Main Street on Sunday night with the other students, walking among the demonstrators at noon on Monday, and, later, jogging on the grass at the far end of the parking lot before he was shot. The defense also unleashed the four-letter words it had been so diffident about repeating in the courtroom by asking him about his participation in the Sunday night march on the president's house.

"At that time obscenities and chants were made?"

"I heard chants. I didn't hear any obscenities . . . at that time."

Fulton asked him if he had "heard the one, two, three, four business," Sunday night.

"Yes, I did."

"You heard the 'One, two, three, four, we don't want your f-u-c-k-i-n-g war'?"

"Yes, I did."

"And you, yourself, made some of those chants, didn't you?"

"Yes, I did."

That's why my boy got shot, John Kahler said to himself, because he said "f-u-c-k-i-n-g" to a bunch of weekend warriors. Kahler was sitting next to his wife in the front row of the spectators' seats. On the other side of Elaine Kahler sat Florence Schroeder and Elizabeth Lewis. Of the mothers, Florence was the most knowledgeable about Kent State. She had read everything. As she told Elaine Kahler, "I don't have my Bill to tell me what happened." The three glanced at Fulton, conveying their disapproval.

"And when you threw the stones, were you angry?"

"I was frustrated, I was upset," Dean replied. "I was in a situation where I had come to discuss a situation or an issue peacefully, calmly, and in a rational manner, as we had been told to in my first five weeks of college education, and it was being denied me on a college campus. I felt this wasn't the way things should be handled."

10

The Man Who Shot
Joseph Lewis, Jr.

<hr>

Peter Davies and Galen Keller worked until half past four one morning to finish an analysis of the twenty-eight guardsmen who had fired from the hill. They huddled over Ohio Highway Patrol reports, National Guard firing incident reports, FBI and Ohio Bureau of Criminal Information statements, grand jury testimony, and the files of the Kent State University Police, assembling all the information on each of the twenty-eight shooters: where he had stood and aimed, what he said he had done on Blanket Hill, and what others said he had done. Of the twenty-eight, only eight—those indicted by the federal grand jury—had admitted firing in the direction of the students, and of the eight, only Sergeant Lawrence Shafer had admitted shooting anyone. He had told the state grand jury that he had deliberately shot Joseph Lewis, Jr., who, he said, was only 35 or 40 feet away and rushing at him.

Shafer was a slender, medium-sized, rather sad-looking man with a reddish complexion, thinning hair, a high forehead, a slightly drooping mustache, and rimless glasses, who worked for the State Highway Department. I had observed him a couple of times in the hallway outside the courtroom, apart from the other defendants, pacing nervously. He looked like a loner.

He did not appear dangerous on the stand. Yet on Sunday night, May 3, 1970, he had struck the driver of a car on the chin with the butt of his rifle, and on Monday he had almost killed Joe Lewis. He claimed to have had his left arm injured by an object thrown at him on the practice field, but there was no record that he had ever received treatment for such an injury.

A photograph taken of Joe Lewis a moment before he was shot showed that

Joe was not moving and that there was not a single person on the slope of the hill between him and the guardsmen. Using this photograph, the FBI had determined that the distance between Joe and the men with the rifles was 60 feet. The first shot he heard, Shafer said, had been fired on his left at the top of the hill while his back was still to the practice field. As he had been close to Taylor Hall, that meant the sound came from the direction of the Pagoda. He admitted he had no fears of anyone ahead of him or on his left, where the bulk of the other guardsmen were, or on his right, along Taylor Hall.

I then asked him what he had seen when he turned around, particularly between himself and the walk that led from Taylor Hall about 50 feet away. (It was behind this walk, we knew, that Lewis had been standing.)

Shafer said he had seen "quite a number there . . . approximately a hundred."

I asked him if he was referring to people up on the terrace, behind the metal railing.

"No," he replied, he meant on the hill, where, he insisted, the closest person was 45 feet away and "a hundred people" were bunched together.

He had fired, he said, after the man on his right fired.

"Did he panic you into firing?" I asked.

"No, sir."

Shafer agreed that two seconds was a fair estimate of the time between the first shot he heard and when he started shooting. It had been the first time he had ever fired an M-1. We knew that a number of men in Troop G had never fired the weapon before; many of them had no conception of the weapon's awesome power. There were reports of their wandering about the campus afterward, shaking their heads at the holes their bullets had made in the metal sculpture and in trees.

"When you turned around," I said, "you saw a young man ahead of you, did you not, in the direction where your rifle was then pointing?"

"My weapon was pointed in the air, sir."

"I see. Totally, you fired five rounds or five shots, is that true?"

"Yes, sir."

I was then able to bring out that he had had two clips of ammunition with him that morning. One was a holdover from his service during a wildcat Teamsters strike during the three days preceding the call to Kent; the other had been picked up from a box of ammunition that the Guard had left open at the corner of Lincoln and Main streets on Saturday night.

I then asked him to take an M-1 from the rifle rack along the wall and demonstrate how he had flicked off the safety switch before firing. The switch,

A few seconds before turning and firing, the guardsmen reach the Pagoda.
(Valley Daily News)

The jurors were not allowed to see this photograph at the time Sergeant Shafer and other guardsmen testified that they were threatened by a mob of students rushing them from 20 or 30 feet away. Joe Lewis, Jr., with his finger upraised (under arrow) stands 60 feet from the guardsmen. No one is between him and the guardsmen, nor is anyone else on the grass for some distance farther down the hill. The guardsmen have turned and begun shooting: hence the panic on the verandah. *(Akron Beacon Journal)*

located in front of the trigger guard, must be deliberately pushed forward before the weapon can be fired.

Shafer released the safety and pulled the trigger. The click echoed through the courtroom.

He said that after firing his first shot in the air he had seen Joe Lewis with his middle finger raised.

"Then I observed the individual coming toward us, and I fired in that direction . . . I believe I estimated his distance as between 35 and 40 feet," he said.

Shafer's story that Lewis was rushing him, closing in from a distance of 35 or 40 feet, and that he was among a hundred others, was refuted by the photograph in my hand. But the judge's ruling would not allow me to show it to the jury. When I showed it to Shafer and asked him to show me the hundred rushing students, Brown objected, saying that it "only show[ed] the terrace" and that the photograph spoke for itself.

Shafer admitted that Joe Lewis had been the closest person to him and that he had previously testified that he had shot in his direction because he had been a danger to his life.

"Because of the way he was coming up, sir, yes, sir."

"Was he moving or standing still?"

"He was moving toward us, sir."

(The photograph showed that Lewis was standing still.)

"Did you see anything in his hands?"

"One hand was upraised giving the finger; the other hand was to his side and partially hidden behind him."

"Show us what he was doing with his finger."

"He was doing this." Shafer put up his right hand, elevating the middle finger.

"Did it present a danger to your life?"

"Not that hand."

"Had you been taught that when self-defense is to be invoked for your own safety it must be based upon reasonable interpretation of the events taking place before you?"

"Yes, sir."

"Well, what instruction did you ever get as to when it is justified to take human life with a firearm?"

"When fired upon, return fire, sir."

"Was this person in whose direction you were pointing when you fired firing upon you?"

"No, sir."

"Had you ever seen that person with a gun in his hand?"

"No, sir."

"A knife?"

"No, sir."

We had learned that the courtroom measured 56 feet from front to back. I pointed out to Shafer that this meant that the "young man in whose direction you fired was . . . four feet further than the length of this courtroom."

I wanted the jury to see just how far from Shafer Joe Lewis had been standing when he was shot, how "dangerous" he had been, so that the only recourse left to Shafer was to shoot him with a copper-jacketed M-1 bullet. I asked Joe Lewis to walk to the back wall and Shafer to pick up a rifle and aim it as he had for his first shot.

Shafer pointed the rifle upward at an angle of about 35 or 40 degrees.

"That's 35, in that area," Fulton said. "Is that fair?" He was walking around, getting into my act.

I agreed that it was fair enough.

I reminded Shafer that he had to release the safety catch when he fired the first shot, about two seconds after he had heard somebody fire on his left.

"How much time did it take for you to get off the second shot after the first shot?"

"Between two and three seconds because the weapon failed to eject, sir." He explained that, although the M-1 was supposed to get rid of the empty shell casing automatically, he had had to eject it manually by pulling the slide back.

"And did that accomplish what you wanted," I said, "namely to get another bullet into the chamber?"

"Yes, sir."

"Because you intended to fire another shot, is that right?"

"I didn't know what I intended to do at that point."

"Show us the position of the rifle as you held it for firing the second shot."

"Something like that." Shafer leveled the weapon.

"And then you pulled the trigger; is that right, sir?"

"Yes."

Shafer tried to deny that he had aimed at Lewis, or that he knew he had hit him, but when I quoted from his FBI report, he admitted, "I did say that the man grabbed his stomach area and fell, but at the same time there was a lot of other firing going on, sir."

I then quoted from his deposition, where he had been more explicit. " 'Then I observed an individual coming toward us with his left hand where he was giving the finger. He had his right hand down to his side partially behind him. I fired at this individual because I felt at that point that, not knowing what he had in his hand, my life was in danger. Then I fired three more rounds in the air.' Is that the answer you gave to that question?" I asked.

Shafer admitted that it was.

"So when you fired at that individual," I said, "you intended to hit that individual, did you not?"

"Yes."

"You knew that he was not armed with a gun at that moment, did you not?"

"No, sir, I did not."

"Had you at any time that day anywhere . . . [seen] anyone other than a national guardsman with a pistol or a rifle or any kind of a firearm?"

"No, sir."

"You felt that this individual with a finger in the air constituted a threat and a danger to your life?"

"Yes, sir."

"And, when you fired at him, was it your intention to hit him with the live bullet that you were firing?"

"Yes, sir."

"And you knew that bullet could kill or cripple; isn't that true, sir?"

"That's true, sir."

"And so when he fell what did you see him doing?"

"I didn't watch him, sir."

"Well, did you see him grabbing at any part of his body as he was falling?"

"When he started to fall I observed him, what appeared, he grabbed his stomach area and fell."

I then read from his FBI statement, in which he had described Joe Lewis as "a white male with long, bushy, sandy-colored hair wearing a blue shirt advance directly at me with one finger upraised in an obscene gesture."

"That was an obscene gesture to you," I asked, "is that it?"

"It's an obscene gesture any place, sir."

"But it's not a life-threatening gesture, is it?"

"No, sir."

"Sort of an act of derision which you don't favor, being addressed in your direction?"

"Doesn't really bother me one way or another."

"It didn't upset you?"

"No, sir."

"Didn't make you angry?"

"No, sir."

"That had nothing to do with you firing at that individual?"

"No, sir."

"All right," I said. "What did?"

This was getting to be too much for Fulton. He stood up and removed his metal-rimmed eyeglasses, revolving them in the air so that the earpieces extended outward.

When I asked Shafer if he could have used his bayonet or rifle butt on Lewis instead of shooting him, he maintained that his injured arm kept him from doing so, even though it did not prevent him from holding the rifle to his shoulder in firing position.

I then got Shafer to testify about the manner in which his weapon had been checked after the shooting. Shafer said that a highway patrolman out of his presence had cleared his M-1 and given him the three unspent shells that he had later handed in. There was no record that he had handed in the second clip, which he had carried in his ammunition pouch; that meant there was no way of knowing that he had not fired thirteen shots rather than five.

Interestingly, the firing incident report that Shafer wrote at six o'clock Monday evening on instructions from Sergeant Pryor made no mention that his life had been in danger, that he had fired in self-defense. It gave no reason for the shooting. I was unable to read it to the jury, however, for after I had put it in evidence, the judge and Fulton again cited the articulate evidence rule.

"It is in evidence," Judge Young explained.

"It is in evidence," Fulton repeated. "It speaks for itself."

"It speaks for itself," Judge Young said. "No need to read it"—thereby converting evidence into nonevidence. It was a device that George Orwell would have appreciated, one similar to that of the "memory hole" in *1984.* Presumably, records were remembered by the "hole" in the process of being destroyed. Evidence that "spoke for itself" disappeared, upon being accepted as evidence, into an "evidence hole."

I asked the judge how the jury would be able to relate the report to Shafer's testimony if they wouldn't see it until the conclusion of the trial.

"There isn't any need for them to know it until the conclusion of the case," Judge Young replied.

Betty Lewis thought Shafer was sly. She had been attending the trial almost daily out of a sense of duty toward her son, hoping to demonstrate to him her faith that justice would prevail. She and her husband, a lumber salesman, deeply regretted not having urged Joe to accept a scholarship to Notre Dame. If he had gone there in 1969, he would never have been shot.

Betty got the bad news late that Monday afternoon. She had been waiting
at their home outside Massillon for her husband to come with the car, so that

she and her sister could drive her father to the hospital. At five her sister, a nun, telephoned. She said she was glad Betty was so calm.

"Why shouldn't I be calm?" Betty asked.

"Don't you know your son Joe's been shot?"

Betty found this difficult to believe. A neighbor had told her earlier about the shootings, but the news hadn't worried her. She had seen Joseph the previous afternoon at Kent, when she and her husband had dropped off a package of bread, meatballs, and fruit—something they often did on Sundays because the campus cafeterias were closed.

When the Lewises got to Robinson Memorial Hospital, they were taken to the intensive care ward. More than fifteen feet of Joe's intestines had been removed, and peritonitis was to be expected. The surgeon was pessimistic. It wasn't until they spotted the bandage on Joseph's ankle that they knew he had been shot twice.

On Wednesday Joseph's eyelids flickered. He opened one eye and looked at his parents.

"What did you do, Joe?" Betty Lewis asked.

Her son's eyes closed.

Joseph, Jr., the oldest of seven children, had turned eighteen on August 6, 1969, nine months before he was shot. He had paid for his schooling at Kent State with his earnings from the post office, where he worked during vacations. Joseph loved Kent State. He was fascinated by anthropology, particularly the idea that morals were relative. He had never had such freedom; he had even hitchhiked east to New Jersey and, in late February, south to the Gulf of Mexico, where he picked up on a beach a wave-smoothed stone as a talisman.

On Friday night, May 1, Joseph had remained on campus. Saturday evening he had been on the fringes of the crowd that threw rocks at the ROTC Building. When he left with his girlfriend, Sue Tardiff, to follow the crowd, the building was not yet on fire. As they proceeded along Main Street toward President White's house, he saw those in the lead setting trash cans on fire. Others were dragging a big air compressor onto the road when National Guard trucks and jeeps appeared behind them, coming from the direction of Ravenna, carrying men in helmets with guns between their knees.

The next thing he knew there was tear gas and the crowd was breaking up and running. Joseph and Sue ran to Johnson Hall.

Watching the blazing ROTC Building from a friend's room gave him a sick feeling. Later, sitting in his room, telling Sue how he felt about crazy destructiveness, his telephone rang. It was his parents, warning him to be careful. Joseph promised to heed their advice.

Sunday morning the guardsmen were everywhere. That afternoon his par-

ents dropped off the food. That night he was talking to a graduate counselor outside Johnson Hall when a crowd of screaming students approached, pursued by guardsmen with bayonets and helicopters with flashing lights. He ran with them into the dormitory and saw a steel bayonet thrust deep into the door.

Joseph decided he would attend the Monday noon rally protesting the presence of the Guard. He wanted to be there, to add his presence, but he didn't approve of mass behavior, of chanting and waving fists. He was a party of one.

When the jeep appeared and he heard the voice through the bullhorn, "This is an illegal assembly. Return to your dorms," he felt a knot in the pit of his stomach. Rocks were thrown at the jeep. He saw one the size of a baseball bounce off a rear tire before the jeep drove away to return to the guardsmen lined up in front of the remains of the ROTC Building. Some of the guardsmen stepped forward, carrying weapons; there were popping sounds, and tear-gas canisters fell on the grass. The wind blew the white smoke away across the Commons. Some of the students ran out, picked up the canisters, and threw them back toward the guardsmen. There were cheers.

More tear gas came, closer now, and the guardsmen moved in a long line, abreast of one another, toward the students. Joseph stayed at the edge of the dispersing crowd. He watched the guardsmen as they marched with rifles and fixed bayonets, and he saw the drama on the practice field, the guardsmen kneeling and pointing rifles in the direction of Prentice Hall and the hill. He saw students in the parking lot run forward and hurl stones. One student picked up a stone and threw it from the hill. "Don't be an idiot," Joseph said.

The guardsmen were milling around. He thought a couple of shots were fired in the air. Students, scattered on the hillside near Joseph, were jeering and laughing.

As the guardsmen moved up the hill from the practice field, Joseph moved across the hill to Taylor Hall. He was next to the sidewalk, 60 feet from the corner of the building, when the guardsmen passed. He gave them the finger, and several of them looked at him through the goggles of their gas masks. This is from me to you, he thought.

The guardsmen wheeled. Joseph thought the move was a threat, like the leveling of guns on the practice field. He continued to give the troops the finger, looking down the barrels of several rifles as he did so. He interpreted the sound of gunshots as the firing of blanks.

My God, he told himself when grass kicked up, there really are bullets. Then he felt a blow in the abdomen.

A young man on his left and a young woman on his right were trying to help him. As he was lifted into the ambulance, he opened his eyes. A friend from Central Catholic High School waved, and Joseph waved back. John Cleary, riding in the same ambulance, screamed every time the ambulance lunged.

Joseph, thinking he was dying, felt calm in the emergency room as his clothes were cut away.

As he lay in bed in the room he shared with Dean Kahler, Joseph kept thinking. He could not conceive that anyone had shot him on purpose. He told himself it had been a warning shot that had gone astray. It was easier to think that it was an accident than that someone had wanted to hurt him. But was the bullet through his ankle an accident? Could he have been shot twice by accident?

Shortly after the shooting Betty's youngest child, five-year-old Jimmy, told his sister Mary that he had been playing National Guard at kindergarten.

"How do you do that?" Mary asked.

"The soldiers shoot the students," Jimmy replied.

As their son slowly improved, the Lewises were left with the problem of reconciling what had happened to Joseph with their expectations of the world. They wavered back and forth, thinking at times that their son was withholding information, at other times that there was something wrong with Ohio and the nation. The two ideas were equally repellent.

Nothing would ever be the same. Friends—and most of their relatives— thought that Joseph had disgraced himself and that the rest of the Lewises shared his guilt. Joseph never again settled down to college studies; eventually he became a factory worker in Oregon.

I had been outside the courtroom preparing some other witnesses during Brown's cross-examination of Joe Lewis. When I returned and Galen Keller whispered that Joe Lewis had been questioned about his opposition to the Vietnam War, I was incredulous. I couldn't believe that any judge would permit such blatantly prejudicial questions.

Later, in the plaintiffs' room in the courthouse, Robbie Stamps told me, "The judge is strangling us. Don't you see?"

Several of the plaintiffs wanted me to defy the judge and take the photos to the jury.

"Those defendants are lying and getting away with it," Robbie said, "because they know the judge isn't going to let you show what's in the pictures."

"You want me to get cited for contempt?" I asked.

"Would he do that?" Robbie asked.

"He can clap me in jail for not following his orders," I said.

"If he puts you in the can," Robbie said, "then everyone will know there's something wrong here."

"Maybe," I said, "but that's not the way you win a case."

"You can't win anyway," someone else said.

"If I didn't think I could win," I said, "I wouldn't be here."

11

The Steel Helmet

████

A procession of former enlisted guardsmen, ranging in age from their mid-twenties to their mid-thirties—truck drivers, salesmen, welders, draughtsmen, butchers, forklift operators—in sport shirts or business suits that were far removed from the awesome helmets, gas masks, and green fatigues of May 1970, took the stand to deliver testimony that was, for the most part, repetitious. When we examined them, they uniformly claimed to have been fearful of being overrun by hundreds of students closing in from 30 feet away. And their lawyers drew from them descriptions of their suffering, in hot gas masks that obscured their vision, as they underwent rock barrages and were terrified by the threatening shouts and actions of the students.

There were some exceptions. Lloyd Thomas of Troop G testified that he could not say rocks were falling when the shooting started, that there had been no need to shoot, and that the guardsmen had continued firing for seven or eight seconds at retreating students. James Farris, a member of Company A who had inadvertently wandered into the middle of Troop G during the hill climb, admitted the accuracy of the Joe Lewis photograph, said that he had seen no more than three or four students in front of him, that they had been standing still, and that not only had none of them carried rocks, he hadn't seen any from the time he left the football field.

First Sergeant Myron Pryor of Troop G, a middle-aged, full-time guardsman, denied firing his pistol either on the practice field (as another guardsman, Sergeant Barry Morris, had stated) or on Blanket Hill, despite the suggestiveness of some photographs (one of which revealed the barrel projecting beyond the slide, a position it assumes either when firing or when all its rounds have been fired) and despite the testimony of several student witnesses, some of whom had served in the military and who claimed to have seen the .45 recoil as Pryor squeezed the trigger.

"When you say you saw the men turn," I asked Pryor, "you turned at the same time?"

"Yes, sir."

"You mean you were playing follow the leader to men who were under your command and under your orders?" I asked.

"I did not give any orders there, sir."

"Were you in full possession of your faculties then?"

"Yes, sir, I was."

I asked Pryor what he did with the pistol.

"I pointed it, sir."

"Pointed it where?"

"At no one in particular. There was a tree, I remember there was a tree in front of me. I was just pointing it."

"Anybody order you to point it?" I asked.

"No, sir."

"Did that on your own?"

"I did, sir."

"Did you point it before you saw other men pointing any firearms?" This was important because Major Harry Jones had stated in his deposition that pointing a pistol could be interpreted as a hand signal to fire.

"I couldn't tell if they were pointing or not, sir. My back was to them."

"And the shots that you heard came from right nearby where you are on that line of men; is that right?"

"Yes, sir, it came from behind me."

"Not any distant shots that you heard, right?"

"No, sir. Just what was in my close proximity."

"You had no suspicion that anybody was firing any sniper bullets at your line of men at that time, did you?"

"No, sir."

"When you wheeled around, sir, did you . . . hear shots immediately or did you move forward from the position that you were in when you first wheeled around?"

"I don't remember moving forward, sir."

I had now reached one of the important props of Peter Davies' theory. In studying one of Ruffner's pictures, he had noted that Pryor was standing on a patch of ground where the grass was worn away. In John Darnell's *Life* magazine photograph, presumably taken after Ruffner's photo, he was standing on grass several feet in front of the worn patch. The advance of Pryor and his men several feet closer to the parking lot was an indication of a deliberate attempt to fire at the distant students.

I showed him the two photographs, but I was not permitted to ask him whether they showed the movement because Fulton evoked the "evidence hole" and "articulate photograph" rules.

Pryor testified that he had kept pointing his weapon from about one second after the shooting began until it ended, or for about eleven seconds, and that he knew live rounds were being fired.

Even if Pryor did not shoot, what difference did it really make? The stance of the senior noncom of Troop G, pointing his weapon at the students, appeared to be an invitation to his younger, less experienced subordinates. We would bring out repeatedly that his behavior was contrary to proper practice.

Sergeant James Pierce of Troop G interested us because after the shootings he had told Guard officers that Pryor, while on the practice field, had said, "If they rush us, shoot them." On the witness stand he could no longer remember this, but he could remember having been struck between one and one hundred times by rocks on various parts of his body.

Many of the enlisted men had poor eyesight (one of them, without his glasses, could not even correctly count the fingers I held up a few feet away), and several were poorly trained. One had had no riot control training at all, and another had just finished basic training prior to the May 1 weekend. We dropped our complaints against Farris, who had admitted seeing no danger, and against several other men from Company A who claimed to have fired in the air and not to have been menaced by students.

It was hard to believe that men wearing steel helmets on their heads and gas masks over their faces could at any time have felt seriously threatened by rocks. I was able to demonstrate this when Sergeant Leon Smith of Company A took the stand. Smith had admitted firing three rounds from a 12-gauge shotgun. A big, heavyset man who drove a coal dump truck, he was asked by Brown to put on his helmet liner, helmet, and gas mask in order to demonstrate the impaired perceptions of the guardsmen.

"Can you hear me now?" Brown asked.

It was uncertain whether Smith, inside the gas mask, had replied. "Speak as loudly as you can," Judge Young suggested.

"I said," came Smith's muffled voice, "he is a lot softer than what he was. I can barely hear him."

When it came my turn to question Smith, I reminded him that he had just told the jury that he had been in fear of his life at the time the shooting started.

He agreed that he had.

"The only time you were ever struck that weekend was when a stone struck your shoe, is that right, rolled against your shoe?"

"That is the only time I was struck, that's right."

"Now sir," I said, "will you put on this gas mask and the liner and the helmet." I handed Smith the equipment. "First, do you know what this helmet is made out of?"

"It's called a steel pot. I don't know what it is made out of."

"A steel pot," I repeated. "Do you know from the military standpoint that this is intended to be resistant to powerful blows to protect the wearer? Is that right, sir?"

"To the head area only," Smith replied.

"Sir," I asked, "the gas mask also constituted a protection to the balance of your face, did it not?"

"Can also be used to strangle you, too," Smith replied.

"Sir, I didn't ask you that. Won't you just answer my question? I am trying to be polite to you. Will you put the gas mask and the helmet and liner on again, sir?"

Smith did so. He looked pretty funny sitting there in goggles and helmet, like a giant toad.

"Sir," I said, "I promise I am not going to hurt you. Would you mind stepping down, sir? Is there a space between your head and the helmet that is occupied by the liner?"

"Yes, there is."

I had a large rock in my hand. I suddenly fetched him a resounding blow on the helmet. One of the jurors gasped.

"What happened to the helmet when I struck you just now with the stone?" I asked.

"You just made a sound," Smith replied.

"Made a sound," I repeated. "As a matter of fact, the helmet was rolling with the blow of the stone," I said, "isn't that true?"

"That is right, sir."

I said a little prayer of gratitude. Courtroom demonstrations such as this are always risky, and they can boomerang. If Smith had complained that the blow hurt, Krause and the other clients would have roasted me alive.

After Smith had reseated himself, I had him describe the rest of his equipment—his shirt, his leather belt, his boots. Then I asked him if he had really feared for his life in all that equipment.

"I most certainly did," Smith asserted, his voice still muffled by the mask.

"You did? From what, sir, were you afraid for your life?"

"From the student that was coming at me with the rocks."

"A hundred feet away with a rock in his hand?" I asked.

"That is right. He was ready to throw it at me."

I invited Smith to remove the mask and helmet, remarking on the thickness of the mask's rubber.

He admitted that he had been struck on the helmet before, while on duty, and that it had never hurt him.

"Were you ever struck as hard as this, sir?" This time, I really clouted the helmet, which he was holding in his hand, with all my might.

"Yes," Smith said.

"Did it ever so much as make a dent or a bend in the helmet, sir? Look at it."

Smith examined the helmet. "I can't see any," he said.

Sergeant William Herschler of Company A had reportedly collapsed after the shootings, saying that he had shot two teenagers. We had the depositions of two other defendants stating that he had fired at students and a Justice Department report showing that the M-1 signed out to Herschler had been fired.

However, when we produced the documentary evidence that his weapon had been fired, Herschler testified that after signing his rifle out on April 29 he had made several exchanges of weapons with other guardsmen. He had first, he said, swapped his M-1 for a shotgun, then swapped the shotgun for another M-1, and then exchanged the second M-1 for a third with Ronnie Myers, a guardsman who admitted firing.

In addition to the photographers, we had a number of other nonplaintiff eyewitnesses to the May 4 events, former students and members of the university faculty. Professor Gerald Kamber, a Marine veteran of Iwo Jima, described General Robert Canterbury's aggressive behavior after the shooting, when he threatened to order his men to rush weeping, hysterical students if they did not clear the area of the Commons in five minutes. Kamber testified that it was only Professor Glenn Frank's tearful appeal to the students that prevented more bloodshed.

Deborah Denton told how she had become mixed up in the teargassing and dispersal while on her way across the Commons between classes. Bill Denton told how he had been assaulted by a guardsman while walking Sunday night from one building to another.

The experience of the plaintiffs on the stand was the reverse of that of the guardsmen, with us trying to show them in the best light and Fulton and Brown trying to show them in the worst.

The plaintiffs were a representative group of young men who would have been leading uneventful lives had it not been for the events of May 4. Several had vulnerabilities—which Fulton and Brown, of course, sought to exploit. Doug Wrentmore, dazed and frightened in the hospital after the shootings, had told television newsmen that the students were to blame for the shootings. Tom Grace and his roommate, Alan Canfora, had been members of SDS. Robbie Stamps had written a bitter, antiestablishment letter that had been found in his room during an illegal search of the dormitories several days after the shootings. Several had taken part in antiwar demonstrations.

And when they had nothing else to use, Fulton and Brown could always ask a plaintiff's opinion of Jerry Rubin, who, a couple of weeks before the shooting, had given a speech at Kent in which he was said to have suggested that his generation could liberate itself only by killing its parents.

Donald Scott MacKenzie was a tall, handsome young man who had transferred to Kent State from a small college in Iowa in the fall of 1968 and became an active participant in moratorium marches. On Saturday night, May 2, he went around the campus urging others to go to the Commons, and later he observed the burning of the ROTC Building. Sunday, as he walked on the campus, he sensed that his fairly long hair and wispy beard aroused hostility among the guardsmen. That night, approaching President White's house, he got his first dose of tear gas. Later he took part in the Main Street sit-in.

His memory of what happened on Main Street did not quite coincide with Dean Kahler's. Dean recalled an announcement that the students were violating the curfew while they were waiting for Mayor Satrom. As Scott remembered it, a National Guard officer had told them that the mayor would come if they first cleared the street. In any case, he was chased through the campus.

When his second Monday morning class was canceled because of a bomb scare, he sat on the grass near the tennis courts, north of the Commons, waiting for the noon rally. He kept a good distance between himself and the guardsmen, and as the guardsmen wheeled near the Pagoda he was on a lot behind the Prentice Hall parking lot, heading in their direction.

He thought he saw someone in the front group of guardsmen fire a pistol before a bullet knocked him down. He got to his feet as the barrage continued, ran, and threw himself into a ditch. When the shooting stopped, he got up, frightened at the blood pouring from his neck.

"Help, help, I've been shot, I need help," he shouted, *running toward the tennis courts. Someone drove him to the campus health center a few blocks away, and from there an ambulance soon took him to St. Thomas Hospital in Akron, where he was eventually joined by Jim Russell.*

The bullet had entered Scott MacKenzie's neck an inch and a half from his spine and exited through his cheek, pulverizing a portion of his upper jaw. Dr. Joseph W. Ewing, who operated on him, told reporters that Scott had not been struck by a military bullet—an opinion based on the absence of fragments and the small size of the entry wound. This story was seized upon by the Guard as evidence that weapons other than their own had been fired on the Kent State campus. The Akron Beacon Journal *soon cast doubt on Dr. Ewing's theory by pointing out that he was an old golfing chum of General Del Corso.*

When Scott learned that the FBI had questioned his girlfriend's family about his political beliefs, he ceased expecting justice. He returned to Kent State in the fall and received his degree in June 1971.

Scott MacKenzie had thought a great deal about what had happened and decided that human nature was at fault. He tried to rid himself of bad thoughts through meditation and yoga. He gave the impression of one who had suffered and made his peace with the world.

12

Witch Hunt

———

Steven Sindell had discovered on the list of defense exhibits a reference to a violent letter that had been found in Robbie Stamps' dormitory room shortly after the shootings. Stamps was frightened that it would be used against him when he testified. Mike Geltner thought he could prevent its admission as evidence on the ground that it had been seized during an unlawful search of the dormitories by the Ohio Highway Patrol. A federal suit won by Geltner and the ACLU had condemned the search, but we couldn't be certain that our unpredictable judge would rule out the use in our civil suit of evidence obtained during that search.

Before Stamps took the stand, Geltner brought up the matter with the judge at the bench. In a manner that was becoming increasingly familiar to us, Judge Young waxed eloquent on the importance of Fourth Amendment protections against illegal searches and seizures, but when it came down to Stamps' letter, he left the door open to possible use of the document.

Robbie Stamps had no confidence in the jury. He knew well the thinking of such people. His mother had been born and raised in the Cleveland area, and both of her sisters were convinced that he had done something to deserve being shot; the doctor who ran the TB clinic where his mother worked made jokes about her "hippie" son; and his father, who had been a career Army officer, heard abusive comments from the customers of his auto-leasing agency. Their neighbors in Euclid treated Robbie like a pariah, and despite his excellent qualifications, he was unable to obtain a decent job anywhere in the state. His parents were so disgusted that they were making plans to move to California.

Robbie Stamps, a handsome young man with delicately chiseled features and jet-black hair, about five feet nine inches tall, had been friendly with three of the other victims, Sandy Scheuer, Jeff Miller, and Allison Krause. Perhaps the most intellectual of the living victims, Robbie had graduated summa cum laude from Kent State in the summer of 1972 and then taught Spanish at the University of Hawaii. At the time of the trial he was completing his work at Kent State for a master's degree in sociology.

In May 1970 Robbie Stamps was finishing his sophomore year at Kent State. He spent Saturday, May 2, in his room in Tri-Towers, studying for a mid-term examination. That night he was on the Commons during the attack on the ROTC Building. When he saw flames, he returned to his dormitory.

His first reaction to the presence of the national guardsmen was that they would keep the campus peaceful. He recognized one of the men in uniform as Robert Heffelfinger, his biology laboratory mate, and gave him a sandwich. He sensed that everyone was jittery, even the guardsmen, who stood in doorways with the butts of their rifles resting on the ground, pretending not to hear blaring from windows overhead the raucous, provocative words of the Rolling Stones' "Street Fighting Man."

> *Ev'rywhere I hear the sound of*
> *marching, charging feet, oh boy.*
> *'Cause summer's here and the time is right*
> *for fighting in the street, oh boy.*

Sunday night, with helicopters pulsating overhead, searchlights sweeping, whiffs of tear gas floating on the air, and frightened students begging to gain the shelter of Tri-Towers, he decided that the Guard was making things worse.

Monday morning he walked onto the Commons shortly before noon, carrying his books, a bag of potato chips, and two pretzels, planning to protest the presence of the guardsmen at a safe distance—for, unlike most of the other students, he assumed the guardsmen's weapons were loaded. When a tear-gas canister landed nearby, he went to a washroom in Prentice Hall to bathe his face and his tear-filled eyes in water.

He left Prentice on the parking lot side, intending to return to Tri-Towers before going to a 1:10 psychology class. (Among other members of that class were Allison Krause and her boyfriend, Barry Levine, Jeff Miller, and Bill Schroeder.)

When Robbie reached the parking lot, stones were being thrown at the guardsmen by several students on the practice field. He watched from the

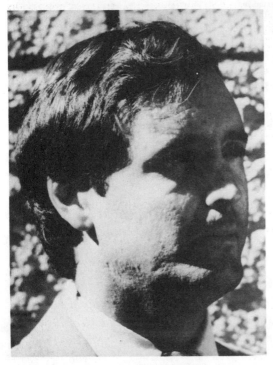

Robert Stamps *(Floyd Stamps)*

Until the summer of 1970, Jan Wrentmore was an ardent supporter of President Nixon. *(James Munves)*

Charlotte and Floyd Stamps moved from Cleveland in disgust. *(James Munves)*

Albert Canfora and his son Alan. Albert lost his seat on the Barberton City Council and the vice presidency of his union local as a result of his son's misfortune. *(UPI)*

Thomas Mark Grace (center, with arm raised), Alan's roommate, a few minutes before he was wounded. *(T. M. Grace)*

back of the lot, and when the guardsmen arrived at the top of the hill, he resumed his walk to the dormitory. He assumed that the incident was over and that the guardsmen were on their way back to the ROTC Building. He had his back to the guardsmen, who were about 600 feet away, and was handing a pretzel to a young woman when a bullet hit him an inch below the belt line and an inch and a half from his spine.

The ambulance that took him to Robinson Memorial Hospital also carried Jeff Miller, Allison Krause, and Barry Levine.

Robbie Stamps got a first look at some of the guardsmen who had fired at him when he testified at the criminal trial in the fall of 1974, and he found them difficult to confront. He couldn't escape the feeling that he had deserved to be shot. He was kept from complete hopelessness by his visits to the psychiatrist he had begun seeing several months after the shootings.

Fulton and Brown zeroed in on Stamps' political beliefs, branching out from peace marches in Washington to rallies for Israel (apparently to show the jury that the plaintiff was Jewish). I had been routinely objecting to all questioning about political beliefs, but when Fulton alluded to the illegally seized letter and the judge allowed Fulton to continue probing the matter, I told the judge that regardless of how he ruled on admissibility, the real issue was that the state of mind or political beliefs of a person who was hundreds of feet from the Guard when he was shot had no relevance to the issues in the case.

The judge replied that the political beliefs of the witness were a legitimate avenue of inquiry because they "may throw light on the witness's credibility."

I could hardly believe my ears. "Sir," I said, ". . . wouldn't there have to be a showing of a criminal conviction or some other aspect that could reflect on the credibility . . . ?" Personal political beliefs, I argued, could not be relevant to the justifiability of the shooting.

"I don't really see it, Judge," I said, "and I don't think it can come in on credibility."

"I think it can," Judge Young said. "I think we have to recognize, palatable or unpalatable as it may be, *this trial involves political issues.* Some writer said that the American people have never been very good at handling political trials, and I suppose maybe we aren't. In modern times we get into them because people no longer use the traditional political processes of our system of government to the extent they did. I can't help those things. But I think this is a proper question. I don't think you have a right to interrupt it."

This was the most revealing statement the judge had yet made. It showed that he had no conception of what this trial was all about. By definition, any civil rights case concerned with the First Amendment right of assembly would involve dissent. What the judge was saying, I believed, was that the First Amendment was unenforceable, that he wouldn't even try to give dissenters a fair trial.

I made a strong objection, stating that to permit such questioning could lead to a miscarriage of justice. "We could have an Al Capone shot down against a wall, and whatever his beliefs are, that would have utterly no relationship to the justifiability of the shooting."

Judge Young stuck to his position, and the question was reread.

"Have you ever made any statement about the police being pigs and having also beaten you?"

"Yes, I have."

"Were you receiving psychiatric care on May 4, 1970?"

This was another outrageous question, but it was allowed.

The question was repeated: "On May 4, 1970, were you under treatment by a psychiatrist?"

Stamps, relishing the situation, waited as the courtroom grew perfectly quiet, until Fulton was almost out of patience.

"No, sir," he replied truthfully.

At the end of the interrogation Brown referred to an unpleasant incident in which someone had smeared blood on the door of Robbie's dormitory room. He wanted to know whether the perpetrators had ever called him a Communist or a Commie sympathizer.

"Yes, sir," Robbie replied, "they did."

Robbie Stamps was disturbed at "being treated like a goddamn guilty party or defendant," as he put it when we conferred in the plaintiffs' room.

"The judge was wrong to allow it," I told him.

I was jumped on by Tom Grace, Alan Canfora, and several of the others. "If they're going to ask us about our political beliefs," Tom said, "you can ask them about their political beliefs. The next time you have one of those trigger pullers from Troop G on the stand, ask him if he favored shooting students and antiwar demonstrators."

"You want me to stoop to their level," I said.

"Fight fire with fire."

"The jury will never buy that," I said. "If the judge is wrong, he won't get away with what he is doing."

"That's what you think."

"There's no question that he's wrong to allow political questioning. We're doing some research to present him with a motion."

"No one ever said this was going to be easy," Reverend John Adams cautioned the young people.

That weekend Geltner and Engdahl drew up a motion to prevent further questioning about political beliefs. They had found a Supreme Court opinion, *Griswold* v. *Connecticut,* that held that "prying into political or social philosophies would be irrelevant to the issues in a case involving invasion of constitutional rights." In addition, they would show that the new federal rules of evidence, scheduled to go into effect on July 1, specifically contradicted the judge's argument that beliefs, principles, or opinions had a bearing on a witness's credibility. The new rules stated that *it was impermissible to inquire into religious beliefs or principles or opinions for the purpose of questioning credibility.*

"What is being done here by defendants' counsel," I told the judge Monday morning, in submitting the motion, "is an attempt to equate . . . holding nonconformist views, if they be such . . . with some theoretical contributory negligence aspect of the case."

I reminded him that every American has a right to hold whatever views he or she pleases, and I requested that he instruct the jury to disregard any political questions and answers they had already heard and, further, that he prohibit any repetition of such matters.

Fulton and Brown had no real argument to offer in reply; the issue was really between us and the judge. All Fulton could do was to insist that he had a right to attack Stamps' credibility, while Brown tried to argue that he had a right to go into "why the plaintiffs were defying the law. . . ."

I pointed out that not a single plaintiff had been shown to have acted contrary to law, and that consequently the defense had no legal basis for going into the broader issues of their motivation.

Judge Young returned to his idea that this was a political trial. Our argument, he said, "that affiliations, beliefs, and opinions on political and social matters have no relevance to any of the substantive issues in this litigation" was contradicted by our own claims with respect to the conduct of some of the defendants.

He was referring, he said, to our claim that Governor Rhodes' involvement in a primary campaign had been a factor in the rhetoric he had employed during the May 3 press conference and in his handling of the National Guard. The judge said that if he granted our motion and kept the defense from questioning the plaintiffs' beliefs, we would also be kept from inquiring into the governor's motivations. Another element in the pattern of protecting Governor Rhodes had emerged. Judge Young had already indicated that we could keep out testimony on the events of Friday night and most of Saturday by dropping Rhodes as a defendant; now he was telling us that we could avoid prejudicial questioning of the plaintiffs by emasculating our case against the governor.

He added that he believed the plaintiffs' motivations were inseparable from their actions. If we were to try to leave out discussion of their motives, he said, "I think we would have to terminate this trial at this point."

I looked at Geltner, and he looked at me.

The judge was now talking as though the plaintiffs were defendants. He went on to equate interest in the mental states of the guardsmen with interest in those of the plaintiffs, telling us that if we were justified in inquiring into the motives of the guardsmen—as to whether or not they were in fear of their lives—the defense lawyers were justified in inquiring into the reasons the plaintiffs had attended a rally or thrown stones.

The judge was legitimizing the defense strategy of using the unpopularity of the demonstrators' ideas as a justification for the shooting.

Judge Young closed by saying that he hoped he would be able to instruct the jury properly, "so I can guide them in using their own commonsense judgment to make and interpret this great distinction between the people's rights to hold beliefs and people's rights to act upon beliefs."

I felt a chill. *The plaintiffs were on trial for their beliefs.* What the judge was doing in the courtroom was as great an affront to civil liberties as what the guardsmen had done on the campus.

During the recess that morning, before Judge Young made his ruling, Robbie Stamps and several of the other plaintiffs had discussed the motion and were heartened to learn that there were laws to protect them against unfair questioning. They were gaining a practical education on our Constitution and legal traditions. Unfortunately, the lessons were not turning out as I had hoped. When we returned to our anteroom with the adverse ruling, for the first time since the trial began I could not look the plaintiffs in the eye.

Dave Engdahl eased my position by telling them we had lost the motion.

"You mean the judge won't stop them?" Alan Canfora asked. "Jesus!"

"Not only won't he stop them," Engdahl said, "he said that your motives are as important as the guardsmen's."

"It's an absolute denial of the Constitution," I said. "You could be the worst criminals in the world, and you would still have a right not to be summarily shot in that situation."

"What are we going to do about it?" Tom Grace asked.

"We're going to go on as we have been," I said, "and see this trial through. I've faced biased judges before, and I've won in spite of them. Just remember, in spite of everything they can do, we are getting the truth across."

The judge had confirmed the worst suspicions of these young men, that they would never get a fair trial, certainly not from him. I had put myself on the line by assuring them that they would. I was beginning to feel that my exhortations to keep the faith sounded to them like whistling in the dark or, worse, that I sounded like an apologist for the system that was destroying them. Were they right? Was I deluding myself? Was I hooked on the system merely because it had worked well for me, bringing me comfort and reputation, and was I now in the grip of something that would chew me up as it had them? As Robbie Stamps said, this wasn't another automobile accident case.

Doug Wrentmore was a tall, well-built young man with light-brown hair and wide-spaced eyes set in a trusting face, the most gentle and soft-spoken of the plaintiffs. His father, a former president of the Kent State Alumni Association, was assistant secretary-treasurer of the Ohio Bell Telephone Company.

> In the spring of 1970 Doug was living in an apartment in a small house on South Water Street, a few blocks west of the campus, with his brother Hal, who had just started his first semester at Kent State five weeks before. Hal was a political activist who in the fall had attended a peace march in Washington despite the objections of his parents.
>
> Doug and Hal stayed out of trouble Friday night. Saturday evening, before driving to a campground on the Lake Erie shore, they took a look at what was happening on campus. They joined the crowd, watched the attempts to burn the ROTC Building, and left shortly afterward, assuming that the fire was out. Leaving town, they passed guardsmen approaching the city from Akron and were astonished to see the sky behind them become bright with flames.
>
> They returned to their Water Street apartment Sunday afternoon to find Kent an occupied city. Heavy military vehicles passing by made the house shake. That night, noting the searchlights and helicopters at the campus, and in defiance of the eight o'clock town curfew, Doug, Hal, and some friends walked to the campus to see what was going on. When they reached Lincoln Street, they saw students sitting down in Main Street and guardsmen with guns and bayonets in the shadows of the trees on campus, where the students could not see them. Doug and his friends quickly turned and went home.
>
> On Monday Doug decided to skip his 12:05 American literature class and attend the noon rally. He had made an arrangement to meet Hal and two friends in front of the Student Union, at the foot of the Commons, near the ROTC Building. Hal was not there, and Doug decided to look for him near

the Victory Bell. Because he didn't want to cross the Commons between the Guard and the students, he walked around behind the ROTC Building and came out on the hill near Johnson Hall. He still could not find Hal, but he stayed there as the jeep appeared and the students were dispersed with tear gas. After the guardsmen had passed and gone down to the practice field, he slowly approached them.

Several students were throwing rocks from the Prentice Hall parking lot. He watched as the guardsmen knelt and aimed their rifles, some at the parking lot and some at the hill, in his direction. He had never had a weapon aimed at him before.

When the guardsmen ascended the hill, Doug backed out of their way and went down to the parking lot.

It appeared to him that the guardsmen were returning to the ROTC Building. He thought that the best way to avoid them on the way to his one o'clock class would be to follow a circuitous route that would take him in back of the practice field to the Memorial Gym and behind Johnson Hall. He was walking away from the guardsmen, crossing the parking lot and glancing over his shoulder occasionally to see what they were doing, when he heard what sounded like firecrackers. He turned, took a couple of steps toward the guardsmen, then felt a pain in his right leg.

He jumped behind a parked car and ducked down, then stood to see what was happening. He was standing behind the trunk of a car that came only to his chest when someone shouted, "Get down! Those are live bullets!" As he ducked again, a hail of lead cannonaded into the car and smashed the window of another behind him. They're shooting at me! he thought. Then he realized that he had been the only person standing in the parking lot; everyone else was hugging the ground.

When the shooting stopped, and in the first moments of silence, he stood again and noticed the hole in his trousers below his knee.

A couple in a green Chevrolet drove him to the hospital in Ravenna. Sitting in the back seat of the car, he saw that blood was coming out of the back of his leg. The bullet had gone completely through.

He was the first victim to arrive at Robinson Memorial Hospital. "I guess you won't be taking part in any more demonstrations for a while," a doctor said coldly. Doug sat in a wheelchair in the admitting room while the bodies of Allison Krause and Sandy Scheuer were brought in. It was his first experience with death.

He felt they all had done something wrong to deserve to have been shot and killed. The following day his image appeared on television screens throughout the country and his voice said that the guardsmen had been provoked by the students.

Under repeated questioning at the trial, Doug Wrentmore would say only that he hadn't seen anyone advancing toward the Guard just before the shooting.

"Do you recall . . . ever stating that just prior to the Guard shooting that you saw approximately fifty students behind them as they went up that hill?" Fulton asked.

"Do I recall stating that? No, I don't."

"You recall, do you not, that you did talk to the FBI?"

"Yes."

"And did you tell them that there were students following the Guard toward Taylor Hall?"

"I don't remember saying that."

Jan Wrentmore found the trial a shattering experience. It had taken her several years to appreciate why Doug wanted to sue the guardsmen, and it was only when she saw some of the guardsmen on the stand that she finally understood that *these men had meant to shoot her son.*

Doug's injury had proved to be only the first of a series of shocks. Her husband died before the end of 1970; then she was confronted with the draft problems of her sons and the divorce of her daughter. Attending some of the parents' meetings arranged by Reverend Adams, she found that she felt herself closer to Florence Schroeder than to the friends with whom she played tennis and golf.

13

The Plaintiffs as Defendants

—

Five of the nine wounded plaintiffs had now testified. Of the remaining four, James Russell's and John Cleary's cross-examinations would be relatively uneventful; Tom Grace's and Alan Canfora's were to be dramatic.

Evidently the defense found nothing that they could use to arouse the jurors' prejudices against Russell and Cleary.

Jim Russell, an anomaly among the plaintiffs, was representative of the "silent majority" of students who looked on college as a place to have a good time. His life at Kent State centered on the Tau Kappa Epsilon house on fraternity row, on Lincoln Street at the western border of the campus. He was among the "Greeks" who derided political demonstrations and attended them only to jeer and call the participants Commies.

After a weekend away, Russell returned to Kent State Sunday night to take part in a singing practice session at the fraternity house. He was surprised to find the campus occupied by guardsmen. The demonstration that night near the fraternity house, at the corner of Lincoln and Main, was the first he had ever taken part in. When the troops attacked, he ran back toward his fraternity house and found it blocked by several guardsmen. Russell insisted that he had a right to proceed; an officer told him he was an insult to the Army fatigue jacket he wore and struck his left knee with a baton.

At 12:25 P.M. Monday he was halfway down the hill, among the trees, when the guardsmen turned around. Shotgun pellets struck his forehead and thigh.

John Cleary, had gone to Kent State to become an architect. He had been upset by the attack on the ROTC Building and afterward had picked up trash cans that had been thrown into the street and, using a fire extinguisher, helped to put out small fires that had started in two sheds.

Monday afternoon he was shot while standing near the metal sculpture in front of Taylor Hall, as he advanced the film in his Instamatic camera to take another picture of the guardsmen. The bullet just missed his heart.

Tom Grace had been in favor of United States participation in the Vietnam War when he arrived at Kent State in the fall of 1968, fresh from the Christian Brothers Academy in Syracuse. The events in Chicago during the Democratic convention, and Nixon's reelection, changed his views, and in 1969 he joined the SDS.

He was downtown Friday night and on the Commons Saturday when the ROTC Building burned. On Monday he was following the guardsmen up Blanket Hill when they wheeled and fired. He was running away from them, downhill, and had put about another five yards between himself and the rifles when a shot knocked him off his feet. Not thinking, he struggled to get up until he heard his roommate, Alan Canfora, yell at him to stay down. Alan, crouching behind a tree to one side of him, had probably saved his life.

Tom stayed down, digging his fingers into the grass while bullets buzzed over his head. A few yards before him—he was facing downhill—he saw someone at the roadway at the foot of the hill spin and fall and bleed. It was Jeff Miller, although Tom did not know it then.

After the shooting had stopped a young woman applied a tourniquet to his leg. Tom rode to Ravenna in the lower of two berths in the ambulance. Sandy Scheuer's blood dripped on him from above. He heard the attendants struggling to save her, then a groan, "She's gone." He saw the sheet being pulled over her head.

We had prepared Tom Grace for a tough grilling by Fulton and Brown, especially with respect to his former SDS membership. That had nothing to do with the case, of course, because the guardsmen had no more right to shoot a member of SDS than a member of the Salvation Army. But our refusal to drop our allegation that Governor Rhodes had been politically motivated in his get-tough attitude toward the students had lost us any chance of limiting the questioning regarding the political beliefs of our shooting victims. We figured that Fulton and Brown would try to introduce statements that Tom had made after the shooting, when he had become far more radical and outspoken, and we sought to exclude such questioning before Tom took the stand by asking the judge if he would keep out anything concerning beliefs that the witnesses had embraced *after* May 4, 1970.

The judge refused to commit himself, stating he would rule on a question-by-question basis. This would have virtually the same effect as allowing the prejudicial material into evidence, for allowing the jury to hear the questions was as damaging as allowing them to hear the answers.

"Well," Fulton asked, "have you ever made statements regarding the fact that everyone ought to be armed to defend themselves against the imperialistic government? Have you made statements like that, Mr. Grace?"

"Your Honor," Sindell said, "my objection only goes to time, and the question is unclear."

"All right," Judge Young said. "We are going under the assumption that it is on or prior to May 4." He was telling Fulton that as long as he *assumed* that Tom had said something before May 4, he could ask about it.

However Grace answered, he would be damaged. If he said no, the jury would interpret his reply as meaning not that he had not made the statement but only that he had not made it before May 4.

"Did you ever make a statement like that?" Fulton repeated.

"No, I didn't."

"Do you deny it?"

"I don't know what time you are referring to, Mr. Fulton," Tom said.

"He is referring to any time prior to May 4," Judge Young said.

"No," Tom Grace said, "I didn't."

"Have you made those statements since May 4?" Fulton asked. He knew he was not supposed to ask that. And our objection did not prevent the jury from assuming that Tom had made the statement after May 4. Fulton also asked Grace what SDS stood for and why he had refused an FBI interview.

Tom Grace was thoroughly disgusted with the trial when he left the stand. "Is this the system of laws that works?" he asked me.

"He's going beyond the bounds," I replied. "He's letting them make you guilty by association no matter what you say."

"What are you going to do about it?" Tom challenged me.

The suggestion was made that I retaliate by asking the next guardsman whether he believed that kids with long hair should be shot, or what his opinion was of the My Lai massacre.

"He can't do that," Robbie Stamps said. I was surprised to hear him come to my defense. "I think Joe is doing a good job, showing them how a trial should be conducted."

"What does that matter if we lose?" Tom Grace asked.

"We won't lose," Robbie said. "If you listen to the evidence, they haven't got a leg to stand on."

"I'm glad I told my father not to come and hear this garbage," Tom said.

"I know it's easy to lose heart when you are treated as you have been treated," John Adams told him. "But you must remember things are not always what they seem. In trying to hurt you, they may be hurting themselves more."

That day Tom walked out of the courtroom and away from the trial and spent most of the rest of the summer touring the British Isles.

The defense counterattack went into high gear when Alan Canfora took the stand. Of all the plaintiffs, Alan had been the most active demonstrator; he was portrayed in at least a dozen photographs, taunting the guardsmen with his black flag.

When Alan testified on Monday morning, June 23, Brown and Fulton brought into the courtroom their *pièces de résistance,* three potato sacks full of rocks to which large tags bearing the word "evidence" were affixed.

The Barberton Food Cooperative was on Alan Canfora's mind as he sat in the witness box. Alan had started the cooperative a year before; every morning at four he drove an old truck to Cleveland to buy fresh fruit and vegetables that he sold to the poor for just enough extra to keep the truck running. He sold potatoes for eight cents a pound, half as much as the supermarket price, and fresh tomatoes, lettuce, carrots, eggplants, oranges, and bananas—whatever was in season.

The truck was always on the verge of breaking down. He had made a round trip to Cleveland that morning before coming to the courthouse, and he hadn't liked the way it sounded when he shifted into second. If the transmission went, there would be a lot of disappointed people in Barberton.

A handsome young man with brilliant blue eyes and bright copper-colored hair, his pigtail hidden under the wig he wore as a compromise, Alan waited for Fulton to do his worst. *Maybe*, he thought, *Fulton will snatch off my wig in the middle of a question and expose me.* He nervously wiggled his toes in his shoes.

During his cross-examination of Canfora, Brown asked about his conviction for possession of marijuana, about the effect of the drug on the senses, about his political philosophy, his attendance at SDS meetings, his opinion of Jerry Rubin, and why he had carried a black flag instead of an American flag on May 4.

"What were your philosophies in May of 1970 in as far as your activity in political affairs?" Brown asked. "Were you a political activist?"

"Yes," Alan replied. "In fact, I was even more active, I would say, due to the fact that I had attended the funeral of a friend of mine who was killed in Vietnam the week before that."

"You had been to a number of rallies before May of '70?"

"I had been to a few, yes."

"What kind of rallies?"

"Antiwar rallies to protest the U.S. involvement in Southeast Asia."

"Did you go to the peace march in Washington?"

"In November of '69, yes, I did."

A number of Alan's friends had come to watch him on the stand. When Brown asked him why he had not prevented the burning of the ROTC Building, they laughed. Brown glared at them, and the judge admonished them to be quiet.

"Had you ever driven an automobile where you had your windshield broken by a rock, a crowd, a hostile crowd?" Brown asked.

"I don't think so, no."

"Had you ever had any kind of assault?"

"I had been shot," Alan interrupted.

During our direct examination the jury had not been allowed to see photographs showing Alan's position at the time of the shooting. Predictably, Fulton now tried to make the jury doubt that Alan was behind a tree 200 feet from the guardsmen by drawing from him an admission that the only person who could support his testimony was his roommate, co-plaintiff Tom Grace.

Fulton drew from Canfora an admission that he had never registered to vote. "Have you ever thought it might be appropriate to make a protest at the ballot box?" he asked.

"I think that is a legitimate way to exercise your democratic rights in this country," Alan said.

"Do you think it is as legitimate as throwing a stone?"

"I think it is more legitimate, yes."

"And you threw some stones, didn't you?"

"I threw a single stone," Alan said, "but it fell far short."

This was Fulton's cue for his rocks. "I have some stones in a briefcase, Your Honor," he said. "I have them here. I picked them up from the marshal."

We objected that, without identification, the rocks could have come from anywhere. But Fulton explained that all he was going to do was use them to help Canfora identify the size of the rock he had thrown.

He then spent ten minutes showing Canfora bigger and bigger rocks, despite Alan's insistence that he had thrown "a relatively small rock, perhaps an inch and a half in diameter, two inches." Major Harry Jones, sitting among the spectators, was grinning from ear to ear.

This got to be too much even for the judge, who advised Fulton that he ought to try showing smaller rocks.

"How about this size, is that too big, too?"

"I would say that's closer, but it is still probably too big. Smaller than that . . . about three-quarters that size, two-thirds."

"So it wasn't an inch and a half?"

"It wasn't exactly round, it was more of a . . ."

"Jagged?"

"Perhaps oblong."

"Oblong rock. Sort of like a touchstone?"

"It was relatively small. I couldn't throw it that far."

"Tell the court and jury why you threw it."

"Do you want me to explain?" Alan asked.

"Yes," Judge Young interjected. "He asked you why. When he asks why, the door is open, tell whatever you want to tell."

"I threw it as a gesture of frustration towards them and not intended to hit them."

"Was that a pacifist gesture?" Fulton asked.

"It was a frustration and anger after being teargassed and chased by bayonets."

"Chased by bayonets?"

"That's right."

Albert Canfora had taken a day off from his job at the union office at Goodyear Aerospace to see his son on the stand. He was proud of Alan, who had been an honor student throughout grammar school and high school in Barberton. A small, sharp-featured, volatile man, he fidgeted in his seat in the courtroom and worried about the wife of one of the jurors, who sat with the guardsmen's wives and who had been heard referring to Tom Grace as a "little Commie."

Tom Grace, Sr., sitting beside Albert Canfora, thought the antics of Brown and Fulton disgraceful. It was not just the business with the rocks, it was their side remarks, their pulling chairs and pushing the table, Brown's walking around while the plaintiffs' lawyers examined witnesses, and Fulton's sweeping his glasses off with his two hands, perhaps to distract the jury, and popping up from his chair whenever he felt like it.

Tom had come to Cleveland to see Alan Canfora testify; he was fond of the young man, and he felt he could use some moral support. He himself had joined the civil lawsuit in the hope that his son would receive some recompense for his injury, but most of all, he wanted to learn exactly who had taken a bead on his son. He wanted to find out just what had been in the mind of a man who had fired at an unarmed student at least fifty yards away from him.

On the night of the shooting, Tom Grace, Sr., drove from Syracuse to Ravenna arriving at two in the morning to find his son in shock and under heavy sedation. He spent the next two weeks in his son's empty apartment, wondering how long Tommy would keep his foot. Gangrene had set in, and the doctor wanted to amputate. Tommy refused. But with his son unconscious much of the time, he might have to make the decision.

"Awful sorry this happened," Tom told his father during one coherent interval. "I don't like to put you to this trouble."

Tom, Sr., reassured him that he was glad to be there.

A week later, when the gangrene had cleared up, Tom, still full of morphine and Demerol, was taken to a hospital in Syracuse, where an orthopedist grafted some skin from Tom's thigh to his damaged foot. It was during the plastic surgery, with operations every four or five days, that the pain was at its worst.

14

The Defense's Jugular

—

Our case was now moving into the higher echelons of the Ohio National Guard, to the commanding officers of Company C, Troop G, and Company A, Snyder, Srp, and Martin; three lieutenants, Stevenson of Troop G and Kline and Fallon from Company A; Major Jones of the 145th Infantry; Colonel Fassinger of the 107th Cavalry; Assistant Adjutant General Canterbury; and Adjutant General Del Corso.

With the exception of Sylvester Del Corso, who was in Columbus, all these officers were on Blanket Hill at the time of the shooting. All were culpable, in our view, at least for having failed to control their men. Moreover, some of them were suspected of having fired weapons, and Major Harry Jones had carried a nonmilitary pearl-handled .22 caliber Baretta automatic in violation of regulations.

Raymond Srp, a tall, stringy gentleman with a crewcut and a long nose, was now a major. Unlike the enlisted guardsmen defendants, he had never admitted firing a weapon, nor was there any evidence to indicate that he had fired one. He had been named in our suit because he had been on Blanket Hill, in command of Troop G. If an order to fire had been given to those men, it should have passed through him. If such an order had not been given, then our claim was that he had not exercised proper control over his men.

We called him first because he had one supremely important piece of testimony. He had told the FBI, "The lives of members of the Guard were not in danger and it was not a shooting situation."

To ask his opinion on the danger to the Guard, we had to qualify him as an expert. We did so. Then, on the witness stand, he expressed a different opinion, talking about a threat of danger "around the corner of Taylor Hall."

When I tried to use photographs to refute this, the judge prevented me from getting anything across to the jury.

When Judge Young said my questioning was repetitive, Fulton commented, "Do they do it that way back east?"

I replied, "If you try to inject any more prejudice, I will have to say that I was born in Russia, and maybe that will give you a few more grounds for prejudice, but I wasn't born there. I was born across the lake [In Des Moines, Iowa.]. . . ."

I was awakened at midnight on the last Sunday in June by my son Bob. Galen Keller was on the phone and wanted to speak to me. She was breathless with excitement. She had been reading the federal grand jury testimony of James Ronald Snyder, the former captain of Company C who was scheduled to go on the stand in the morning, and she had found an admission by Snyder that he had perjured himself in telling the state grand jury that he had found brass knuckles on a student whom he had beaten with his baton, and a pistol on Jeff Miller's body. Snyder had confessed to federal prosecutor Robert Murphy that these stories had been invented as possible defenses against criminal prosecution, or a civil suit; and he had described meetings with other guardsmen at which these fabrications were discussed.

I was excited, and I asked Galen to bring the testimony to my apartment at seven. This was the big break I had been looking for, the one that could crack the case wide open for us. I had been trying, without success, to get various defendants to tell about the discussions they had had with other guardsmen and the instructions they had been given on writing their firing incident reports (which uniformly parroted their fears of students and rocks and, I was certain, had been prepared as a coverup).

There was a question as to whether or not the testimony could be introduced into the trial as direct evidence, but the federal rules were clear that it could be used indirectly, as a way of impeaching witnesses. I would be able to ask Snyder whether the guardsmen had agreed on a common story after the shootings. If Snyder answered yes, a coverup would be revealed to the jury. If he answered no, I could show the grand jury transcript to the judge and then read Snyder's inconsistent grand jury testimony to the jury.

James Ronald Snyder was a short, stocky, hypertense individual with regular features and large, wide-spaced, haunted eyes. He had been released from the Guard after the shooting and was now a detective for the Portage County Sheriff's Office.

I could see that Fulton was nervous that morning even before I put the former captain on the stand. He kept pulling his glasses from his head and fidgeting in his seat. He must have known what we had on Snyder.

After the dispersal at the Victory Bell, Snyder had moved his men to the area between Taylor and Prentice halls, and they had stayed there. They had been neither on the practice field nor on Blanket Hill. Snyder, we knew, had been very aggressive on May 4. We had photographs of him beating a student on the head with a baton (near the Victory Bell, ten minutes or so before the shooting) and of some of his men leveling rifles. But Snyder explained that he had cautioned his men against overreacting. In his view, he said, a guardsman had cause to fire in self-defense if a person tried to take away his weapon to use it against him. I was hitting pay dirt with him.

He stated that a rock thrown from a distance of 60 feet was no justification for shooting.

I soon reached the fringes of the main track. "Is it a fact," I asked, "that in your testimony before an investigative agency, you said about a student you struck on May 4, Monday, that you had found brass knuckles on him?"

"Yes," Snyder admitted.

Fulton and Brown tried to head me off by getting the judge to rule that I could not develop anything beyond the bare words of the grand jury testimony. I could ask Snyder whether he found brass knuckles, or a pistol on Jeff Miller, but not what his purpose was in telling a grand jury that he found such things.

This meant that I could show Snyder up as a liar for having told the state grand jury one thing and the present jury another, but I could not demonstrate that he had lied for the purpose of creating a coverup.

I couldn't believe that Judge Young intended to go so far, and I approached the bench to confer with him.

"He admitted that he lied . . . for the purposes of framing up a defense and helping to frame up a defense," I told the judge. "This is certainly crucial to our case."

The judge said that I could go into that as long as I stuck to the questions and answers contained in the federal grand jury record. That sounded a little better; I could go beyond asking if he had in fact found the knuckles and the pistol. But what if I wanted to bring out more detail than was recorded in the minutes?

I returned to the witness and got Snyder to admit that he had made up the story of finding the brass knuckles on one student. Then, to get at the real issue, I asked why he had done it. He explained that he had first told the story to a Captain Thompson in the Company C orderly room in Akron.

"And you were afraid at that time that there might be assault charges brought against you because someone had taken photographs of you striking this boy with a stick, is that right, sir?" I asked.

"No," Snyder said.

"What was your reason for inventing this brass knuckles thing?"

"Well, this was a conversation between two or three people in the orderly room, and there was some kidding going on, and I think I made the statement at that time, 'Well, I got the answer to that problem, it is self-defense.' I was kidding about it at the time. However, I didn't hear nothing more about it at that time and went on about my business. Some time later I found myself locked into a story, and that's how that came about. But this business with that in the orderly room started out as a kidding kind of thing, because everybody was quite concerned about legal actions against them."

"Let me understand this," I said. "In June, in the orderly room, how many people were present when you brought out these brass knuckles?"

"It would be myself and Captain Thompson and probably somebody else, I can't remember now."

"You say people were worried about being sued or other proceedings against them, is that it?"

"Yes."

"You said, 'I have the answer to the whole thing, look at what I have found, brass knuckles and a gun,' is that right?"

"Yes," Snyder replied.

"You brought out not only the brass knuckles, but you brought out a gun at that time, claiming that you found it on the body of Jeff Miller, is that true?"

"Yes, sir."

At this mention of a gun found on her son's body, Elaine Holstein felt faint. She clutched her husband's arm, and he led her from the courtroom. She had never before heard this story, which was first published in 1971.

"And at that time did you say in words, almost in these words, 'I have got the answer to this whole situation. It's going to be self-defense and we will claim that we were in fear for our lives.' Was that it in substance, sir?"

Fulton objected.

"Sustained," Judge Young said. "This is repetitive. He has already said that."

He had said part of it, that was true; he had said nothing about being in fear for their lives.

The judge stuck to his ruling, confining me to the federal grand jury testimony and not permitting me to probe one inch beyond it, into the territory of the coverup. When I tried to find out exactly who had participated in the discussions, or whether anyone from the Guard inspector general's office had attended, the judge said that I could not ask about events that had occurred after the day of the shootings.

I asked if I could question the witness about the meetings at which this claim of self-defense was actually used to prepare a defense which had no merit.

Fulton objected that Snyder's Company C had fired no weapons and asked that my remarks be stricken.

Judge Young told the jury to disregard my remarks and announced again that he was not concerned with anything that happened after May 4. "This other matter is totally beyond the scope of this trial, in my opinion . . . it can't be involved against other witnesses or other defendants."

"Unless others were present and there was complicity between them," I said.

The judge had forced me to desist from this line of questioning; yet I still had another string to my bow, another grand jury question that got to the heart of the matter. It laid the lack of meritorious defense on the table so plainly that the judge would be hard put to find a rationale for keeping it out. I asked Snyder if he could think "of any common story that was decided on by the Ohio National Guard subsequent to the shootings."

"Or maybe he can't," Fulton blurted out.

"I suggest counsel is suggesting to him how he might answer," I said. "I think it is improper."

Fulton stalled by raising several objections to the wording of the question, which was finally rephrased.

"Sir, do you know of any common story that was decided on by the Ohio National Guard subsequent to the shooting?"

"You may answer that yes or no," Judge Young reminded the witness.

"Can I explain?" Snyder asked.

"No, you may not," Judge Young said. "First you have to answer it yes or no, and then I will determine whether or not you can explain."

"Yes," Snyder said.

"Your answer was yes?" I asked.

"Yes." There it was; the guardsmen had decided on a common story.

Now, of course, I wanted the jury to hear what that common story was.

The judge, however, permitted Snyder to obfuscate by replying that the only common stories he knew about were those he had read of in the *Akron Beacon Journal,* "about snipers and self-defense." The judge would not agree that this was impeached by his grand jury testimony—which, consequently, was kept from the jurors.

15

The Master of the Rocks

▬

"Why don't we go home?" Libbie asked in our apartment the night after Snyder's appearance on the stand.

"What do you mean?" I asked. "It's Tuesday."

"I mean this is killing you, Joe. It's no good."

"I can't quit," I said.

"I know you're tough," Libbie said, "but there's nothing to be gained beating your head against a stone wall. I see what it's doing to you, and I can't stand it. I can't sit in that courtroom day after day, seeing you get slapped in the face. They're just not giving you a fair trial. They're fixing it so you'll lose."

"You're the eternal pessimist," I said. "Listen, Libbie, Judge Young is not going to get away with this. I just know in my bones that if we play by the rules, we can't lose."

To my surprise, the plaintiffs were all optimistic when I met with them the following morning. They thought that in showing up Snyder as a liar we had put the case on ice.

"Everybody could see how nervous Snyder was," Robbie Stamps said, "and that's the first time I've seen Fulton scared."

I patted Robbie's shoulder. I had become fond of him during the ordeal, and it warmed my heart to see that his initial cynicism and despair had been softened by a more positive outlook.

Yet I had misgivings. The clients couldn't know—any more than the jury could—what was in the federal grand jury minutes. They couldn't know how close I had come to demolishing any semblance of a defense. I had had

Snyder on the ropes. He knew what he had told the federal grand jury, and he knew that I knew. I could have kept him on the stand for two days, telling the jury about the meetings and the discussions about making use of the brass knuckles and the planted gun. Any guardsman who followed him on the stand and talked about menacing students and abject fear would have sounded ludicrous.

The judge's tremendous powers were tying our hands while not restraining the tactics of the defense. What other devices, I wondered, was he going to throw at me to suppress the truth?

Lieutenant Alexander Stevenson of Troop G was another nervous witness, a small, sharp-featured, hard-hat construction worker. He denied firing his rifle despite Captain Srp's testimony that he had done so.

Captain John Martin, the commander of Company A, was a corn and soybean farmer from Wooster. He testified that he had seen no reason for any weapon to be fired on May 4, that he had felt no concern for his life, that he hadn't seen any guardsman hit with a rock after leaving the practice field, and that the guardsmen had not been assaulted.

Through Martin we were able to approach for the first time the issue of the National Guard's rules of engagement (and the responsibility of Del Corso and Rhodes for those rules).

Nelson Karl asked Martin to describe the circumstances, other than an order to fire given by an officer, under which weapons may be discharged by someone on National Guard duty.

"In cases where one's own life is in danger. In the case when another person's life is in danger. Another circumstance would be in the case of arson of an inhabited building. And there may be more, that's all I recall at this time."

"Isn't it a fact, Major [he, too, had been promoted since 1970], that you personally instructed your men that they could only fire as a last resort to protect that individual's life or the life of a fellow guardsman?"

"That's correct, sir."

Martin had testified previously that the first shot was fired by a guardsman. "I submit to you, sir, isn't it a fact that your first thought at that time was, 'What idiot is firing with a weapon in this situation'?"

When Martin gave an indirect answer, Karl approached the bench to show Judge Young that the witness had given this precise reply to questions asked on previous occasions. I joined Karl, pleading with the judge that he permit us, as he had originally agreed, to use prior testimony to impeach witnesses.

Fulton objected to our use of previous testimony. The judge, as usual, agreed with Fulton and echoed his arguments.

With Major Harry Jones the trial reached a new phase. A high-ranking officer of the 145th Infantry Regiment, he was the first witness with important testimony on the roles of the two generals, Del Corso and Canterbury. For the first time we would be getting away from the shooting aspect of our case and on to the reasons for the dispersal of the noon rally and the Guard's mission on the campus.

Yet Jones would also have testimony regarding the shooting. For he had been on Blanket Hill—indeed, photographs showed him at a good vantage point, near the Pagoda, when the firing started—and he had stated elsewhere that he saw no reason for the shooting.

He was important to the defense, too; as the officer in charge of rock collecting, he would be used in an attempt to place the sacks of rocks in evidence.

Major Harry Jones, a five-foot-nine, loose-limbed Tennessean with a long, equine face and a "lazy eye" that required him to wear dark glasses in the courtroom, was the training officer of the 145th Infantry, a regimental staff man. On May 4, at the request of Major Arthur Wallach, commander of the First Battalion of the 145th (which included companies A and C), Jones had joined the men at the ROTC Building and moved out with them. He had gone with Company C to the area between Taylor and Prentice halls and then joined the other troops on the practice field. As he followed them up Blanket Hill, he became involved in an altercation with a rock-throwing student, during which he drew his pearl-handled .22 caliber Baretta pistol.

Photographs show him standing, hands on hips, at the Pagoda, wearing a soft cap and fatigues, without a gas mask, facing downhill, looking past the members of Troop G, who have just turned. He remains in the same position while the Troop G guardsmen take several steps in the direction of the parking lot and open fire.

In connection with the Guard's role at the university, Jones testified that when he arrived on the campus at midnight Saturday, Del Corso and Canterbury told him that their mission primarily concerned the security of the buildings. The first discussion about dispersing crowds occurred in the middle of Sunday afternoon, following Governor Rhodes' visit.

Jones was instrumental in drafting the Matson-Frisina letter. He testified that he had met with Vice President Matson on Sunday afternoon and shuttled between him and Major Wallach, obtaining information on the Guard's authority to disperse crowds. He also admitted that the firing on May 4 was indiscriminate—that it had not been at definite targets and thus was against Guard regulations—and that Pryor's pistol pointing could have been interpreted as a signal to fire.

Like Srp, Jones had stated elsewhere that the shooting was unjustified, but we were unable to get him to testify accordingly.

When Engdahl had qualified Srp as an expert in order to question him about the justifiability of the shootings, the judge told him—erroneously—that we could not impeach our own witness. Since we now planned to make Jones an expert in order to ask him a similar question, we anticipated the same roadblock. Therefore we tried to head the judge off by showing that the new federal rules of evidence, slated to go into effect the following day, July 1, specifically provided for the impeaching of one's own witness.

Judge Young read from the book: "Rule 607, 'Credibility of a witness may be attacked by any party including the party calling him.'

"Nevertheless," he said, "I am going to stand to my guns on this thing . . . I am not going to permit [it]."

I had thought I could no longer be surprised by anything Judge Young said, but this floored me. Apparently he didn't think he had to abide by the rules. When we asked quietly that he explain his reasoning, the judge became more temperate, suggesting that we wait and see what happened when Jones testified the next day. "At the moment," he told Sindell, "you are yowling before you know whether you are hurt."

He then gave a little speech, stating his concern that the truth was not coming out and indicating that mere technicalities, such as the new federal rules of evidence, were not the essence of the law. "We got a lot of theorists that have never been in a courtroom, and they spend all their time determining the law by reading books about it. I don't propose to govern [my trial] by listening to a bunch of theorists and their attempts to reduce the law to something that you can put into a computer. . . ."

The question of whether or not the judge would follow the new rules of evidence did not come up the next day because the defense permitted Nelson Karl to question Jones on his opinion of the shootings without making him an expert. When Jones gave a different opinion on the stand from the one he had formerly expressed, we ran into the same old roadblock against using the federal grand jury minutes for impeachment purposes.

"Is there any way that you can suggest," I asked the judge, "to avoid a miscarriage of justice, where we have diametrically opposed bits of testimony, to establish what the truth is?"

"In the first place," Judge Young said, "I don't think we have diametrically opposed bits of testimony on this matter, so I am not going to worry about that.

"Again, as I say, this federal grand jury stuff, I let you have it for discovery, that's as far as I'm going to let you go with it."

I told him it was a miscarriage of justice.

When it came their turn to examine Jones, Brown and Fulton moved to the center ring of their circus, unfolding and brandishing a long FUCK MURDERS banner and bringing out all the bags of rocks.

Brown first had Jones describe the continuous barrage of concrete-filled Styrofoam cups, bricks, coat hangers, and nail-studded golf balls that menaced him as he climbed Blanket Hill; then the student shouts, "Something like, 'We've got them. Get them' . . . 'Get the weapon. We have to get them. Take them. Kill the green pigs, get them off the campus.'

"That was continuous the whole time that we was going up the hill. There was a large number of the missiles." It was, Jones said, the worst riot he had ever been in.

Fulton had several color photographs of the tables on which the Guard had displayed, for the press, the missiles it claimed to have found on the campus, and Jones described how his men had searched the area of hostilities Monday afternoon.

The judge would not accept my argument that such stuff should be admitted only when it could be connected with the plaintiffs, but I was able to knock out a great many of the items anyway. The color photographs had admittedly been taken days after the Monday events, and Jones was unable to specify exactly when or where most of the objects had been found. He did say that he had picked up rocks on Blanket Hill and marked them with his initials.

Jones couldn't say that he had seen the FUCK MURDERS sign before the shooting. I then asked him to locate among the rocks on the floor some that bore his initials, but after several moments of searching he couldn't find a single one that he had picked up. He also conceded that rocks occurred naturally on terrain like that of Blanket Hill, which meant that any of the rocks might have been there before the May 4 confrontation.

16

Practicing on
the Practice Field

▬

Major Jones had admitted, under Nelson Karl's questioning, that a national guardsman was not permitted to "discharge weapons into a crowd at undesignated targets." That the guardsmen had fired weapons contrary to their own regulations had only an indirect bearing on our case. The testimony helped us to influence the jury—assuming that it believed the shooters had broken Guard regulations—just as, in an accident case, jurors might be more inclined to find against a motorist who struck another car after passing through a red light.

Actually we offered two arguments involving Ohio National Guard regulations. First, we claimed that the guardsmen had violated their own regulations at Kent State. Second, we claimed that the regulations were themselves deficient. To prove this second point, which made its first appearance in the trial during the testimony of Lieutenant Colonel Charles Fassinger, we compared Ohio National Guard regulations with those of the regular Army and we introduced experts on methods of civilian crowd control.

In the past sixty years the regular Army has been used only twice in domestic situations. The most recent employment was in Detroit in July 1967, following the disastrous intervention of the Michigan National Guard. As a consequence of this experience, the Army changed its crowd control procedures. In 1968 it issued Field Manual 19-15, *Civil Disturbances and Disasters* (revised on October 23, 1969).

The philosophy behind FM 19-15 is one of restraint. It points out that the commitment of military forces is a drastic last resort and that the guiding principle is "minimum force, consistent with mission accomplishment."

Recognizing that the mere appearance of troops could be provocative, it counsels moderation in displays of force and lists six graduated steps in troop employment. The last of these, full firepower, is to be used only when the alternatives are "imminent overthrow of the government, continued mass casualties, or similar grievous conditions."

The manual prescribes rigid rules for the loading of weapons and gives six different ways of carrying rifles and bayonets—only two of which contemplate the presence of ammunition in rifles, and only one of which permits a round in the chamber.

The 1969 revision is more specific on shooting. In addition to the restriction on full firepower, it only authorizes shooting when (1) lesser means are unavailable, (2) the risk of harm to innocent persons is not incurred by its use, and (3) its purpose is any of four listed purposes: self-defense, prevention of a lethal crime such as sniping, prevention of destruction of public utilities, etc., and detention of persons guilty of the activities mentioned in the other three purposes. It also prescribes other restrictions such as the use of expert marksmen against snipers. These conditions *all* have to be present. The absence of any one of them—for example, the possibility that innocents might be hurt—forbids the use of shooting.

Although the Ohio regulations echoed the Army's requirement of minimum force and described a fixed sequence of six steps to be used in dispersing rioters, the rules for the final step, "Weapons," departed significantly from Army regulations. First, there were no rigid restrictions on the conditions under which rifles could be loaded. Instead, the Ohio regulations promulgated under Del Corso and known as OPLAN 2, stated that "rifles will be carried with a round in the chamber in the safe position." Worse, the OPLAN provided that shooting was justified when "rioters to whom the Riot Act has been read cannot be dispersed by other means" and specifically immunized any guardsman who shot anyone. "When the Riot Act has been read within hearing," it said, "and you are engaged in dispersing or apprehending rioters, using necessary and proper means, then you are declared by Ohio Statute (RC 3761.15) to be guiltless if any of the persons unlawfully or violently assembled is killed, maimed or otherwise injured in consequence of resisting."

The OPLAN reads like an outline of what happened at Kent State on May 4; it is a prescription for disaster. The six-step procedure for dealing with rioters is:

a. Issue a military request to disperse.
b. Riot formation—show of force.
c. Simple physical force if possible.

d. Rifle butt and bayonet.

e. Chemicals.

f. Weapons.

On the Commons on May 4, the Guard under Canterbury's direction followed a and b and skipped c. Step d was employed only to the extent that bayonets were fixed to the rifles; but bayonets and rifle butts were not used to repel any students allegedly rushing the guardsmen or stoning them. Step e was employed only to the extent of using tear gas when the assembly was first dispersed, although when the shooting began some of the guardsmen still had tear-gas canisters.

The OPLAN rules thus provided the basis for a number of charges we could make against the Guard. To the extent that the OPLAN authorized shooting to disperse a mob, we could show that such authorization illegally departed from Army regulations. As such, the OPLAN implicated Rhodes and Del Corso as the persons responsible for its publication.

At the same time, we could show that the Guard had leapfrogged over the same rules by firing weapons before exhausting lesser means. Canterbury, all the officers on Blanket Hill, and the men who fired shared liability for the failure to use nonlethal alternatives.

Lieutenant Colonel Charles R. Fassinger, the first witness questioned about these regulations in any detail, had served as a noncom during the Korean War and received a direct commission following the conclusion of hostilities. In 1975 he was forty-five years old and the head of a welding corporation. A stocky, fair-skinned individual with graying blond hair, he lived with his wife and children in the expensive Cleveland suburb of Northfield and shared a number of friends and acquaintances with Jan Wrentmore.

Charles Fassinger was one of the few defendants who attended the trial almost every day. The others were Del Corso and Canterbury, who usually sat apart, as though they were not overly fond of each other, and Ralph Zoller, a big truck driver, one of the four Troop G men who had admitted shooting at students.

Fassinger, the commander of the 2nd Squadron of the 107th Armored Cavalry, had arrived at Kent State at midnight Sunday, to be told by General Canterbury that all rallies on the campus, peaceful or not, were prohibited. He had been in front of Troop G, about ten yards past the Pagoda, with his back to the practice field, when the shooting began. Like Major Jones, he admitted on the witness stand that the firing had been indiscriminate.

He also stated at one point that the students on the Commons were not nice people—a remark that drew sympathetic titters from many of the jurors and from Canterbury and the other guardsmen in the room.

When Sindell tried to question him on the difference between Army regulations and the Ohio OPLAN, he was severely handicapped by the "evidence hole" rule, which prevented him from reading any part of the documents to the jury. All he could do, when Fassinger had testified that they were the same, was to ask the witness to read FM 19-15 to himself and find the passage which, for example, authorized shooting to disperse a mob.

Even after Sindell had given Fassinger overnight to find the justification in the Army field manual, the colonel insisted that the meaning of the Ohio OPLAN paraphrased in one sentence the paragraph in FM 19-15 titled "Application of Force."

"That's your testimony?" Sindell asked. "The meanings are the same?"

"Yes, sir."

This testimony was belied by the documents that the judge was preventing the jurors from hearing read. Later the judge would even prevent Del Corso, the issuer of the OPLAN, from testifying about it.

Major John Whiton Simons was the only National Guard officer who testified as a witness for the plaintiffs.

Simons, chaplain of the 107th Armored Cavalry, had been at Kent State on May 4 and had witnessed the dispersal of the students but not the shootings. He had remained on the Commons, near the Victory Bell, and had seen a few of the guardsmen reappearing over the crest of the hill just before the shooting began.

We called him because he was the only Ohio National Guard officer who had ever spoken out against the shootings. He had told the *Akron Beacon Journal* that the killings should not have occurred, and several months later he had stated in an interview on Walter Cronkite's evening news show that the shootings sprang from a "mistake made at the state level with the adjutant general and the governor, who apparently feels that every campus disorder is another Normandy invasion, so you go in with the weapons loaded with rounds."

On the witness stand Simons testified that before the jeep moved out to read the riot act the students were "milling around [in] a kind of picnic, festive atmosphere."

A picnic, festive atmosphere is a peaceful assembly in anyone's lexicon.

Was the jury buying this? I kept watching Stanley Davis, Jr., the assistant engineer whose presence on the jury had been the subject of so much discussion. He had no poker face. As I read his expression, he was not with us.

As the guardsmen kneel on the practice field, supposedly at a time when the barrage of missiles is at its worst, no one is within 200 feet of them in any direction. *(Beverly Knowles)*

PLAINTIFF'S
EXHIBIT

5002

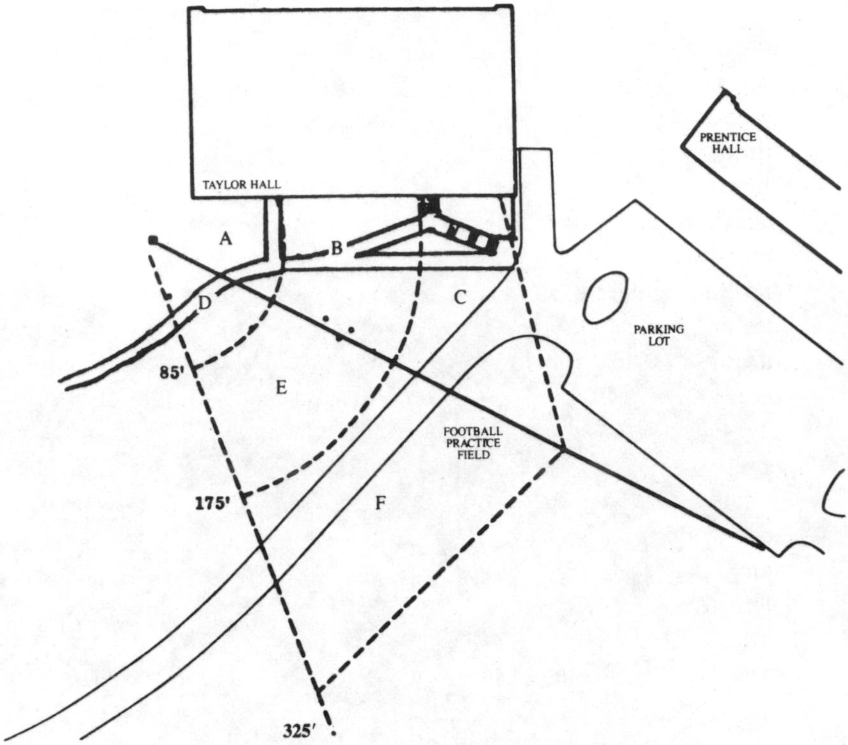
TAYLOR HALL
PRENTICE HALL
A
B
C
D
E
F
85'
175'
325'
PARKING LOT
FOOTBALL PRACTICE FIELD

Detected Movements* of Students in Designated Areas

	Time from Beginning of Film Sequence								
	0 Seconds				3 Seconds				6 Seconds
Area	Total Students	Movement Toward Guard	Movement Away From Guard	Nondetectable Movement	Total	Toward	Away	No	
A	5	---**	3	2	---	---	---	---	All movement at this time is generally away from guardsmen except for fallen and other stationary individuals
B	25	7	2	16	35	3	5	27	
C	30+	10	---	20+	30+	5	---	25+	
D	10	---	---	10	12	---	---	12	
E	15	10	---	5	16	5	2	9	
F	20	5	---	15	20	2	---	18	

• = Trees

***Rate of movement variable (3-10 mph estimates) and not accurately determinable.**

****Dashes (---) mean none detected.**

Several of the other men impressed me as being equally unsympathetic to our position.

Interspersed among the Guard officers as witnesses were several Kent students, one of whom, Sharon Jacobs, had been with her roommate, Beverly Knowles, when she had taken two remarkable pictures from Prentice Hall at the time the guardsmen were on the practice field.

Since the "evidence hole" rule kept us from showing the photographs to the jury and Miss Knowles was unavailable, the only remaining way of informing the jury what the photos showed was the testimony of Mrs. Jacobs.

Had the jury been permitted to see these photographs in conjunction with the testimony of certain guardsmen, the photographs would have been eloquent indeed. They spoke for themselves, if any photographs ever did.

Here is the sort of testimony that the Knowles photographs, kept from the jury by the "evidence hole" rule, impeached:

Sergeants Okey Flesher, Barry Morris, William Perkins, and Lawrence Shafer described vividly the missiles falling on them from all directions on the practice field.

Major Jones said that he had told the guardsmen to kneel in order to present smaller targets.

"When we reached the practice area," Sergeant Myron Pryor told Fulton, "we were receiving pieces of stone, rock, brick, wood, anything they could throw at us. And at that time we stayed there, we received bricks, stones, and shouting and obscenities."

"I had been pelted in the preceding period," Sergeant James Pierce said, "with enough rocks and knocked down and beaten around to the point where I feared for my life. . . . There we were. The students were regrouping and forming around us, and it was continually bombardments, we were trying to face movements, we were moving around. You couldn't hear . . . you were yelling, 'There is one coming in from the left' and 'One coming in from the right.' . . . Missiles, bottles, bricks, stones, whatever, chunks of wood." He had been bruised on his "arms, back, neck, groin, legs."

Lieutenant Howard Fallon said that the Guard was "to all intents and purposes enveloped" on the practice field. "It seemed that the entire tempo of the thing shifted into a higher gear. The volumes of stones and bricks and thrown missiles increased. They were throwing the tear gas back. Their proximity to the Guard changed, they got closer."

The Beverly Knowles photographs, taken while the guardsmen kneel (presumably at the time of maximum danger), give a panoramic view of the practice field and its surroundings. One shows everything from the foot of

Blanket Hill and the access road separating it from the practice field to well beyond the fence, and includes the eastern end of the parking lot, where the rock throwers had been. The other overlaps the first and shows the rest of the parking lot and a portion of Blanket Hill.

The photographs reveal not a single student within a couple hundred feet of the guardsmen.

When James Michener came upon the Knowles photographs in the course of researching his book, he was astonished.

> To the south, there are no students for at least two hundred yards; much of the field is visible and completely empty. To the east, not one student can be seen behind the fence. And where the mob was supposed to have been there was seen only empty space for at least forty yards, then the high steel fence of the baseball diamond, then the famous parking lot. On or near it could be counted about a score of students, five of them with books under their arms, walking away from the Guard. One researcher, an excellent baseball player, went down to the scene and placed a student where the Guard had been. Picking up what rocks he could find, he retreated behind the fence and tried to throw them at the supposed Guard. His conclusion: "Joe DiMaggio couldn't have reached them."*

The jurors, deprived by the "evidence hole" rule of seeing the photographs in the course of the trial or hearing testimony about what they showed, were unable to reach any such conclusion. Would they, several weeks later, at the end of the trial, remember their significance among the hundreds of other photographs?

---

*James Michener, *Kent State, What Happened and Why* (New York: Random House, 1971).

17

The Adjutant General

By now, seven weeks into the trial, our meetings with our plaintiff clients had become harmonious. A kind of euphoria had set in. In spite of Judge Young's obstructionism, they believed we had discredited the guardsmen's stories of their fear of rushing students. They had seen the defendants twist and turn on the stand, nervously watching Fulton and Brown for possible cues. Their one remaining complaint was that I was letting Fulton get away with his continual prancing around and his triumphant grins.

"What else can I do?" I asked them, recounting how I had often brought Fulton's antics to the judge's attention and how my motions had been ignored.

What the plaintiffs really worried about was the effect of the judge's permissiveness on the jury, who might assume from it that the judge was on Fulton's side.

"You have to realize," I said, "that some of the jurors may resent the unfairness just as much as you do. Look, I can't expect you to agree with everything I do, but I haven't lost a case in three years, and I'm not going to lose this one."

"Remember," John Adams said, "it is very hard for us to sit in that courtroom day after day and be objective."

"There is just no case for the defense of those men," I said. "Now all we have to do is to tie in Del Corso, Canterbury, and Rhodes."

I didn't let on that I had, in my apartment, a secret weapon, a blockbuster that was going to level what was left of the defense. It was nothing less than the previous sworn testimony of Adjutant General Sylvester Del Corso, the highest-ranking officer of the Ohio National Guard in 1970, on the justifiability of the shooting.

All I had to do was to qualify Del Corso as an expert, just as we had done with Captain Srp, and ask his opinion of the shootings. If he gave different answers from those he had given the federal grand jury (and I expected he would, for he had taken a different line in his deposition), I could then confront him with what he had earlier told an investigative body. He would then either have to admit his earlier testimony or find himself lying under oath.

Judge Young, of course, had been making conflicting remarks about our use of the federal grand jury minutes. But Del Corso's testimony would really put him on the spot; it was so powerful that he would be able to keep it out only by abusing his discretion.

If he tried (as he had before) to rule inadmissible any question on the justifiability of the shooting, or if he repeated that we could not impeach our own (expert) witness, we could show that such rulings ran counter to the new federal rules of evidence, which we had called to the judge's attention during our interrogation of Major Jones and which were now in force. We were counting on the new rules, which were more liberal than the old rules, and we assumed that the judge would adopt them by observing the provision that they be used in trials already in progress unless such adoption were to work an injustice. (The judge himself had first mentioned the new rules in early June, during Fulton's cross-examination of Professor Robert Dyal. At that time, ruling in my favor under the old rules, he had said, "Starting on the first of July it's going to be a whole new ball game"—an indication that he, as well as we, looked with favor on the coming change.)

Sylvester Del Corso had attended the trial every day and had listened attentively to all the testimony. He seemed troubled.

A self-made man, Del Corso was born on the wrong side of the tracks, in the Berea section of Cleveland, and he attended Baldwin-Wallace, a local college, on a football scholarship. He had joined the Ohio National Guard at fifteen, lying about his age, and he was commissioned a second lieutenant eleven years later, in 1939.

The Ohio National Guard was nationalized at the beginning of World War II, and soon he found himself commanding an infantry company in the "Buckeye" 37th Division, which fought in the South Pacific on Guadalcanal, Bougainville, and New Georgia. As a full colonel and commander of the 148th Regiment, he received the surrender of the Japanese forces in northeastern Luzon. He was one of the very few guardsmen defendants who had had any combat experience, and he was the only one with any sort of record as a leader of men under fire.

THE ADJUTANT GENERAL   143

Del Corso had found a home in the Army. He returned to active duty status as commander of an Army disciplinary barracks during the Korean War. He served in Army Intelligence in Europe, as a military adviser in Vietnam, then as a property officer and National Guard adviser in Ohio.

On April 4, 1968, he was invited by Governor Rhodes, then in his second term of office, to take over the Ohio National Guard. Del Corso was an active adjutant general. He traveled around the state giving speeches, warning of potential trouble, and encouraging mayors to ask for the Guard. He also circularized Ohio's guardsmen and Guard officials in other states, at Ohio's expense, urging them to write President Nixon in support of his Vietnam policy and to condemn the peace movement.

During the two years Del Corso served preceding the Kent shootings, the Ohio National Guard was called out on 31 occasions, six times as often as it had been summoned in the preceding five years of Rhodes' incumbency and more than any other National Guard outfit in the country. Del Corso attributed this circumstance to the fact that there was more unrest in Ohio, but his claim was not borne out by statistics. (The American Insurance Association reported that in the year ending February 28, 1970, Ohio ranked fifth among the states in the amount of property damage claims resulting from riots. Indiana, with a smaller population, had more than double the claims of Ohio, and while Ohio had suffered outbreaks in 18 cities, Indiana had had trouble in 27, California in 40, and New York in 24.)

Of the 31 call-outs between April 1968 and May 4, 1970, 14 were for civil disturbances, 5 of them in April and early May 1970. Between April 8 and May 2, 1970, Del Corso dispatched 952 guardsmen to Cleveland State University, 561 to Ohio University in Oxford, 96 to Sandusky, 2,861 to Ohio State University in Columbus, and 1,196 to Kent State.

Del Corso, who called himself a military man and not a politician, regarded SDS and the New Mobilization Committee to End the War in Vietnam as instruments of an international Communist conspiracy, that is, enemies of the United States.

We suspected that Del Corso's political views had contributed to the guardsmen's behavior being harsher toward the Kent students than it was, for example, toward the striking wildcat Teamsters, against whom the units that served at Kent had been called out on April 30. (There had been testimony that the guardsmen had not loaded their rifles while on duty against the Teamsters, despite the fact that they had actually been fired upon.)

Del Corso went with the troops to the Kent State campus on Saturday night and was with them when they dispersed the crowd around the fire, marching across the Commons, over Blanket Hill, and down to the practice field in a maneuver that paralleled the one they were to make on Monday. Along with

Canterbury, he picked up and threw back some rocks that had come in his direction from students.

Sunday morning Del Corso attended a meeting at the Kent firehouse—the temporary city hall—that was presided over by Governor Rhodes. Here Rhodes, after meeting with the mayor and other local law-enforcement people, made an aggressive, table-thumping public statement in which he said that the campus violence was caused by vicious elements who were trying to "destroy higher education in Ohio" and who were "worse than the brownshirts and the Communist element and also the night riders and the vigilantes. They're the worst type of people that we harbor in America. . . . I think that we're up against the strongest, well-trained, militant revolutionary group that has ever assembled in America. . . . We are going to eradicate the problem. We're not going to treat the symptom."

Del Corso left Kent with the governor and was in Columbus when the shooting occurred. He was with Rhodes an hour later when the governor called Vice President Agnew, told him about the shootings, and asked that federal investigators be rushed to Ohio.

In December 1970, after attending a review of Guard civil-disturbance policies in Washington, Del Corso abandoned the routine gun-loading policy and instituted a new set of riot control drills that emphasized the use of clubs.

We began by asking the Guard's highest-ranking officer about the unusual practices of weapon swapping that had been described by Sergeant Herschler and Lieutenant Fallon. Del Corso said that it was against regulations because "the individual in the military is taught that he and his weapon are inseparable and he should take good care of it and it will take good care of him."

Now we came to the nitty-gritty. I thought, in view of all the fireworks that would accompany an attempt to use Del Corso's federal grand jury testimony, that I would first try to get a statement from him on the justifiability of the shooting.

"Based upon your years of crowd control experience and handling of disturbance," I asked, "where you have a large number of people in a crowd, [isn't it true] that a certain percentage you might expect would be bystanders, curiosity seekers, passersby, and innocent of any criminal act?"

"He is getting into opinion testimony with respect to acts that he wasn't even there to witness," Fulton objected.

"He was there," I said. Fulton thought I was referring to the crowd at the shooting, but I could have been talking about the Saturday night fire. He had tipped his hand; he was going to object to Del Corso's being asked his opinion of the shooting on the basis that he had not been present.

"Is it a fact, sir, that you did testify before the federal grand jury, the state grand jury, and have been interviewed by the FBI and others?"

"Yes."

"And you have had access to photographs and have had access to various official documents and investigative reports concerning this incident, is that right, the shooting incident?" This would be the basis for an expert opinion; an expert did not have to be present at the scene—in fact it would be highly unusual if he had been.

"Yes," Del Corso answered, "limited access to some of the photographs."

"And you have spoken, I dare say, to General Canterbury many, many times concerning the events that occurred, is that right, sir?"

"Yes."

"Now, sir, did General Canterbury tell you that the closest student to the Guard at the time of the shooting was 20 yards?"

"I recall that something, the closest student to him, I think, is what he said. I don't recall, I recall something about 20 yards."

At this point Judge Young stopped me from qualifying General Del Corso as an expert or using the federal grand jury testimony to impeach him. He used a variety of arguments: that making an expert of a defendant would confuse the jury; that I would have to frame hypothetical questions (I was prepared to do so); and that I could not make him an expert over his counsel's objection.

I pointed out that in malpractice cases it was common to call doctor defendants as experts on their specialties, a situation exactly parallel to this one with Del Corso. I also reminded him that he had already let another defendant, Captain Srp, testify as an expert.

Judge Young wouldn't budge. We were at the jugular of the defense contention that the shooting was justifiable, and the judge was holding us back.

During the lunch recess my colleagues and I discussed the quandary we were in.

"Maybe I'm wrong," I said to Fred Mandel. "In New York we put opinion questions to adverse witnesses and defendants. Maybe you don't do that in Ohio?"

Fred Mandel and Steve Sindell said that it was commonly done in the Ohio courts. They were, they assured me, just as astounded by the judge's ruling as I was. This was significant because under the federal rules of civil procedure, the Ohio law on this matter was supposed to control what happened in any federal court within the boundaries of the state.

Sindell went to his office and got an Ohio ruling on this question. In 1965 the Ohio Court of Appeals had ruled that "the examining party [was allowed] to compel all testimony relevant to the issues in the case, and there is nothing in the statutory language which indicates that expert testimony is not included. An adverse party called to testify under this section may be examined as to any relevant matter [in] issue in a case whether or not it involves expert testimony." In the same decision the Ohio court had also said, "A civil defendant has no protection against subjecting himself to liability. If his testimony will provide facts which will aid the court in arriving at a just decision, he has a duty to testify."

Nothing could be clearer than that.

There was no reason to think that Judge Young was not as familiar with Ohio law as Sindell and Mandel. When we returned to the courtroom, and before the jury was brought in, Mandel and I moved that various types of testimony, such as the federal grand jury minutes, be admitted into evidence under the new rules that had gone into effect on July 1, 1975, and that were supposed to prevail at this trial; indeed, they were admissible under the old rules as well.

Judge Young replied that he had the option of following the new rules or not and that he did not intend to bind himself by them.

Mandel then reminded Young that six weeks before, on June 10, when Professor Dyal was on the stand, he had said, "Starting on the first of July it's going to be a whole new ball game." When Mandel reminded the judge that he had to apply the new rules where possible, the judge replied that he had explained how he felt about the use of federal grand jury testimony "until I am blue in the face," and he added that he did not think that Del Corso's grand jury testimony was impeaching because of the trivial nature of the differences between what it contained and what the witness said on the stand. "I don't think," he said, "that every trivial variation in language between what a witness says at one hearing and what a witness says at another hearing involving the same subject is to be considered as being an impeachment of that man's testimony. . . .

"If a man makes a radical departure, if he suddenly changes his story, that is a horse of another color. Certainly the jury should know about that."

The federal grand jury testimony, I told the judge, "establishes the facts, that's why counsel have been quick on the trigger to try to head me off . . . because they know, and I can show the Court, this witness has testified to repeated questions . . . that . . ."*

I asked the judge's permission to put in the record Del Corso's answers to the questions of the grand jury.

Judge Young told me that he didn't "think this is in the interest of justice"

*Testimony deleted pursuant to prohibition by Judge Young.

but that I could read the grand jury testimony to the court reporter when no one was around to hear it. This meant it would go into the trial transcript for use on an appeal, but it would not be given to the jury. The judge refused to listen to it himself, and he suggested that I read it to the court reporter during his lunch hour. "Let the poor court reporter starve," he said.

I did just that, and the court reporter did not starve.

Six weeks after the end of the trial, on September 29, the *Cleveland Plain Dealer* published an article containing what it claimed were excerpts from Del Corso's federal grand jury testimony:

> Sylvester T. Del Corso, adjutant general when the Ohio National Guard shot and killed four students at Kent State University in 1970, repeatedly told a federal grand jury that the guardsmen were unjustified in their actions, the *Plain Dealer* has learned.
>
> The *Plain Dealer* has been shown a copy of Del Corso's secret testimony to a federal grand jury in Cleveland. In that testimony, given last year, Del Corso stated 16 times that the guardsmen were not justified in shooting, or even aiming at, the students at an anti-war rally on campus. . . .
>
> During his grand jury testimony Feb. 26, 1974, Del Corso not only said repeatedly that the guard was unjustified in shooting, but also said:
>
> The Kent State University administration was "very, very negligent" and should have permitted the students to hold a protest rally on the university Commons on the day of the shootings. . . .
>
> Based on pictures of the shootings and reports received, the guardsmen were not surrounded by the students at the time of the shootings and were not threatened by the students.
>
> None of the students was close enough to the soldiers to endanger their lives.
>
> There was no sniper fire before the shooting. . . .
>
> In his testimony before the grand jury, Del Corso faced intense and repeated questioning about the shootings. Jurors asked him repeatedly if the shootings were justified.
>
> After what appeared to be an initial effort to sidestep the question, Del Corso clearly and consistently told the grand jury that the guard was wrong to shoot.
>
> "I say it was unjustifiable, because as I see it, I can't see how it can be justified," he testified. "And to me, overall, like I say, I can't see any justification in it."
>
> Later in the day, concluding his six hours of testimony with a voluntary statement to the grand jury, Del Corso said, "I can't for the life of me find any real justification for the shooting there." . . .
>
> To another question, the general, a 42-year military veteran, said, ". . . many of these individuals that fired their weapons, there is absolutely no justification to fire, no justification."

When a grand juror asked, "With the distance the students were at, the closest one . . . was 60 feet and the other was 700 feet away, do you think they were justified in aiming at the students?"

Del Corso responded: "No, I don't think they were at all." Del Corso continued, "Because certainly someone 100 feet or even 200 feet away, I don't think creates a danger to the man's life unless he has a gun or something and is charging at him with something that could threaten his life.

"But certainly anyone that far away, there is no justification to shoot." . . .

After looking at pictures of the shootings, Del Corso, who was in Columbus the day of the shootings, was asked, "Does the guard appear to be surrounded at all in those pictures?"

Del Corso answered, "No, they do not." . . .

In his closing, voluntary statement, Del Corso said that guard officials had initially believed there had been a sniper on campus but had later changed that position after investigation.

". . . we could substantiate no sniper fire," he said. "There wasn't any."

I was no more successful in getting sensible testimony from Del Corso on the differences between Ohio Guard and Army regulations. The "evidence hole" rule was used to prevent me from reading from or even referring to the OPLAN and the Army field manual when I asked Del Corso about the differences between them. The judge would not even allow Del Corso, who had issued the OPLAN, to be considered an expert on the document! Consequently, replies by Del Corso that misstated the facts remained unrefuted.

18

The Matson-Frisina Letter

The witnesses who testified as to who was in control of the campus on May 4, 1970, were three officers of the university, David Ambler, Robert Matson, and Robert White, and General Robert Canterbury. White was president of Kent State in 1970, Matson was vice president for student affairs, and Ambler was Matson's assistant. White had left the campus Friday afternoon for Iowa and returned at noon on Sunday after being informed of the ROTC fire. During his absence Matson had been in charge of the university administration.

The question of who controlled the campus turned on two events and one document. The events were the meetings at the Kent fire station on Sunday morning and Monday morning; the document was the Matson-Frisina letter.

At the Sunday meeting Governor Rhodes indicated what he wanted done about Kent State. At the Monday meeting General Canterbury made the decision to disperse the noon rally. The letter was an information directive to Kent State students issued by Vice President Matson and Student President Frank Frisina late Sunday afternoon. It read:

> During the last two days, the disruptive and destructive activities of a dissident group comprising students and non-students, and numbering 500 to 600, escalated from a peaceful rally through illegal threat to life plus property damage leading eventually to the Governor's imposition of a state of emergency encompassing both the city of Kent and the University.

The Governor, through the National Guard, has assumed legal control of the campus and the city of Kent. As currently defined the state of emergency has established the following:

1. Prohibited all forms of outdoor demonstrations and rallys—peaceful or otherwise;

2. Empowered the National Guard to make arrests;

3. A curfew is in effect for the city from 8 P.M. to 6 A.M. and an on-campus curfew of 1 A.M. has been ordered by the National Guard.

The above will remain in effect until altered or removed by order of the Governor.

The campus at the present state is calm. Several hundred National Guard and state police are presently on campus to maintain order. They are under the direction of Governor James A. Rhodes and will remain on alert on and around the campus until normal conditions return.

We plan to resume our normal class schedule on Monday with the exception of classes scheduled for the floor of Memorial Gymnasium. Currently the gym floor is being used to provide barrack facilities for the National Guard troops. . . .

The letter describes a state of martial law. However, it was not signed by Governor Rhodes or by anyone claiming to represent him; it was signed by a vice president of the university and a student leader. One can question the wisdom of the university putting out such a letter and cooperating more than was necessary. Nevertheless, one must ask: Who was the source of the information? Did Matson and Frisina make it up out of their own heads?

Major Jones testified that the letter had been drafted by Matson after Matson consulted him and after Jones had checked with Major Wallach (who, there was reason to believe, had talked with General Del Corso).

The jurors, of course, because of the "evidence hole" rule, had not seen this letter or heard its contents. Yet the defense lawyers, using the Big Julie (unseen dice in the hat) corollary, had referred to it numerous times as a *university* directive prohibiting rallies.

Now that we were reaching the end of our case we knew it was imperative that we bring the letter's contents into the open so that the jurors could learn exactly what it said.

We planned to do this while examining the two university officials who had framed the letter, Vice President Matson and his assistant, David Ambler. The two officials would also explain the role of the Guard in providing the information contained in the letter, thereby elaborating on Major Jones' testimony.

Objections from the defense and rulings by Judge Young, however, prevented us from developing the evidence. After revealing that Rhodes had told him at the Sunday morning meeting that the university's role had been superseded, Ambler was kept from testifying on the origin of the letter on the grounds that he no longer remembered the name and rank of the officer who had told him what to put in it. Then, when Matson took the stand and remembered the source as Major Jones, the judge stated that whatever Jones had told Matson was of no value because he had "no control over the university."

I asked the judge if he was ruling that Major Jones had no authority to transmit orders to Matson.

"I certainly am," Judge Young said. He added that it didn't make any difference where Matson had gotten the information. "He put out the letter, and the letter speaks for itself, and it is what it is."

Despite his insistence that the letter "speaks for itself," the judge refused to let the jury hear it speak. At the bench Karl told the judge that in keeping the letter from the jury he was permitting it to be misled on a very important issue.

"Judge," I added, "this paper is already in evidence. There have been repeated references to [it]. . . . Up to this time the jury . . . hasn't the remotest idea that the following statements appear in this exhibit: 'The Governor, through the National Guard, has assumed legal control of the campus and the city of Kent——' "

"I have read that thing," Judge Young interrupted me. "There is no particular reason why you should read it over to me again."

I told him that we were entitled to have the jury know that the governor did assume legal control.

The judge again cut me off, maintaining that Ambler could testify to what he did but not to "why they put the things in it they put in."

Of course, if all the jury heard was that Ambler had typed the letter, they would assume that it was, as the defense contended, a university directive.

"If some student and some vice president of student affairs determined that the governor had taken control of the campus," Judge Young said, there was no real evidence "on the very serious issue as to what the governor did."

Blakemore, White's lawyer, spoke up. "It does," he said, "if they were advised."

Judge Young just wouldn't hear that.

When I asked the judge's permission to read the letter to the jury, he told me that its words would give them a false impression. In other words, reading it to the jurors was deceitful, but Brown's and Fulton's repeated assertions that the letter showed that the university, acting on its own, had banned all rallies were not.

When the letter first surfaced weeks before, Alloway objected to its reference to the governor. It seemed obvious to me that Judge Young was refusing now to let the jury learn what was in the letter in deference to this objection; but in doing so he was allowing the issue to become distorted.

The question of the origin of the letter—whether or not the governor and/or the Guard was responsible for it—was a question of fact for the jury to decide. However, the judge was in effect deciding it for them by keeping its contents from them, by preventing us from bringing in testimony on the Guard's role in framing the letter, and by insisting that the only way to learn the governor's intention was to ask the governor himself.

Usually when a document says one thing and a witness says another, the burden of proof is on the witness. Judge Young had already rejected a prima facie case, based on the governor's own proclamation, that the governor had invoked martial law, and since then he had thwarted every attempt to show the governor's role in the shootings.

I wondered, in view of all the obstacles, whether we would be able to show any case against Governor Rhodes by the time he reached the stand.

Robert Matson looked uncomfortable on the stand; obviously he would have preferred not to testify. He confirmed that the university administration had been superseded, testifying that at the Sunday morning meeting Governor Rhodes "said something to the effect that the university types . . . should move aside on this one and he would handle it or they would handle it." Although he was the highest-ranking official of the university at the Sunday meeting, Matson said, he was not asked to participate.

The Monday morning meeting, at which the decision was made to disperse the rally, entered the record for the first time in the course of Matson's testimony. He told Karl that it was attended by himself, President White, and representatives of various government agencies and was presided over by General Canterbury. Among the topics of discussion had been the rumor of a noon rally on campus.

"Do you recall at this time whether any decision was reached with regard to that rally at noon?" Karl asked.

"I believe that we left the meeting with the understanding that the general procedures under which we had operated the day before would continue, that would apply to any rally. That's what I remember now."

General Robert Canterbury, assistant adjutant general of the Ohio National Guard, was the highest-ranking officer on the Kent State campus on May 4. In 1975 he was no longer in the National Guard, having been replaced, along with Del Corso, by Governor John Gilligan in January 1971, at which time he had retired to a small town in Arkansas. He was a blunt-featured, medium-sized man with rather sparse crew-cut hair and a weatherbeaten look.

Canterbury left the Kent State campus late Saturday night and then returned at midnight Sunday after receiving a telephone call from Del Corso, who said that trouble was brewing again. On Monday he marched down to the practice field and back up Blanket Hill in a business suit, a gas mask perched atop his head. When the firing began, he was in front of the troops, heading down the far side of the hill toward the Commons, about 35 yards from Taylor Hall. He turned and ran back to stop the shooting.

Canterbury had told the FBI that the Monday crowd on the campus was hostile, intended to burn other buildings, and threatened the guardsmen; that he had been operating under the martial law statute when he dispersed the students; that he had at all times followed the OPLAN; and that the guardsmen's lives had been in danger.

He claimed that the windshield of the jeep from which the dispersal announcement was made had been broken (this was denied by both Colonel Fassinger and Sergeant Haas of the Troop G motor pool) and that he had seen two students get hit by the rifle fire when they were about 15 to 20 feet in front of the guardsmen and running toward them (Canterbury had in fact been on the other side of the hill when the shooting started).

There had been considerable testimony about General Canterbury. Captain James Ronald Snyder called him aggressive and bullheaded and recounted how, late Saturday night, he had dissuaded Canterbury from sending him and his men into a glassed-in rotunda in the center of the Tri-Towers dormitory complex to arrest more than a hundred students.

Chaplain Simons stated that he did not think Canterbury knew what he was doing when he led the guardsmen over the hill after having dispersed the students from the Commons. Several other witnesses described Canterbury's intention to unleash his men against the hysterical students on the Commons after the shooting.

On the stand Canterbury admitted to me, as he had in his deposition, that he had conceived his mission on May 4 to be to disperse the rally whether or not it was peaceful, and that he personally had told campus policeman Harold Rice to read the riot act through a bullhorn from a National Guard jeep.

The suppression during the trial of the Matson-Frisina letter assumed even more ominous dimensions with Canterbury on the stand. Although he claimed not to have read it before moving his troops against the students on Monday, he cited it as the civilian authorization that gave him the right to do so.

Thus, by the magic of the Big Julie corollary, the letter was transformed into its opposite: from a statement of military control on the campus, it became a civilian authorization for the Guard to undertake the dispersal of a peaceful assembly.

Canterbury's version of the Monday morning meeting was that everyone present had discussed the events of the past twenty-four hours and that he was compelled by the Matson-Frisina letter to disperse any assembly.

"There was a discussion entered into by just about everyone there . . . and the decision was made by the mayor, by the sheriff, by the chief of police, by everyone including the university people, that the rallies should not be permitted."

"Well, sir," I said, "let's get down to the discussions. . . . Who was the spokesman for the university there?"

"Well, certainly the president of the university would be normally the spokesman."

"Are you saying," I asked, "that he specifically said, 'We want all assemblies, peaceful or not peaceful, to be dispersed,' yes or no, sir?"

"I can only reply in terms of the letter——"

"But you didn't see that letter at that time, did you?"

"No, but——"

"And we are past that. I want to know what happened at the meeting."

"We were informed the letter prohibited assemblies," Canterbury said.

"When you saw Dr. White at the meeting on Monday," I asked, "did he specifically say, 'I agree, I want all assemblies, whether peaceful or not, at Kent State University, to be dispersed'?"

"After informing us of the letter," Canterbury replied, "and after the matter of assembly had been discussed, I asked Dr. White if the assembly was to be permitted, and his response was that it would be highly dangerous."

"Did he say that he wanted you or the Guard to disperse any and all assemblies?"

"I have given you the total of that conversation."

Canterbury's own career had been in the restaurant business; he had become a National Guard general through years of continuous Guard service. Pushed along by the gung ho speeches and attitudes of Del Corso and Rhodes, he had apparently overreacted at Kent State, wanting to arrest hundreds of students who were only "milling around" in a rotunda, dispersing a "picnic, festive" assembly, leading his troops aimlessly over hill and dale on the Kent campus, and threatening to move again on the hysterical, grieving students after the shooting. I looked on him as a pathetic would-be military hero.

When former university president Robert White took the stand, Fred Mandel asked him whether he could confirm Canterbury's testimony that at the Monday morning meeting White had said "it would be dangerous to permit a rally on Monday, May 4."

"No, sir," White replied.

"Did General Canterbury ask you whether or not you wanted to have the assembly dispersed?"

"I don't recall any such question." He had left the meeting, White said, believing that "the earlier established ban on gatherings would be continued."

Robert I. White was a heavyset man whose features resembled those of General Canterbury. He had come to the university's graduate school of education in 1951 and assumed the presidency in 1963. His policies had gradually become restrictive when, in the late 60s, militants began staging sit-ins.

When on Sunday morning he returned to Kent on the university plane, he found Governor Rhodes waiting for him at the airport to tell him that the university was confronted with a law-enforcement problem caused by 400 troublemakers who had descended on his campus with a view to closing it. The governor told White that the matter was out of White's hands.

From the time of his return to the campus early Sunday afternoon, President White kept mostly to his house on Main Street. When the Monday morning meeting broke up at 11:20, he returned briefly to his office, then went to the Brown Derby restaurant on Main Street, east of the campus, in the direction of Ravenna. He was lunching with Matson and three other vice presidents when he received a telephone call informing him of the shootings.

Under Mandel's questioning, White explained that the typical noon rally dispersed harmlessly after about forty-five minutes because the students would go to classes or return to their rooms.

"Is it fair to say," Mandel asked, "on the basis of what you have just told the jury, that your experience was that by letting people get the steam out and have their rallies, you had no disturbance?"

"Generally, yes."

Later testimony by White, when he appeared on the stand during the defense phase of the trial, showed that he never doubted that the Guard had taken over the campus. On Sunday afternoon he issued a mimeographed statement to the effect that the Guard would stay until its leadership decided the campus would remain peaceful in its absence. "Events have taken the decision out of the university's hands." (He told the Scranton Commission that he believed that he retained control only of "academic operations.")

Blakemore tried to introduce some cryptic notes that White had made during the Monday morning meeting, to show that he had actually opposed dispersal of the noon rally. The notes, which would probably have proved useless in any case, were not admitted as evidence. Our discussion on this point, in which we cited the new federal rules of evidence in favor of the notes' admission as "present sense impressions," occasioned one of Judge Young's more memorable statements on the new rules, which he called "a wonderful thing. They say the judge doesn't have to pay any attention to them, but if he wants to, he can.

"I am like the judge with the deck of cards, I can use the new rules; if you would rather have the deck of cards, you probably better bring in a new deck."

I looked at Fred Mandel, and Fred looked at me. This was a most frivolous statement for a federal judge to make.

Dr. White impressed me as a well-intentioned but weak man who had yielded to the aggressive conduct of Governor Rhodes in the takeover of the campus. I do not envy him his memories.

19

What Price Power?

▬

Governor James A. Rhodes, the person who in our minds bore the main responsibility for the shootings, made his appearance on Tuesday, July 29.

James Allen Rhodes was born into the family of a Welsh coal miner in southern, Appalachian Ohio in 1909. He had to shoulder responsibilities early, for his father died when he was eight years old. To help support his mother and sisters, he took odd jobs, working as a golf caddie and a janitor. He graduated from high school at the age of twenty; in 1930 he pawned his golf clubs to enroll in the School of Journalism at Ohio State University.

Exhibiting a natural flair for politics, he organized Young Republicans on campus and was elected mayor of the university's mock government. Soon after dropping out of school in 1931, and with the help of a friend in the local Republican organization, he opened a campus restaurant. He became a precinct captain in 1933, and eight years later he was elected auditor of the City of Columbus. Eventually he became the city's mayor and, after that, state auditor.

Rhodes was regarded as something of a maverick by the state Republican organization, but he could hardly be ignored when, in 1960, he was reelected state auditor by a 700,000-vote margin, half a million more votes than Nixon had garnered in carrying the state against Kennedy.

Running for governor two years later, Rhodes called for bold and imaginative social programs without specifying how they were to be financed. As governor he slashed social expenditures, fired state employees, canceled construction projects, and drove a small car. The result of these policies, as a

Columbus newspaper that had supported him pointed out, was that Ohio, the sixth wealthiest state in the union, ranked near the bottom when it came to services.

In the spring of 1970 he was in the final year of his second term, barred by the Ohio constitution from reelection. On May 3, 1970, when the governor went to Kent, he was campaigning for the Republican nomination for the U.S. Senate and the primary election was just two days away. Despite Rhodes' outstanding record as a vote getter, polls showed him trailing his opponent, Robert Taft.

Governor Rhodes flew to Kent by helicopter with his aide John McElroy. For several weeks he had been threatening to use "all the force that was necessary" to end the campus disturbances in various parts of the state.

At a conference with General Del Corso, Guard officers, and local law-enforcement officials, Rhodes claimed to have been informed by the Ohio Highway Patrol's "Intelligence" that the campus disturbances were being caused by the same group of troublemakers traveling from campus to campus with the aim of closing down universities. He also said he had been told that four Kent State SDS leaders, who had been released from jail on April 30 after completing six-month sentences resulting from the occupation of a building the previous fall, were behind the present Kent State disturbances.*

At about ten that Sunday morning, when the press had arrived at the firehouse, Rhodes repeated the rumors and said, "We've seen here in the city of Kent, especially, probably the most vicious form of campus-oriented violence yet perpetrated by dissident groups and their allies in the State of Ohio. . . . They're the worst type of people that we harbor in America. . . . Now there's no, there's no place off limits at this hour."

After stating that he would "apply whatever degree of force is necessary to provide protection for the lives of our citizens and their property," the governor added: "When the technique of the Weathermen and the SDS and Student Mobilization Committee, when this is employed and firebombing and violence and let me also say that death is not going to stand in their way to assure their purpose and we are going to employ everything that we possibly can do to protect the buildings."

Kent Chief of Police Roy Thompson followed by saying, "We can't tolerate this burning and threatening of our merchants and our citizens as well as our schools. I [will] be right behind the Ohio National Guard giving our full support, anything that's necessary even to the point of shooting."

*The FBI investigation failed to discover any connection between any of the four and the events of that weekend.

The governor, without disavowing Chief Thompson's statement, then said, "Let me say this, that if they can intimidate and threaten, jowl the merchants of this community and other people . . . I do not believe that people understand the seriousness of these individuals organized in a revolutionary frame of mind."

In May 1970 Rhodes was a big, bluff, hearty man, sixty years of age, six feet tall, with a full head of hair and weighing about 200 pounds. He had a passion for sports; he served as president of the National Amateur Athletic Union and as a member of the Advisory Committee of the American Olympic Committee. When campaigning statewide, he liked to be found shooting baskets in parks or high school gymnasiums.

I knew I faced a formidable task in trying to bring out Rhodes' part in the shootings. His role as commander-in-chief, sharing responsibility for Del Corso's hair-trigger OPLAN regulations, automatically made him a defendant —but that was far from being the heart of our claim. He had acted overtly to displace the university's authority, incited the guardsmen and placed himself in personal command of the Guard by invoking martial law. And, in 1975, he was governor again, having been elected to a third term in the fall of 1974.

Unlikely as it may sound, Rhodes and McElroy claimed that their citation of the martial law statute had been a mistake. We thought we could show that this was not so. In support of his contention that his use of the martial law statute was a mistake, Rhodes had deposed not only that he had not employed martial law at Kent State but that he had never proclaimed it elsewhere (in fact he had proclaimed it on May 22, 1970, in calling the Guard to Ohio State University). In addition, we were confident that the governor was aware of the difference between the two statutes used for calling out the Guard: the martial law and the aid-to-civil-authorities statutes. The martial law statute had been passed in 1967 during his own administration, and he had signed eighteen proclamations that cited the aid-to-civil-authorities statute.

Furthermore, we could show that Rhodes had violated the Constitution no matter which statute he claimed to have used. The martial law statute had been illegally employed because the civil courts, which must be shown to be incapacitated before martial law may be imposed, had been operating normally in Kent and in Portage County. On the other hand, if Rhodes tried to say he had intended only to call the Guard to aid the civil authorities, we could show that his April 29 proclamation, instructing the Guard merely to "consult" with the civil authorities, leaving "the procedure of execution to the discretion of the commanding military officer," gave the Guard far too much authority. If there was any doubt that this was so, a decision arising from an 1897 Ohio

National Guard case stated that guardsmen were to be considered no more than armed police,

> subject to the absolute and exclusive control and direction of the magistrates and other civil officers . . . nor can the sheriff or magistrate delegate his authority to the military force *or vest in the military authorities any discretionary power, to take any step or do any act* to prevent or suppress a mob or riot. [Emphasis added.]

We had the two proclamations Governor Rhodes issued on April 29 and May 5, the statements he made to the press on Sunday, May 3, and the secret instructions he gave the Guard the same day, before the press conference. We had physical evidence of all but the last, and for that we had the testimony of Michael Delaney.

The first proclamation, which the governor claimed authorized the call-out of the National Guard at Kent, said:

> WHEREAS in northeastern Ohio, particularly in the counties of Cuyahoga, Mahoning, Summit and Lorain, and in other parts of Ohio, in particular Richmond, Butler and Hamilton Counties, there exist unlawful assemblies and roving bodies of men acting with intent to commit felony and to do violence to person or property in disregard of the laws of the state of Ohio and the United States of America; and
> WHEREAS these unlawful assemblies and bodies of men have by acts of intimidation and threats of violence put law-abiding citizens in fear of pursuing their normal vocations in the *transportation industry* . . .
> NOW, THEREFORE, I, JAMES A. RHODES, Governor and commander-in-chief of the militia of the State of Ohio, do hereby order into active service such personnel and units of the militia as may be designated by the Adjutant General to maintain peace and order and to protect life and property throughout the State of Ohio. . . . The military forces involved will act *in aid of the civil authorities* and shall consult with them to the extent necessary to determine the objects to be accomplished, leaving the procedure of execution to the discretion of the commanding military officer designated by the Adjutant General. [Emphasis added.]

The second proclamation, issued the day after the shooting, said:

> WHEREAS, on April 29, 1970, the Governor of Ohio as commander-in-chief issued verbal orders to the Adjutant General of Ohio directing him to call up such units of the Ohio National Guard as in his judgment might be necessary or desirable to meet disorders and threatened disorders relating to wildcat strikes in the truck transportation industry, and to meet disorders or threatened disorders on campuses of Ohio State University in Franklin County, and campuses of other state-assisted universities; and

WHEREAS, pursuant to Section 5923.231 of the Ohio Revised Code, the Governor of Ohio thereafter on April 29, 1970, issued his Proclamation ordering into active service such personnel and units of the militia as the Adjutant General might designate "to maintain peace and order and to protect life and property throughout the State of Ohio"; and

WHEREAS, pursuant to the verbal orders aforementioned, the Adjutant General of Ohio called to active service units of the Ohio National Guard and assigned them variously to service in the City of Kent and on the campus of Kent State University in Portage County, and on the campus of Ohio State University in Franklin County, in addition to divers specific assignments related to restoration of order in the truck transportation industry; and

WHEREAS, it is desirable to make a written record, both of events and the derivation of authority exercised by personnel and units of the Ohio National Guard in Portage County and Franklin County,

NOW, THEREFORE, I, JAMES A. RHODES, Governor and commander-in-chief of the militia of the State of Ohio, do hereby supplement my Proclamation of April 29, 1970, by specifying that personnel and units of militia as may or may have been designated by the Adjutant General to maintain peace and order in the City of Kent and on the campus of Kent State University in Portage County, and on the campus of Ohio State University in Franklin County, are included in the call of active service hereinbefore referred to . . .

The two proclamations possessed a number of curious features. That of April 29 mentioned seven counties but not Portage County, where Kent is situated; it referred only to trouble in the transportation industry; and it did not specifically cite the Ohio statute under which it had been invoked.

(On April 29 there had been disorders at Ohio State but none at Kent State. The reference to "disorders or threatened disorders on . . . Ohio State . . . and [other] campuses" implied that the Guard had been called on April 29 to confront, among other things, "threatened disorders" at Kent State. Yet there was no evidence that on April 29, two days before the downtown trashing, there had been any hint of a threat in Kent.) The proclamation of May 5 sought to remedy the earlier proclamation's deficiencies by saying that it had been issued under the martial law statute (5923.231) and encompassed "verbal" orders given on April 29 regarding "disorders or threatened disorders on campuses of Ohio State University in Franklin County, and campuses of other state-assisted universities." Kent and Kent State University were mentioned in the third paragraph as places to which National Guard units had been sent "pursuant to the verbal orders aforementioned." The May 5 proclamation also explained the need for its existence, stating that it was "desirable to make a written record, both of events and the derivation of authority exercised" by the Guard in Portage and Franklin counties.

Obviously John McElroy, in drafting the May 5 proclamation, had been faced with the problem of showing—after the event—that the Guard had been acting in some legal manner at Kent State on the previous day. He did this by claiming that its activities were covered by verbal orders issued in conjunction with the April 29 proclamation and asserting that both proclamations were issued under the martial law statute. The difficulty, of course, lay in presenting a plausible verbal order that, given on April 29, could cover events that did not take place until May 2. He did this by claiming that the April 29 verbal orders referred to "disorders or *threatened* disorders on campuses of Ohio State University in Franklin County, and campuses of other state-assisted universities." (Emphasis added.)

On its face the May 5 proclamation was a coverup document intended to justify the shootings. We speculated as to why, after invoking martial law, the governor and McElroy later denied having done so. The most plausible explanation was that the invocation of martial law, in addition to being illegal, would have made the governor personally responsible for everything that had happened in Kent after the Guard arrived.

Originally we sought to have the judge declare that Rhodes invoked the Guard in an illegal manner, but the judge had refused, passing the issue on to the jury as a matter of fact (whether or not Rhodes and McElroy had lied in maintaining that the reference to martial law was an error).

When we tried to read to the jury the Matson-Frisina letter, showing that the governor had taken over the campus, we were told that we could learn his intentions only by questioning him in person.

I fully intended to cross-examine the governor, using the two proclamations as supporting evidence.

Promptly at 9:30 on a Tuesday morning, Judge Young opened the oak door in the back of the courtroom, turned right, and climbed the stairs to the bench. "Good morning, ladies and gentlemen," he greeted the jury as he sat down.

"Good morning, Your Honor," the jurors chorused.

"Ready to go?" Judge Young asked.

"Yes, sir," the jurors murmured.

"Very well," Judge Young said. He turned to me. "Call your next."

I was standing beside our table on the floor of the courtroom, below the judge and about ten feet from the jury box. "We call the defendant James Rhodes to the witness stand."

Judge Young watched Rhodes as he walked through the gate that separated the spectators from the arena. "Your Excellency," he said, "if you will come forward and raise your right hand, the clerk will swear you in."

At the words "Your Excellency" I caught Fred Mandel's eye. He was shaking his head in wonderment.

Rhodes took the oath, a figure in blue: dark blue suit, blue shirt, striped tie, and blue-gray brilliantined hair. He sat heavily in his seat in the witness box.

While Judge Young cautioned him about keeping the microphone close to his mouth, I was trying to size up the governor. I knew he would be an evasive witness, but this would present no problem as long as the judge required him to respond directly to the questions.

The judge did everything but that. I was prevented from referring to the two proclamations by the "evidence hole" rule. For the rest, Rhodes was either silenced by objections from Alloway, almost invariably sustained by the judge, or permitted to reply to my questions with speeches instead of answers. My objections, instead of curbing this improper behavior, brought him only encouragement from Judge Young.

I was not permitted to elicit from the governor that, as he had averred in his deposition, he did not know that the guardsmen's guns were loaded. When I asked whether he had ever considered that the Guard required special training to prevent the shooting of civilians, he replied, "I think the National Guard was operated well. We had called the Guard out to other campuses and had no trouble. Called the——"

"Sir," I tried to halt the irrelevant speech.

"——called the Guard out for riots," Rhodes continued.

"Sir," I started again, "I am interrupting you because you are not answering the question."

"We called the Guard out for riots in Cleveland, Youngstown, Akron, Toledo," Rhodes continued, "that's in the northern section, which was civil disobedience and unrest. We had no trouble at any one of the places where the mayor asked us, and we performed our duty as governor and called out the Guard. We had no trouble. So there would be no reason that I would discuss, after successful operations, the detail concerning the Guard."

"So your answer to my previous question would be no?" I asked Rhodes.

Fulton got up. "Well," he said, "objection again to what his answer is. His answer is what his answer is."

"Sustained," Judge Young said. "He has given his answer." He told me to move on to the next question.

"In the truckers' strike," I asked, "is it a fact that there was some shooting, if you know?"

"In the truckers' strike," Rhodes replied, "there was shooting, and the——"

Okay, that was the answer. There was shooting. I cut him off.

"Let him finish," Brown said.

"Let him finish," Fulton echoed.

"You may finish your answer," Judge Young said.

"We had met at the downtown airport with the officials, the mayors of the respective communities that were involved," Rhodes said. Supposedly he was still answering my question about whether there had been shooting during the truckers' strike. "I remember very vividly we had probably twelve mayors. At that time they asked me to call out the Guard, and we did, and we had extreme violence in the way of shooting, and they also shot at the Guard, shot at the highway patrol, shot at competitive truckers. It was a disturbance of proportion, and they needed the Guard and I called the Guard out."

"Sir," I asked the governor, "my question is, did you have trouble and shooting at that particular time, the truckers' strike? That was my question."

Fulton got up. "And that was his answer," he said.

"The question has been answered," Judge Young said.

"Now," I asked Rhodes, "how about at Hough? Did you have some shooting or some physical violence on one side or both sides of any confrontation there? Won't you please answer that directly, sir?"

"In Hough, Cleveland, Ohio?" Rhodes asked.

"Yes."

"Excuse me, Your Honor," Fulton said. "I object to Mr. Kelner's remark, 'Answer directly.' I think the witness has been very direct."

"I am trying to be very explicit," I said, "and move along, and if he would answer directly I would appreciate it."

"Well, again," Fulton said, "ask that his remarks about 'answer directly' be stricken."

"Mr. Kelner," Judge Young said, "as I have told you time and time again, you are asking questions which, while they are permissible on cross-examination, make it difficult because they do not call for simple direct answers, and you cannot ask a question and then require the witness to make an answer that he cannot properly give to it. If you don't want him to give that kind of an answer, you shouldn't ask that kind of a question."

"I will rephrase my question," I said, "with Your Honor's permission." I turned to the witness and asked, "Was there physical violence and/or shooting in the Hough disturbance?"

That was a question that could be answered by two yeses or two noes or any combination thereof. Rhodes' answer consisted of 98 words.

I requested that a tape recording of the May 3 press conference be played so that everyone could hear it, and afterward I offered it in evidence. As the tape was played, Rhodes leaned forward, listening intently to every word. His voice on the tape was loud and angry.

The scene here that the City of Kent is facing is probably the most vicious form of campus-oriented violence yet perpetrated by dissident groups and their allies in the State of Ohio. . . . Now it ceases to be a problem of the colleges of Ohio. This now is the problem of the State of Ohio. Now we're going to put a stop to this, for this reason. The same group that we're dealing with here today, and there's three or four of them, they only have one thing in mind. That is to destroy higher education in Ohio . . . Last night I think that we have seen all forms of violence, the worst. And when they start taking over communities, this is when we're going to use every weapon of the law-enforcement agencies of Ohio to drive them out of Kent. We have these same groups going from one campus to the other, and they use the universities that are supported by the taxpayers of Ohio as a sanctuary. And in this they make definite plans of burning, destroying, and throwing rocks at police and at the National Guard and the Highway Patrol . . . They're worse than the brownshirts and the Communist element and also the night riders and the vigilantes. They're the worst type of people that we harbor in America . . . It's over with in Ohio. . . . I think that we're up against the strongest, well-trained, militant revolutionary group that has ever assembled in America. . . . We are going to eradicate the problem. We're not going to treat the symptom.

"Is it a fact that you did deliver your remarks in a very forceful manner by pounding the table with your fist and by various emphatic gestures?" I asked.

"About like this," Rhodes said, tapping his index finger on the desk in front of him.

"That's your best recollection of the physical manifestations of your feelings at that time, sir?"

"I didn't think it was a matter of feeling," Rhodes replied. "This was almost a state of war."

"You mentioned during the course of your remarks that they cannot continue to set fire to buildings that are worth five and ten million dollars. Sir," I asked, "were there any buildings that were worth five and ten million dollars that were set on fire at Kent State University?"

"Our intelligence——"

"Were there," I asked again, "not what your intelligence said, were there?"

"The answer is no," Rhodes replied, "but I would like to amplify what the intelligence showed."

"Your counsel will have that opportunity, sir," I said. "Please be patient with me, so I can continue. You mentioned there were certain groups going from one campus to the other and that they use a university, state-supported by the taxpayers, for the purpose of burning, destroying, and throwing rocks. You recall those remarks in substance, don't you?"

"Yes, sir," Rhodes said.

From this point on, Alloway objected to every question I asked, usually on the grounds that it was argumentative. All but a few objections were sustained by the judge.

"Now, sir, are you aware that all of the youngsters shot were actually students registered at Kent State University?"

Objection sustained.

"Are you aware that there were three students or three individuals who may not have been students who were arrested for the burning of the ROTC Building?"

Objection sustained.

"Sir, under your concepts of procedures as commander-in-chief and as governor, what is your opinion: that only those who are guilty should be brought before the bar of justice and none others?"

Objection sustained.

I looked intently at Rhodes and paused to let the jury savor the effect this roadblock had in barring me from getting pertinent answers. Rhodes wore the studied expression of a man being protected from an annoyance. His face was flushed and set in a hard glare.

I wondered what this man was *really* thinking now about his role in the deaths and maiming of thirteen unarmed young students. I regarded his Sunday speech as gasoline poured on a smoldering fire.

Rhodes was allowed to answer one question about who it was that he had referred to as moving from one campus to the other and terrorizing a community.

"The leaders of the SDS and Weathermen and the Student Mobilization."

"Did you have evidence that they were engaged in any criminal activities?" I asked.

"I had information from the intelligence that they did."

"Did you, as chief executive officer of the State of Ohio, order their arrest if there was evidence of criminal activities?"

Objection sustained.

"Did you order an investigation of any criminal activities and insist that the law be enforced against such persons?"

Objection sustained.

I reminded the governor that he had been heard on tape to say, "We will apply whatever degree of force is necessary to provide protection for the lives of our citizens and their property." I asked him to explain the degree of force he was talking about.

Objection sustained.

"Well," I asked, "did it include shooting, sir, under any circumstances?"
Objection sustained.

"Sir," I asked, "do you remember in the tape recording you made this statement: 'Let me assure everyone that there is no place, there is no sanctuary, no place off limits, and we are going to disperse crowds.' Do you remember that statement on the tape?"

"Yes, sir."

"Did that include the dispersing of crowds whether they were peaceful or not peaceful?"

"I referred to the crowds that took over the City of Kent and I think in essence that we were concerned with the agitators going from campus to campus and trying to have some control on the crowds, that if we could give assistance to the local public officials."

I thought that we could bring out the governor's belligerence and his attitude toward shooting by showing that, when he heard Chief Thompson pledge that shooting would be used if necessary, he had uttered no disclaimer that he had not intended matters to go that far.

I asked him if he had heard Del Corso make the remark, rather than Chief Thompson, because in his deposition he had acknowledged hearing it and mistakenly attributed it to Del Corso.

"I did not hear General Del Corso say that," Rhodes replied. "I think that was the voice of the chief of police of Kent."

Judge Young called us to the bench. "I am going to make this statement for the record so there won't be any doubt about it," he said. He was furious. "This trial is a search for truth." He was raising his voice. "Somebody, some inefficient public servant in making a transcript, which everyone relied upon, made the transcript incorrectly, and as a result many people have been misled into making statements which were not true. I am not going to permit you," he told me loudly, "to clutter up this record under the pretense that you are impeaching the witness by that sort of deceit and trickery."

"On my part, sir?" I asked the judge.

"I am not claiming it is deceit and trickery and anybody's fault," the judge amended his previous statement, "but the fact of it is, it is not true."

He cut me off, then, on the grounds that Del Corso hadn't made the remark.

At the recess, after Rhodes had stepped down from the stand, Arthur Krause told me that he had heard the judge accuse me of deceit and trickery. "If I heard it where I was sitting," he said, "you can be sure the jury heard it."

This was disturbing news. Judges are supposed to be careful about any words or actions that might indicate their feelings about any of the parties involved or the evidence. In my view, this was a serious matter, coming on top of all the judge's other prejudicial expressions and actions, and I intended to call it to his attention.

Michael Delaney, our key witness on the governor's off-the-record words and intentions, had been a headquarters noncom of the 145th infantry in 1970 and was in charge of press relations.

Delaney left the Guard a year after the shooting, when his six-year stint ended. In 1975 he was employed by the public relations department of the American Banking Association in Washington, D.C. He was a bearded, dark-haired, serious-looking man of thirty-four who, while in the Guard, had taken part in a number of peace marches. Several weeks after the shootings Delaney had told a *New York Times* feature writer that he thought Rhodes' order "to break up peaceful and legal assemblies" had made the situation explosive.

Under Sindell's questioning, Delaney revealed that he first saw Governor Rhodes on Sunday, May 3, when he joined a small automobile procession that followed the governor through the campus for an inspection of the burned ROTC Building. Afterward, he said, they all went to the Kent fire station. There, before the press conference, Governor Rhodes called a private meeting that was attended by Prosecutor Ronald Kane of Portage County and an assistant, and representatives of the National Guard, Kent State University, the law-enforcement agencies, the Kent fire department, and the State of Ohio.

I noticed that Governor Rhodes, in the audience, was listening intently to every word of the former Guard sergeant.

"Were there any Guard officers that you observed?" Sindell asked.

"Yes, sir."

"Now, were there any members of the media present in this room prior to the press conference?"

"There were not."

"How many people outside of yourself and Governor Rhodes were in this room?"

"Probably close to fifteen."

Delaney testified that the governor addressed this small group in private for about fifteen minutes.

"Mr. Delaney, I would like you to tell the Court and the ladies and gentlemen what you heard Governor Rhodes say in that room prior to the press conference."

"The governor," Delaney said, "said that the meeting was off the record and that no notes should be kept."

Rhodes' face was flushed. He clasped his hands in front of him and stared at the witness.

Delaney continued. "He said that he was there to assume full command of the situation. He told university representatives that the campus was under Guard control and that they should stay out of it. He asked the fire chief to reiterate what had happened the preceding evening, and then the governor said if the firemen had to be sent in again, they would have the complete Guard support.

"He said as long as he was the governor of the State of Ohio, the campus would remain open. There were groups of students, SDS, brownshirts, Weathermen, which were part of a conspiracy to close down the campus and to disrupt the system and that he intended to keep the classrooms open if it meant keeping an armed guard in each classroom.

"He said the National Guard should use whatever force was necessary to disperse any student rallies or meetings, and he did not want to see any two students walking together. He said it was a martial law situation and that when he returned to Columbus he would issue a proclamation to that effect."

For a man who claimed he did not know the guns were loaded, to say the Guard under his command should "use any force necessary" to disperse assemblies was, to me, the ultimate in irresponsibility and recklessness.

In his cross-examination, Brown challenged Delaney's memory of the details, but he was unable to shake him.

Alloway, the governor's lawyer, asked whether Delaney had heard the governor issue any orders.

"Yes," Delaney replied.

"What?"

"That the Guards were to use any necessary force to disperse any meeting, any gathering of students."

"Mr. Delaney, to whom did he issue such an order?"

"It was to the Guard representatives present in the meeting and to the meeting in general."

"Can you name any of the Guard officers who were present?"

"No, sir."

"Were they in uniform?"

"Yes."

"How many of them were in uniform?"

"As I recall, there were three or four Guard officers there."

Alloway asked whether the Guard officers had responded to the orders.

"There was one question that I recall that was asked."

"What was that?"

"It was a question from one of the Guard officers about the legality of the situation, and the governor responded that he would take care of it when he got back to Columbus, would issue a proclamation."

"All right now," Alloway asked, "I believe that you said the governor said something about martial law; is that correct?"

"In substance, yes, sir."

"In substance?"

"Yes, sir."

"Did he use the words 'martial law'?"

"I don't recall him using the specific words, no."

"Well, then, how do you know that he said anything about martial law?"

"In regard to the question, the question was on martial law, and that's when he said he would issue the proclamation to that effect when he returned to Columbus."

"All right. Then what you are saying is that martial law in effect then had not been proclaimed; is that correct?"

"That is correct."

"And do you know whether martial law ever was proclaimed?"

"I was never told that it was. I don't believe it was."

Delaney also testified on the injuries sustained by guardsmen on May 4. He had checked both with the hospital in Ravenna and with the Guard medics in the bivouac area in the parking lot near Bowman Hall. He found that no guardsman had been injured other than one who was emotionally upset. He had found this man (probably Sergeant Herschler) at Robinson Memorial Hospital and had driven him back to Kent State in his jeep.

At the end of the afternoon I told the judge that his criticism of me as "deceitful" had been heard in the rear of the courtroom.

"I know Your Honor's meticulous attention to the concept of fair trials," I said, "and I know you did not intend to raise your voice, but it is obvious the jury heard it, because persons toward the back of the room heard it.

"Is there anything that can be done, sir?" I asked. "I know Your Honor would not want to convey any impression to the jury. . ."

"Whatever the Court may or may not have said," Charlie Brown put in, "I thought was perfectly justified."

Judge Young said that in his general charge at the end of the trial he would instruct the jury to disregard anything they interpreted as expressing his opinion of any of the evidence or anything else. He refused to give such instructions at the end of the day, when the incident was still fresh in everyone's mind.

One morning the film that Clyde Ellis, one of our lawyers, had put together along with William Johnston and Richard Waltz, two of the defense lawyers, from various pieces of television news footage was shown in the courtroom. It contained scenes of downtown Kent after the Friday night rioting; the ROTC Building on fire; the Kent State campus on Sunday, with the remains of the burned building; the confrontation on Monday, with two different sequences showing the guardsmen firing; and Doug Wrentmore in the hospital, telling television newsmen that the students had provoked the Guard.

No matter how many times they saw photographs or films of the campus on May 4, the parents of the four dead students could not get used to them. In some ways the trial was worse for them than the nightmare of the five preceding years: the obscene letters, the telephoned threats, the alienation from neighbors and relatives, and the pain of empty rooms and old letters found unexpectedly at the bottom of a drawer.

Watching the movie, Florence Schroeder wondered whether the pain had purchased anything of value, whether it wouldn't have been easier to pretend that Bill had just been lost in an automobile accident. She had thought the truth would prevent a future shooting, but what was the use when others did not care? Let them find out for themselves that trust was not enough. Let them lose their innocence as she had lost hers.

20

Absolute Proof
in Sight and Sound

—

By the end of July, after more than ten weeks of trial, the jurors had heard sixty-nine witnesses. This number included the deposition of the absent photographer, Terry Norman, who denied firing his pistol, and the testimony of a campus policeman, Harold Rice, who had examined Norman's pistol and confirmed that it had not been fired; two experts, Colonel Thomas McNeal (on weapons) and FBI Special Agent John W. Kilty (who was not allowed to testify on the relationship between certain expended cartridges found on Blanket Hill and certain .45 automatics assigned to some national guardsmen); ten former students of Kent State; three present or former faculty members; three present or former members of the university administration; thirty-six national guardsmen, including thirty-one defendants, twenty-nine of whom had been on Blanket Hill on May 4, 1970 (Captain Snyder had been between Taylor and Prentice halls and Del Corso had been in Columbus); Governor Rhodes; nine plaintiffs; and three photographers who had been students at the time of the shooting.

As was usual in cases in which a number of law-enforcement personnel were charged with having fired at a number of civilians, the jurors were exposed to two conflicting stories. From the guardsmen they heard that a large group of students, shouting imprecations such as "Kill! Kill!" and showering them with rocks, had threatened to overrun them as they neared the top of Blanket Hill, and that the front of this surging mass had been 20 feet or so away when the men of Troop G wheeled and opened fire. From the plaintiffs the jury heard that the students had been from 60 feet to more than 700 feet from the guardsmen, that there had been no surging mass threatening to overrun the guardsmen, and that at the time the shooting started, no one had been closer to Troop G than Joe Lewis.

In other cases—such as those arising out of the Orangeburg, Chicago, and Jackson State shootings—the jurors had had to decide whom to believe on the basis of their experience of human nature and the logic of the facts. In this case, however, photographs had recorded the actual events.

The "evidence hole" rule, by keeping the photographs out of sight during the course of the trial, blunted their value. It was simply not true, as the judge kept saying, that the photographs "speak for themselves." Most of the photographs, taken at fairly close range, showed only part of a scene. It was necessary for us, by questioning the photographers and introducing their photographs into evidence, to relate the pictures to the scene by showing where the photographers had been standing, the directions in which they had aimed their cameras, and the times at which the pictures were taken. What a single picture could not demonstrate, several taken at about the same time could. (One exception was Beverly Knowles' panoramic shot of the practice field with the guardsmen kneeling. The time was fixed by the guardsmen's posture, and the photograph had been taken from far enough away to show all the territory around them in every direction.)

Because the photographs belied their case, the "evidence hole" rule benefited the defendants. The judge, by enforcing that rule, also helped Fulton's effort to challenge the comprehensiveness of the photos. Fulton asked photographers why so many photographs taken on Blanket Hill focused on the guardsmen rather on students, and why none had been taken from just behind the guardsmen as they turned, showing the view down Blanket Hill as it appeared to them. The photographers could provide reasonable answers to these questions, but it was still possible for the jurors to doubt that the photographs of the guardsmen on Blanket Hill showed the entire story of what had happened. What was needed to still such doubts was a panoramic view of Blanket Hill, of the guardsmen and the students at the time the shooting began, taken from a distance, like the Beverly Knowles photograph of the practice field.

Such a panoramic view did in fact exist and, miraculously, it was a motion picture that encompassed the time before, during, and after the shooting. It was introduced as evidence and shown to the jury on Monday, August 4.

The film is not very clear. It was taken with an 8-mm home movie camera from a distance of almost half a mile through a zoom lens that distorted distances. The students appear as small blobs of light moving up the hill toward the guardsmen at the top. Then there is a sudden reversal of the movement, presumably when the shooting begins. As one watches the film, one has no way of grasping the number of persons moving up the hill or their proximity to the guardsmen. The film most emphatically does not speak for itself. It does no more than provide a blank for the projection of one's emotions. Depending on the predisposition of the viewer, it may be cited as depicting a menacing rush by students ("substantial evidence," in the words of James Michener, "that the Guard believed itself to be in mortal danger") or as proof that no one was close enough to alarm any soldier armed with a rifle and bayonet.

To find out exactly what the film showed, the Justice Department, preparing for the criminal trial, paid a photo-interpreting firm $30,000 for a CIA-type analysis. The enhancement of images by digital processing, along with careful frame-by-frame measurements and calculations, revealed the precise movement of the students relative to the guardsmen just before the shooting.

The laboratory report was summarized in a diagram that consists of two parts (see page 138). The top section is a map of Taylor Hall and the area in front of it, including the practice field and the Prentice Hall parking lot. The map is divided into six sectors defined by two arcs and a bent line at distances of 85, 175, and 325 feet from the guardsmen, and a bisecting line defining the cone of fire.

The bottom section of the diagram is a table that shows the number of students counted in each of the six sectors at three different times: at the beginning of the film sequence, three seconds later (at about the time the shooting started), and three seconds after that.

Here for the first time was complete information on the numbers of students on the hill, their distances from the Guard, and the directions in which they had been moving. The table reveals everything one has to know about the positions of the parties to the shooting. It tells us that the total number of students in front of the guardsmen as they fired, to a distance of 325 feet, was between 80 and 143. (The chart gives the number as 113, but the probable error in counting students in the farthest zones, where they were clumped together, was 30 percent.)

Of particular interest are the number, movement, and distances of the students nearest Taylor Hall, those reported by Troop G to have been following them up the hill and threatening to overrun them, the infamous followers of the Guard's right flank. The diagram tells exactly how many students were in the three sectors A, B, and C (which encompassed the cone of fire) and what they were doing.

A member of Troop G, looking over his shoulder and down toward the parking lot, would have seen five students at a distance of 60 to 85 feet, 25 students between 85 and 175 feet, and 30 students between 175 and 325 feet. Of these persons, 17 were moving toward him, 7 of them no closer than 85 feet and 10 no closer than 175 feet. Three seconds later, when the guardsman wheeled, he would have seen a couple of students standing at least 60 feet away and 8 others approaching, only 3 of them closer than 175 feet.

The evidence of the film is that at no time before Troop G opened fire were they being approached by more than 17 students, that none of the approaching students was closer than 85 feet, and that 10 of them were more than 175 feet away.

Their speed, the table notes, was estimated at between 3 and 10 miles per hour.

The film provides conclusive evidence that the guardsmen had not been rushed. We called as witnesses Christopher Abell, the student who took the pictures, and Robert Arnold Johnson, the photo expert who analyzed them.

Defense counsel did not like this idea. They knew what the expert analysis showed, and they preferred to give the jury their own interpretation. They objected on the grounds that the admission of expert testimony would contravene the judge's ruling that pictures spoke for themselves, but we prevailed on the issue. The image analyst was scheduled to appear on Monday, August 4; Abell testified on Wednesday, July 30.

Christopher Abell, a Kent State sophomore in May 1970, had set his camera on the windowsill of his room on the fifth floor of Wright Hall in the Tri-Towers complex. He did not realize that he had captured the shooting sequence until he saw the developed film.

Johnson stated that the Abell film had poor resolution and suffered from "blooming of light-colored images," which made it difficult to identify an object from a single frame.

After the film had been projected in the courtroom, Johnson told how, by digital image processing, he was able "to suppress, somewhat, the noise or the grain structure of the film, such that the images were somewhat more interpretable." He explained that photogrammetry, the measurement of film images, could not provide a general solution as to the locations of all the individuals but "was used to determine the velocity of different identified individuals."

"Was there anything else that you did with the film," Engdahl asked, "different from the ordinary layman's viewing?"

"Well," Johnson replied, "in viewing film of this type you have to be very careful to understand [that] an image that appears too long or too large because of the particular characteristics of the camera and the film would give the false impression that the image was nearer to you." He also explained that with images changing colors as they moved, one had to be careful about confusing individuals.

When Engdahl held up an enlarged version of the diagram, Brown objected to the jury's seeing something that was not in evidence. (If it had been in evidence, of course, they wouldn't have been able to see it either—because of the "evidence hole" rule.)

Engdahl moved the diagram out of the jury's line of vision, and Johnson pointed out the locations of each of the six sectors on the large easel map and began describing the activities in sector A.

Johnson testified that the persons closest to the Guard who could be seen during the first second of the shooting sequence on the Abell film were next to the sidewalk that runs perpendicular to Taylor Hall.

"Was there movement on the part of those closest persons to the Guard?"

"Yes. They were moving across the sidewalk and down the hill away from the Guard."

"In the shooting sequence, is there any point in time at which a pronounced movement of persons occurred?"

"Yes, sir."

"When does that occur with reference to the beginning of the film?"

"Approximately three or four seconds into the film."

"And what is the direction, so far as it is determinable, of that pronounced movement?"

"It is away from the Guard."

After stating that he had not detected any movement of people toward the Guard within 85 feet of the Pagoda, Johnson described the movements in some of the other areas, noting that the speeds toward the Guard "were in the range of three to ten miles per hour"—between a walk and a run.

When Engdahl asked him whether there was any rush of persons toward the Guard in the opening moments of the shooting sequence, Johnson replied, "My opinion is that there was not."

When Engdahl offered the chart in evidence, the judge first ruled it in, then decided to "limit it to some extent. The diagram part of it I will permit," he said, "because I think that is meaningful. The chart that is on the bottom of it will have to be blocked out. . . ."

Of course the table, which the judge was omitting, was the vital part; without it, the jury would not know how many students had been in each zone or what their movements had been.

In addition to conflicting stories about the distances of movements and the numbers of students, the jurors also heard different accounts of the sound of the first shot. Several guardsmen testified that the first shot came from the vicinity of Taylor Hall. However, some guardsmen said that it sounded as though it came from a low-caliber, hence non-military, weapon.

Here again the jurors had independent, objective evidence to assist them in deciding which version to believe, for there existed a tape recording of the entire sequence of shots. And as it had done with the Abell film, the Justice Department had hired a laboratory to make an analysis.

In addition to studying the tape and other recordings made on the Kent State campus at the time, the laboratory conducted test firings of different weapons at the Army's Aberdeen Proving Grounds in Maryland and on the Kent State campus and analyzed the characteristics of the sounds and the manner in which they traveled to the place on the campus where the recording had been made. After six weeks of work, at a cost of $38,000, the engineering firm of Bolt, Berenek & Newman of Cambridge, Massachusetts (the firm that had investigated the famous seventeen-and-one-half-minute erasure on a key Nixon tape), established the nature of the first weapons that were fired and their locations, as well as a number of other things.

The first three shots, it was found, came from M-1 rifles located between the Pagoda and the corner of Taylor Hall. Shots 1 and 3 originated midway between the Pagoda and the hall; shot 2 was 10 feet away, very near the Pagoda. All three shots occurred within three-fourths of a second, with the first two one-third of a second apart and the third almost four-tenths of a second after the second. The M-1 that fired the first shot was discharged five times, and the second and third rifles fired three rounds each. One M-1 fired a full clip (eight rounds), and two others fired seven rounds apiece. The final shot was the last of one of the seven-round sequences.

Altogether, the laboratory detected sixty-seven shots on the tape, at least thirty-two of which came from M-1s. A minimum of three shots were fired from a .45 automatic, and there were at least two from a 12-gauge shotgun.

We were able to put this information before the jury by calling two witnesses, Terry Strubbe, the former Kent State freshman who had made the recording at his window on the first floor of Johnson Hall, and Scott Robinson, one of the Bolt, Berenek & Newman technicians who had studied the tape. However, we were not permitted to let the jury hear the tape until two weeks later, when the defense had completed its case.

The Strubbe tape not only provides incontrovertible evidence of disputed events, its two sides also record the sounds of everything that occurred: Patrolman Rice's warning as the jeep made its first pass; the chants of the students; then and after the second warning, "Here come the pigs!"; cheers and jeers and, through it all, the ominous, monotonous clanging of the Victory Bell; the long stuttering volley of shots; the cheers of "Yea!" when they cease (presumably from those who think they have been hearing blanks). Seventeen seconds after the final shot the bell is heard again, and there is the sound of someone coughing (from tear gas?). Twenty seconds pass; a voice is heard: "They were shot!" There are angry shouts, the bell again for another half minute, and "Help! Help!" A bit more than a minute later there is another voice, "Take your goddamn guns down." It is now two minutes and twenty-seven seconds since the final shot. The bell again; the warbling of an ambulance; finally, almost three minutes after the last shot, a single cry, "Help!"

Terry Strubbe could testify only that he had made the tape recording.

The expert, Scott Robinson, explained how the tape had been analyzed and described the test firings at fourteen locations corresponding to the firing line of guardsmen in the photographs. In each position, Robinson said, blanks had been fired from an M-1, a .45, and a small cannon (simulating a shotgun) in three modes: toward the ground, level, and at a 45-degree elevation. He described how sound travels through the air and bounces off objects, and how its pattern of echoes can be used to identify the path it has followed. He told how they had simulated the conditions of May 4 by placing a line of men where the guardsmen had been, parking cars near Johnson Hall in the positions shown in photographs taken that day, and recording the test shots with high-quality apparatus from the window of Strubbe's former room. He explained how the tape recordings were transformed into graphs that were used to analyze the sound waves.

I asked Robinson where the first shot had been fired from, and he indicated, on the large map of the campus, a point midway between the Pagoda and the south corner of Taylor Hall.

Asked what kind of weapon fired that first shot, Robinson replied, "It is my opinion that it was an M-1 rifle."

"And what was the basis of that, sir?"

"The basis of that was the comparison of the sound of the first shot on Mr. Strubbe's tape with the test sound of an M-1 done for us at Aberdeen."

Robinson then explained how, for confirmation, they had duplicated the original event, using Strubbe's tape recorder.

I asked whether any shot preceding the first shot of the Guard appeared on the Strubbe tape.

"There is none audible on the tape," Robinson replied.

"Now, sir, how much time did the tape run before the sound of the first shot was recorded on the tape?"

"At least ten minutes"—without, he added, any break in continuity.

He described the rest of the shots and said that the entire sequence had lasted 12.53 seconds.

Robinson had testified that no weapon had been heard to fire before the first M-1. Nevertheless, to cover all bases, I asked him whether Strubbe's tape recorder would have picked up the sound of a .38 being fired from the vicinity of Johnson Hall (the location at which the Terry Norman pistol incident had occurred).

Robinson replied that if such a shot "would have been audible to the human ear . . . it would have been audible in listening to the tape. . . . I did not hear on the tape any firing before what has been identified as the first shot and which we have determined was an M-1."

Robbie Stamps was enthusiastic when Robinson finished testifying. "That was great," he told me. "I wish Tom Grace had stayed to hear this."

Even Alan Canfora agreed that Johnson and Robinson had nailed down our case.

"They can't stop us," I said. "No matter how hard they try, they can't keep the truth out of the courtroom."

"This is scientific proof of everything we've been saying," Robbie said.

It is wonderful what a couple of good witnesses can do to restore your spirits. "I want you to know how proud I am of all of you," I told them. "I know it's been rough, but your patience is being rewarded. And our next two witnesses are going to make the Ohio National Guard look sick."

21

A Seminar on Crowd Control

It was not easy to find a military man who would testify against the Ohio National Guard. I spent many hours tracking down generals and talking to several who condemned the guardsmen's performance at Kent State, but all of them balked at testifying in public. The one military authority we were able to get was Colonel Edward King, the highest-ranking officer to resign in protest over the Vietnam War.

It happened that King, during his quarter century of military service, had had considerable crowd control experience, principally as an infantry noncom in Korea and as a military police officer in West Germany. He described three riots he had had to deal with, two in Korea in 1947 and 1948 and one in Germany in 1954, real riots in which he and his men had been exposed to real danger, including being shot at. He explained how the soldiers had protected themselves with their rifle butts and never fired a shot, emphasizing that trained men under such conditions would never shoot, never even load their weapons, without a direct order from an officer.

Brown was unable to think of a way to attack King's qualifications; he even helped us by asking how long it took to remove a clip of M-1 ammunition from a pouch and load a rifle with it.

"About five to ten seconds for a good, well-trained soldier," King replied, thereby destroying the defense's excuse that the routine loading of rifles was needed because of the length of time the action took.

With King we were finally able to bring before the jury the differences between Army regulations (FM 19-15) and the Ohio National Guard OPLAN

2. He quoted the Ohio and Army policies on loading weapons and said that the Ohio rules indicated "a loss of control to the individual . . . in effect, passing on to the individual soldier the option of when he wants to fire."

He also stated that arm waving, chanting, and shouting of obscene words did not authorize dispersal of a crowd in the absence of violence. Such dispersal, he said, "would be contrary to good judgment and proper standards" and would "create violence when no violence was present."

The OPLAN regulation, paragraph 6(f)(c), authorizing shooting to disperse a crowd, he said, violated the principal riot control rule that minimum force be used, and it "risks death and serious bodily injury to persons in the area."

King described the graduated steps that troops could use in dispersing crowds and gave an impressive demonstration of the options available, showing how the nine-and-one-half-pound M-1 rifle with the steel plate in its butt and a bayonet affixed to the barrel could become a club or a spear.

At my request, King stepped down from the witness box and stood before the jury box. Suddenly he jabbed the steel-plated butt of a rifle toward the jurors, who recoiled from the violent movement. The sharp, punching movements of the rifle butt were followed by a quick swing of the bayoneted end of the rifle as King jabbed at the jurors in fast, menacing movements.

The maneuver took only a few seconds and came off even better than I had expected. Everyone on that jury, friend or foe, would have had to conclude that the rifle butt or bayonet offered viable alternatives to shooting.

King resumed his seat, and I continued. "Sir, I am going to ask you to assume there has been testimony to these ladies and gentlemen of the jury that shots were fired without ever using the butt stroke, any variation of the butt stroke which you have just demonstrated to us. . . .

"I ask you whether any shooting done without going through the maneuvers and the procedures that you have just demonstrated would be justifiable under proper standards and procedures of Army or National Guard regulations?"

King replied that such shooting would be contrary to good Army standards. "Why?"

"The Army standards indicate the use of deadly force should be taken only after all lesser means have been exhausted or unavailable, and that certainly would not have been the case if you had not used the butt stroke."

"How about under the Ohio National Guard regulations?" I asked. "Would that be contrary to their own regulations at that time?"

"According to Annex F, OPLAN 2," King replied, "it says, 'Force will be used in sequences listed below,' and the fourth sequence is rifle butt and bayonet, in that order."

King also pointed out that it was improper for men with bad eyesight, and

Guardsmen turning and levelling weapons. Note the three people on the roof of Johnson Hall (southeast wing): from left to right, Joy Hubbard (Bishop), Pat Frank (Rivera), Bruce Phillips. *(Howard E. Ruffner)*

The guardsmen shooting. A close examination of these two pictures convinced Peter Davies that the guardsmen had taken some steps in the direction of the parking lot. (Note the relative positions of the bare patches of ground.) *(John Darnell)*

whose gas masks did not contain corrective lenses, to carry loaded weapons.

With regard to the swapping of weapons that Sergeant Herschler and Lieutenant Fallon had described, King said, "Once you begin switching weapons, then no one knows where the weapons are except the individuals that are not accountable in this circumstance."

King also testified that the intermingling of Troop G with Company A and with two men from Company C resulted in a "loss of integrity of command" and that marching the troops to the practice field had been unnecessary and provocative.

"Sir," I asked, "based upon proper standards and procedures in a riot control situation, civilian riot control, I ask you whether kneeling and aiming in the direction of civilians with loaded weapons is in conformity with proper standards and procedures?"

"It is not in accord with normal standards and procedures. It is indicating a bluff. You normally do not aim a weapon unless you intend to fire the weapon."

Brown then asked King a series of questions designed to show that each individual had to determine for himself when his life was in danger.

King replied, "You do not act individually in military formation. You react to orders."

We followed King on the stand with James Ahern, the second part of a one-two combination that should knock out any remnant of a belief that the guardsmen had acted properly at Kent State. James Ahern had been appointed to the Scranton Commission as an expert in riot control and had directed a lot of pointed questions at Del Corso and Canterbury when they testified in August 1970. What he learned of the Guard's behavior on the campus was contrary to all crowd control techniques developed in the late 1960s, and he was outspoken in his criticism. On Monday, May 3, 1971, on the eve of the first anniversary of the shootings, he had told a gathering of Kent State students that the killed and injured had been "victims of the conscious, deliberate acts of other men."

A big, handsome man, Ahern had worked his way up through the police department of New Haven, Connecticut, from patrolman in 1954 to chief in March 1968. He had been a line police officer during a two-day riot in 1959, a lieutenant in charge of part of the city during a five-day riot in 1967, and chief for several turbulent years. On the first weekend in May 1970, while the National Guard was trying to cope with students on the Kent State campus, twenty thousand persons had converged on the New Haven green to protest the trial of Bobby Seale and twelve other Black Panthers for the murder of

Aftermath. The parking lot, and the dead and wounded. *(Beverly Knowles)*

1. William Schroeder   3. Sandy Scheuer   5. Alan Canfora
2. Jeff Miller   4. Thomas M. Grace

General Canterbury (right) threatens to order his men against the students squatting hysterically on the Commons while faculty members and a graduate student try to dissuade him. *(Akron Beacon Journal)*

Alex Rackley. That crowd had been controlled without any damage to persons or significant damage to property.

In addition to his own personal experience, Ahern had studied crowd control methods in many cities in Europe and America; served as consultant to the U.S. Commission on Civil Rights, the Ford Foundation, and the Justice Department; and lectured at a number of universities and written articles on crowd control.

I asked Ahern to define the difference between a riot and a demonstration.

"A riot can be in varying degrees," Ahern said, "but generally speaking, the best definition that I can give is a group of people or a crowd, either with or without direction, that has done damage to property and harm to people. . . . A demonstration would be a group of people banded together to protest some grievance . . . exercising their right to protest and dissent."

"Now," I asked, "if you have a group of people, hundreds of people perhaps, chanting, singing, shouting in loud voices, gesticulating with arms and arm waving and shouting, assuming obscenities, words which in common parlance are four-letter words . . . but without any physical force, nor rock throwing, nor stone throwing, nor damage to property or persons, I ask you, how would that be characterized in law-enforcement circles with regard to whether or not it is a riot or a demonstration?"

Ahern stated that it was a demonstration.

I asked him whether he thought it would be proper to disperse such a crowd.

"No," Ahern said, "it would not." If you were to disperse that type of crowd, "it would virtually eliminate attendance at football games, labor picketing, almost any kind of dissent."

I then asked him what should be done about such a crowd if there were intelligence reports that violence might develop.

Ahern answered that the role of a prudent law-enforcement commander would be to have available necessary reserves based on the intelligence, adding that he could hardly think of a demonstration in which he had been involved "where there weren't conflicting pieces of intelligence, particularly where it is a . . . politically inspired demonstration. Many times the other side will spread false rumors to provoke an action to discredit the cause.

"So I would say, you don't act on the basis of intelligence, but . . . have the necessary reserves hidden away to handle any contingency. . . . You are there to protect their rights to demonstrate. You are there to protect them and the rest of the population from bodily harm."

I looked at the jury to see what they were making of this idea of the law as *protecting* demonstrators. Several of the women were nodding agreement.

Ahern stated that he would permit chanting to continue undisturbed, as well as talking, milling, and speechmaking, "as long as they want to stay."

"How many hours?"

"It is interminable sometimes."

Ahern described some riots he had been faced with, and the various steps of increasing force, up to the use of tear gas. He said he had never seen tear gas fail to disperse a crowd. During the five-day riot in New Haven in 1967, he said, over five hundred arrests were made and not a single person was shot.

"What were the prevailing procedures and instructions to the policemen with regard to when it would be permissible to actually shoot?" I asked.

Ahern stated that there were many restrictions on the use of lethal force by policemen. "But beyond that, in a crowd situation, basically, the policy of the New Haven Police Department was to use every available means other than lethal force . . . a determination had to be made by a commanding officer at the scene so that individual judgment was not left to the individual police officer . . . his life or the police officer's life in imminent danger . . . danger of death to other persons, a situation of wholesale property damage that would eventually result in physical harm to citizens."

Ahern said that in May 1970, at the time of the Bobby Seale demonstration, his police force of five hundred men had been confronted with twenty thousand demonstrators "on the green in the City of New Haven . . . approximately four square blocks . . . around fifteen acres." He said the demonstrations had lasted two days and ended in a peaceful manner at about five or six in the evening. Yet on both evenings there were disturbances of significant proportions. "The entire police department had been mobilized, specially trained, and additional riot control material was obtained."

Ahern recounted that the National Guard had sent a contingent of about five hundred troops to the city, that state police were also on hand, and that he was in command of all forces, with the others serving "as an extension of the New Haven Police Department." The strategy was to have "low visibility [but] with all kinds of police officers held in ready reserve. . . .

"The theory being that there are many times in tense situations where the police are a . . . part of what is being protested against . . . a very large display of police officers . . . can be very intimidating to a peaceful assembly. In fact, it may be provocative and may precipitate violence."

I asked him about the behavior of the twenty thousand demonstrators.

"It was boisterous, but generally speaking, except for one incident where a group of individuals attempted to leave the green and storm . . . the City Hall . . . there was no need for any police action."

"Was there arm waving and gesticulating?"

"Yes, absolutely."

"Was there name calling against the police?"

"Of the most intimidating kind that I have ever heard, and possibly will ever hear again. . . . 'Off the pigs,' was probably the most common chant during the course of those two days. There were direct appeals on the part of some people to assassinate the police officers, including me, which is extremely upsetting."

"How would you characterize the crowd with the various things you just described, was it a riotous crowd or a peaceful crowd in terms of law-enforcement description?"

"It was a peaceful crowd."

"What did you let that crowd do as they were milling around and name calling?"

"We let them do anything as long as there was no harm to anybody and no harm to property," Ahern said. The national guardsmen were kept out of sight in an armory three-quarters of a mile away, and during the two days of demonstrations not a single shot was fired.

The judge accepted Ahern as an expert witness, and I began my questions to draw out his opinion of the events at Kent State.

I asked Ahern a hypothetical question regarding the dispersal of the noon rally at Kent State. "Assume this Court and jury have heard testimony to the effect that there was a crowd of individuals who met on the campus or Commons of Kent State University on May 4, 1970.

"That some individuals were talking to each other, some were clanging a bell, some were singing, some were gesticulating, moving their arms in various ways, and some in rather forceful ways, some were shouting obscenities and chanting antiwar slogans of various types and the like.

"I am going to ask you to assume that up to a certain point in time, that there was no damage to property on that day, that time; that there was no physical injury [to] any person at that time. I ask you, sir, do you have an opinion, based upon your years of experience in this field of law enforcement and crowd control and riot control, as to whether it would be proper to disperse such a crowd, doing the things that I have just described?"

"It is my opinion," Ahern replied, "that it would be improper and unnecessary . . . to disperse a crowd under the conditions that you stated."

"And will you give us the reasons for your opinion?" I asked.

"The reasons being," Ahern stated, "that there is a constitutional right to protest and to demonstrate against grievances, and also from a more practical point of view, the best kind of dispersal in any kind of crowd situation is a voluntary dispersal, and the rule of thumb and almost a command in terms of crowd control is to use as little force, as little presence as is absolutely necessary to protect that crowd or to protect others against that crowd while it is peacefully demonstrating."

I then asked Ahern whether, assuming he had information that violence of some nature might be expected to occur after this crowd had assembled, it would then be proper to disperse it.

"It still would be improper to disperse that crowd," Ahern replied.

"Why?"

"Because a prudent police commander or law-enforcement commander would, number one, assess the validity of that intelligence, and based on that, he would have ample reserves to handle the situation when it happened if it did happen."

I asked if he had an opinion as to whether, assuming a decision to disperse such a crowd and assuming no evidence of any firearms in the crowd, it would have been proper to move out 116 men with loaded and locked military weapons.

"I would have to know," Ahern told the judge, "whether he is talking about sidearms or shoulder pieces."

I rephrased the question, explaining that some of the men had sidearms and some had M-1 rifles, shotguns, and tear-gas grenade launchers.

Ahern replied that it would not be proper to move against a crowd with loaded rifles but that it was common practice, "because of the nature of urban police," to carry loaded revolvers at all times, including crowd situations.

"And can you tell us what the distinction is," I asked, "as to the propriety of using and carrying loaded revolvers by policemen and the use of loaded M-1 rifles by military people, in such a theoretical riot or crowd control situation?"

Ahern explained that policemen habitually carried loaded sidearms and were often transferred rapidly to crowd control duty and just as rapidly sent out again on their own. (Police, on their own, had enormous discretion in the use of their weapons; but on crowd control duty, in formation, they were under the control of a superior and had no individual discretion.) It was not proper, he said, "for a law-enforcement agency to send their personnel in, in a dispersal action, with loaded shoulder arms."

I then described, using the large map on the easel stand, what had happened after tear gas had been fired and the crowd had been dispersed, and asked if he thought it had been proper to move the troops to the practice field.

"In my opinion," Ahern said, "moving against that crowd, based on the fact that the crowd was to be moved against, it was imprudent, unnecessary, and dangerous to proceed any further than that hill.

"One never takes men into a situation where you can't get out. The whole idea of moving against a crowd is to disperse it as quickly as possible, is to leave avenues of escape, and really the basic question in that kind of a situation is, Where did they hope to drive that crowd?

"The only other place—they are already on campus—perhaps into the buildings. If it were into the buildings, then going down where that fence was on the practice field would just serve no purpose at all. . . .

"They actually split the crowd, without diverting it, and put themselves in an embarrassing position of having to come through without having accomplished the mission, subjecting themselves to more verbal abuse."

I next asked Ahern to assume that before any attempt was made to disperse this crowd forcibly, the troops gave no warning of their intentions other than declaring "the assembly . . . is illegal, has been prohibited, and you are to disperse, and remaining here is illegal."

He was further to assume, I said, "that this was repeated with a person shouting through a bullhorn standing on foot and also in a jeep as it made the rounds; and that no further communication was made to the crowd of any force that would be used against them if they failed to comply with the orders to disperse.

"Sir, I ask you, based upon your years of experience in this field and your expertise in this field, would that be adequate, would that be sufficient in compliance with proper standards of conduct in accomplishing the dispersal?"

Ahern replied that the order was inadequate not only because it failed to specify any threat to shoot but because the Commons area was open to the public and was probably necessary for access to the school buildings for those who weren't even demonstrating.

"So that just a statement of fact that it is illegal may puzzle people . . . it would [affect] a lot of people who had a right to enter and probably a necessity to attend their normal business; in other words . . . those who are not even demonstrating."

Referring again to the map, I asked Ahern to assume that there had been rock throwing on the practice field but none or little as the guardsmen climbed the hill, and that the guardsmen wheeled and fired sixty-seven shots at persons in the parking lot area and in the air or into the ground. "Assume further," I said, "that there has been testimony here by some officers of the National Guard that there was some indiscriminate firing, I ask you, sir, do you have an opinion . . . as to whether such an occurrence would be proper in relation to riot control or crowd control, assuming even that there was a riot going on?"

"In my opinion," Ahern replied, "it would not be proper to fire under those circumstances under any conditions as you described them to me.

"Because fire should only be directed in a very controlled fashion when fired upon." Even if there were a sniper, he said, you would not fire indiscriminately and kill innocent people. "You do not hold the crowd responsible for the actions of one individual. You do not fire except when fired upon."

"Your Honor, I object," Fulton said. "He is going beyond the scope of what was asked."

"Sustained," Judge Young said.

Fulton could claim that I was giving Ahern a biased hypothetical question, based on our view of what had preceded the shooting. I therefore decided to give Ahern the defense version. I asked him to assume the worst, "that there was an avalanche, a tremendous volume of stones, rocks, sticks being thrown even at the moment right up to the time of firing.

"I ask you, do you have an opinion as to whether it would be proper to fire on a crowd and at persons or in the air, including indiscriminate firing, under those conditions?"

"Yes, I do."

"What is your opinion?"

"It is my opinion that to use firearms in the situation as you have just described it would be improper."

"Give us your reasons, sir?"

"Because the use of rocks, bottles, lead pipes is very common and is not considered by law-enforcement people to be putting anybody in grave physical harm.

"There are many ways to dodge a thrown missile, to catch it, to fend it off, to protect each other and give signals when something is coming, people look one way and a fellow officer looks the other way. . . . A great many missiles can be thrown at law-enforcement people and very seldom are they hit. They are very adept at watching out for that. . . .

"I think going up the hill, in my opinion, was the most dangerous point that they had. Having arrived at the crest, they were really home free to bring up more reserves, to take direct physical action against stragglers if it were considered very harmful. Arrest situations.

"People could have been apprehended at that point."

Ahern also gave as his opinion that the events of May 1, 2, and 3 should have had no bearing on the measures taken on May 4.

"When you are dealing with a sustained disturbance situation," he said, "you cannot react to a demonstration because of past violation of law, past riotous behavior.

"It may or may not be the same people, it may be of totally different character, different tenor. As a matter of fact, that particular crowd, the next day, may be protesting something that the demonstrators themselves had done.

"I would say that it would be improper to visit the sins of one action or one crowd upon another."

Fulton began his cross-examination of Ahern in an ingratiating manner, suggesting that a name like Ahern belonged on the letterhead of his law firm. (In other words, what was a good Irish cop doing with a bunch of weirdo hippies, Communists, Sheenies, and ACLU queers from the east?) He made a joke about an expert's being someone from out of town, and then he got to the main thrust of his examination, which was to show that police officers had a right to fire their revolvers in self-defense. In this, of course, he was ignoring the careful distinction that Ahern had made between police acting as individuals and police acting on crowd control duty under the supervision of a superior. Fulton's aim was to show that self-defense was a justification for shooting in any situation.

Fulton then tried to show that the situation at Kent State in May 1970 was more dangerous than what Ahern had been confronted with at the same time in New Haven.

"Tell us about the outside groups that came into the City of New Haven," Fulton asked. "Did it include Weathermen?"

"Yes."

"Did it include SDS?"

"Yes, it did."

"Did it include people who advocated the overthrow of the government?"

"Yes, it did."

"Did it include groups that told the students to go out and kill your parents?"

"I don't think—I don't recall that in particular. I heard a lot of things in those two days, but I don't think I can recall that one."

"There has been evidence in this case that that type of group came into Kent State, they advocated killing their parents."

This circuitous reference to Jerry Rubin was a measure of Fulton's futile attempts to shake Ahern's testimony.

In that Cleveland courtroom, with its sacks of rocks, its restrictions on the display of evidence, and its stories of thousands of bestial students, the testimony of Colonel King and Chief Ahern—voices of common sense and reason —sounded like a revelation.

Ahern told how 500 police officers had controlled crowds of 20,000 without violence—that is, crowds that outnumbered them 40 to 1. At Kent State, taking even the largest crowd estimate—3,000—the odds against the 162 guardsmen who started the dispersal had been 19 to 1. *At the time of the shooting, the highest estimate of students, allowing for 30 percent error in the Abell film count, was 143 unarmed students against 72 armed guardsmen on the top of the hill—that is, 2 to 1.*

Ahern's testimony covered the entire spectrum of responsibility for the shootings:

Rhodes for authorizing demonstrators dispersed instead of protected, for leaving provocative armed guardsmen on the campus, and for inadequate assessment of intelligence.

Del Corso for loaded rifles, for improper training, and for inadequate assessment of intelligence.

Canterbury for improperly ordering the dispersal of a nonviolent assembly, for leading the men to the practice field, for chasing a crowd after it had been dispersed, and for inadequate assessment of intelligence.

The officers on the field for inadequate control of their men.

The enlisted men for unauthorized and unjustified shooting.

In our meeting room in the courthouse that afternoon, the clients, all but Florence Schroeder and Elaine Holstein, were more relaxed than I had ever seen them. Even Joe Lewis was grinning.

"Did you see the way the jury was listening to Colonel King and Ahern?" Joe asked me. "Even Stanley Davis."

"Judge Young's mouth was hanging open," Robbie Stamps said.

"Don't get too happy," I cautioned. "The trial isn't over yet."

"How can you say that?" Robbie Stamps demanded. "You're the one who's been telling us that we could win."

"It's the voice of experience," I said. "I knew the situation was never as bad as you thought. For the same reasons, I know it's not as good as you now think. We've still got a tough fight ahead of us."

Yet I was grinning, too. Privately, I didn't see how Fulton and Brown had a prayer of escaping judgments against their clients unless they came up with a military or civilian expert who would testify that the guardsmen had acted properly in dispersing the noon rally and shooting the students.

Providing, of course, that the jury relied "solely on the evidence," as they were sworn to do.

22

"All the Rights and Privileges of Students"

Florence Schroeder was nervous because she was scheduled to take the stand that week, along with Elaine Holstein. For the three months of the trial she and the other parents had heard their children maligned as troublemakers and bums who deserved their fate. She waited for her chance to tell what her boy had been like—that he had attended Kent State on an ROTC scholarship and had been cadet first sergeant, that he was bright, engaging, and growing in his awareness of possibilities. She had waited five years to tell her story, and now that the time was approaching, she couldn't eat and could barely remain in the courtroom.

A stately woman with the rounded figure and features of a classical Wagnerian soprano, Florence Schroeder had attended the trial every day, anticipating and dreading the moment when she would sit in the witness box and tell the world what she thought of those who had heartlessly killed her son.

> *Bill Schroeder telephoned his parents Sunday night, May 3, to say that he was all right and that he was upset by the burning of the ROTC Building. He thought that destroying buildings was not a sensible way to protest, and he was concerned that if the students drove the ROTC off the campus, he would have to transfer to another school to keep his scholarship.*
>
> *He had already transferred once. He had spent his freshman year, beginning in the fall of 1968, at the Colorado School of Mines. In 1969 he had moved to Kent State because the Colorado school had few courses in psychology. Bill had spent the spring of 1969 with missionaries in Guaymas, Mexico.*

The poverty there, and especially its effect on the young, had somehow rein-forced his doubts about the Vietnam War.

At nineteen he was a strikingly handsome young man with bright blue eyes and a good deal of self-confidence. At Kent State he drove a smart little Fiat, worked at a hamburger joint and an aluminum plant, sent his mother money, spent two afternoons a week helping retarded children, wore a belt with peace symbols, and admired Mick Jagger, who flouted the rules Bill had been taught to obey and lived at the edges of the permissible. He was the outstand-ing sophomore in the ranks of the Kent State ROTC—but, as he told his mother, he resented being taught additional ways of killing people. He ad-mired Don Peters, the Vietnam veteran who was his ROTC adviser, yet worried that Peters made notes on the opinions Bill expressed during their friendly bouts at the pool table.

In April 1970, Bill Schroeder attended an antiwar conclave at Case West-ern Reserve University in Cleveland. Later that month, when Nixon an-nounced the move into Cambodia, Bill asked his roommate Lou Cusella if he thought it meant eternal war.

According to the book Thirteen Seconds,* Bill and a pal, Al Springer, went downtown to a bar on Water Street the first Friday night in May, picked up two young women, and left Bill's apartment at 3 A.M. for Al's home in Akron. They heard about the ROTC fire at half past eleven Saturday night, in a taproom in downtown Akron. Bill drove back to Kent to see the wreckage.*

Bill spent Sunday in Akron and returned to his apartment just before the 8 P.M. curfew. He was upset and frightened by the disturbances, the excess of police, and the Guard.

On Monday Bill's nine o'clock experimental psychology class was canceled; it was near a laboratory that it was feared might be attacked. At eleven he went to North Hall, a building a few yards away from the burnt-out ROTC Building, for an examination on war tactics. When the class ended, he and a friend went to the noon rally.

Bill was wearing a faded denim jacket with small yellow and purple flowers in the lapels, a black-and-red striped shirt, orange bell-bottom trousers, boots, the belt with the peace symbols.

There is a photograph of Bill standing at the edge of a group of students on the Commons, a folder under his right arm. He is perhaps a hundred yards from the guardsmen at the ROTC Building, and his back is to them.

Another photograph, taken some minutes later, after the guardsmen had fired tear gas and moved out, shows Bill climbing the hill toward Johnson

*By J. Esterhas and M. D. Roberts. Dodd, Mead & Company, 1971.

Hall. Some of the students in front of him appear to be running, but he is walking. The folder is now in his left hand.

When the shooting began, he was in the parking lot, a few yards from Sandy Scheuer. He was probably lying prone when hit, facing away from the guardsmen, for the bullet entered the left side of his back at the level of the seventh rib, fracturing five left ribs up to the third and exiting from his left shoulder. "The direction of the bullet," the coroner's report said, "was from left to right, back to front, and below upwards. The body contained fragments of metal particles, one fragment containing copper coating . . . the cause of death was hemorrhage from the left lung."

Bill Schroeder died five minutes after arriving at Robinson Memorial Hosptal, shortly after whispering his name to the orderly, a name the orderly caught as "Bill Schneider."

At four that Monday afternoon Florence heard the name William Schneider on the radio and telephoned Bill's apartment. The lines were busy.

Half an hour later a reporter from the Cleveland Plain Dealer *telephoned to ask if she had a photograph of her son.*

"Why do you want it?" she asked.

Pause. "Oh. Sorry. Must have the wrong Schroeder." The reporter hung up.

Florence and Louis Schroeder were the only Ohio parents who did not go to the hospital. Their minister arranged to have Bill's body taken to a morgue in Akron. Lou Cusella identified the body, the blood-soaked shirt pillowing the pale head.

Lou dropped in on the Schroeders the night after the shooting but was unable to talk. Florence and her husband tried to comfort him.

Louis Schroeder was a quiet man with a massive square jaw and the same brilliant blue eyes as his son. He didn't talk as much as Florence, or read as much, and he was more skeptical.

Florence had expected that the authorities would find out what had happened on the Kent campus. If some students had shot at the guardsmen, the authorities would learn that Bill had not been one of them and that he had been innocent. She was astonished when General Del Corso said there was no proof that a sniper had been on the campus.

That summer Fruehauf closed its Lorain plant, and Louis, who had been superintendent for fifteen years, suddenly became an unemployed fifty-five-year-old making the rounds of personnel offices and contacting friends who might know of openings. Florence followed the reports on the special grand jury called by Governor Rhodes (for whom she had voted). When the grand jury blamed the students and professors, she began to think that she ought

to take Senator Stephen Young's advice and sue the governor and the guards-
men. In December she told Fred Mandel she would join the suit, not for
money but to obtain public acknowledgment that Bill should not have been
shot.

The Schroeders were surprised when no action was taken following the
Scranton Commission's report. They were astounded when Attorney General
John Mitchell announced, in August 1971, that he would not convene a
federal grand jury. They followed each step of the appeal, attending every
hearing in the state and federal courts.

In November 1971, when a professional patriot addressed a Boy Scout
Court of Honor in their Congregational Church and urged them to support
Nixon, the Pentagon, and the boys in Vietnam, the Schroeders found them-
selves resenting the speaker's assurances that everything their country did was
right. When a neighbor asked Florence why she had not joined in the enthusi-
astic applause, she replied that it was persons like the speaker who had killed
her son. She no longer felt that she was part of the majority or that others knew
better.

Perhaps, Mrs. Schroeder thought, God had visited this affliction on her and
Louis and the other parents because they were strong enough to fight back to
make sure that such a terrible thing did not happen again.

She worried now about the jury, but she tried to have faith that the jurors,
in accordance with their oaths, would base their verdicts on what they heard
in the courtroom.

Fulton and Brown seemed particularly worried that Florence Schroeder
would become emotional and attract sympathy in a manner that could prejudice their case.

The judge agreed with them. He ruled that the testimony of the two mothers
bore on damages, which would be handled in a separate part of the trial, rather
than on liability. I argued that because the defense lawyers had related liability
to political activities, it was only fair that the parents of the deceased students,
who could not speak for themselves, describe their children's characters and
beliefs. Certainly Mrs. Schroeder should have a chance to show that her son
had been an ROTC member, especially after all the testimony regarding the
ROTC Building fire.

I also pointed out that if the parents were not allowed to testify, the jury
could draw mistaken conclusions from their silence. I proposed that the parents at least be permitted to state that the four dead students were not members
of any organizations more radical than the Boy Scouts.

The judge offered to make a statement on their behalf.

"You should understand," he told the jury, "that all four of the deceased plaintiffs, plaintiffs' descendants, those deceased children, were in fact students at the Kent State University and had all the rights and privileges of students and were properly on the campus at the time and place of these tragic events. . . .

"The fact that the parents didn't testify and there has been no particular evidence is the reason that I am giving you this statement so you won't feel that something has been omitted . . . or that there is any doubt about the status of those four persons who were killed.

"In addition to that, I should say to you that the deceased student William Schroeder, during his lifetime and during the time that he was a student on the campus of the Kent State University, was there on a scholarship and was a member of the—he was on an ROTC scholarship. . . . and was a member of the campus ROTC."

The judge apparently couldn't bring himself to say that Bill Schroeder had been cadet first sergeant.

In the final hours of the session of Wednesday afternoon, August 6, as we closed our case, the defense moved that the judge direct verdicts in favor of Governor Rhodes, President White, and General Del Corso because of a lack of proof, and in favor of eleven guardsmen whom we had not called.

Fulton also requested directed verdicts with respect to the federal claims, on behalf of all the officers from General Canterbury on down, on the basis that they had violated no one's civil rights. His argument was based on the legality of the dispersal order, but Judge Young responded that the civil rights claims grew out of excessive force represented by the shootings.

The judge gave us overnight to consider dismissing the charges against the eleven enlisted guardsmen who had not been called. The next day we offered to dismiss eight of the eleven plus Paul Naujoks, who had been called to testify. We maintained our stance against the remaining three, Lonnie Hinton, Russell Repp, and Dwight Cline, for others had testified that Hinton and Repp had fired, and Captain Cline had been close enough to the guardsmen to prevent their firing.

Fulton's request for a directed verdict in favor of General Del Corso inspired us to make a counterproposal. We still wanted the jury to hear Del Corso's opinion of the shootings as he expressed it to the federal grand jury; therefore we offered to drop our case against him if he would agree to testify as an expert.

Judge Young left the decision to Del Corso and his lawyers, even though

Fulton and Brown would have a conflict of interest in that Del Corso's expert testimony would be against the interests of their other clients.

A few days later Fulton reported the general's decision to stick it out with the other defendants.

Part Three

THE CASE FOR
THE DEFENSE

23

The Man in the Gold Coat

The defense case took just five days and eighteen witnesses. The witnesses included the three defendants we had refused to dismiss—Hinton, Repp, and Cline—and Dennis Breckenridge, one of the defendants we had dismissed. (Breckenridge, a member of Troop G, had fainted at the ROTC Building after the shooting.) The other seventeen witnesses for the defense were two National Guard officers, a medical expert, a KSU trustee, President White, two members of the Kent City Police Department, a Kent fireman, two Ohio Highway Patrol officers, a Kent merchant, a surveyor, a weapons expert, Kent Mayor LeRoy Satrom, a university administrator, and two former students, one of whom had attended Kent State.

The brevity of the defense's case and the small number of witnesses it called did not at all mean that their case was less elaborate than ours. For most of the defendants had already testified, and the defense had been making its case as we were making ours.

The defense's purpose now was to have their version of the events confirmed by nonparty witnesses who would not be suspected of self-interest, to present once more the horrible events of Friday and Saturday nights—in Panavision, as it were, with drum rolls and flourishes.

They began with four witnesses from the City of Kent: policeman William Sutliff, fireman David Helmling, merchant David Amsel, and Police Chief Roy Thompson.

Sutliff, who was twenty-six years old at the time of the shootings and had been on the police force just one year, gave a stupendous description of the disturbances on Friday night.

"There was two fellows in front of the Portage National Bank," he said, "who were putting a lawn spreader through the front window. I found out later the lawn spreader came from the hardware store across the street, and we . . . went to get him, but he ran into the crowd, which we retreated back to the line of men.

"We marched them up North Water Street, which is, like I say, about five or six hundred feet, which there was a fire in the street. The whole street was on fire.

"They had trash containers, paper boxes that was engulfed in flames in the middle of the street. We marched up there and dispersed the people off the street . . . almost every window we passed was smashed out. . . . A whole bunch of small stores, all those windows were smashed out.

"The whole street was covered with debris and people, and as we marched back down North Water Street, the fellow right next to me—he is a deputy sheriff, Ross Jamerson— . . . he was standing right to my left, and all of a sudden I heard a tremendous crack and he fell to his knees and he went down to the pavement and blood was coming from underneath his helmet.

"When I looked down there was a cue ball there that had split his helmet and the cue ball was on the ground and half of it had turned to dust. . . . Jack Rose—he was a sergeant—he went down. He got a brick on the top of the head and he collapsed to the pavement. We felt it come off a building, which we weren't able to determine. He was down and injured.

"Then the deputy to the right of me, he was another deputy, Mancini I think his name was, he was a special, he is not a full-time deputy, he went down. He got a dislocated shoulder out of it. By that time I think we had fourteen men on the street."

The next evening, Sutliff said, he "was one of nineteen policemen and sheriff's deputies lined up across Main Street to prevent the students from marching downtown.

"They were coming down Main Street, probably half a mile from us at this time, screaming and yelling, breaking windows all the way.

"And, like I say, I couldn't believe it, I looked behind me, and here comes the National Guard. And there was probably ten vehicles, I think probably close to 150, 200 men. . . . They stopped there. A captain came over and asked us where Wall School was. . . . He said that's where they were supposed to meet. And Sergeant Rose, who was next to me, he said if he didn't get off that such and such truck, there wouldn't be any Wall School."

I got up to object not only to such hearsay as what Sergeant Rose had said but on the ground that all these events had already been described many times.

"I have given counsel in this case full latitude to present their cases the way they want to present them," Judge Young said, "because I think at this time we better have all the cards laid on the table."

I could only stare in wonderment at the judge.

The testimony of David Helmling, a handsome volunteer fireman with jug ears and an angular jaw, suggested some of the mystery that surrounded the ROTC Building fire. He revealed, first, that the Kent fire chief had notified his men two or three weeks in advance of May 1 that an attempt was going to be made to burn some buildings on the Kent State campus and, second, that on Saturday the firemen had been called to the firehouse—only a minute and a half from the campus—in the late afternoon, in anticipation of an emergency. Despite the fact that they were ready and waiting and anticipating trouble, he said, no call came until between 8:30 P.M. and 9 P.M., more than an hour after the assault on the building began.

Ever since the events of May 1970, it had been widely publicized that at the time of the ROTC Building fire, students had interfered with the firemen by taking away their hose and slashing it full of holes. It now developed that Helmling had a second hose working by the time the building was actually set on fire (with rags soaked in gasoline from the tanks of motorcycles in a nearby parking lot).

Helmling testified that he was beaten when he approached the burning building with the second hose, that three members of the crowd helped him and returned the hose to him, and that he was able to enter the structure and had in fact reached the blaze with two other firemen when they were ordered to return to the firehouse.

"Was the fire still going when you left?"

"Yes, sir."

Helmling testified that he spent twenty-two minutes at the fire station before being ordered back to the campus and that when he returned, the fire was out of control.

I cross-examined Helmling about the lack of police protection during the seventeen minutes he had spent at the ROTC Building on the first trip to the campus.

He didn't know that the campus police station was only a block from the ROTC Building, and he didn't know whether anyone had radioed the fire department from the fire truck to request police assistance when the first hose was taken.

During the afternoon recess several of the clients asked me if I knew where the campus police were when the firemen arrived at the ROTC Building. I referred them to Galen Keller, who explained that they had been standing in a parking lot a few hundred yards away, dressed in riot gear.

"What?" Arthur Krause exclaimed. "They were all suited up and did nothing?"

"It's worse than that," Galen said. "I think there were a lot of provocateurs in the crowd that night, in the pay of the National Guard, the highway patrol, the police, the FBI, the CIA, and military intelligence."

"We've heard all this before," Krause said, "but where's the proof?"

"It's hard to prove who was in that crowd," Galen admitted, "but there were a lot of suspicious things about the fire that came out at the trial of Jerry Rupe."

"Who was Rupe?" Doug Wrentmore asked.

"He was indicted along with me by the state grand jury," Alan Canfora said. "He was one of the few who were actually brought to trial for interfering with a fireman and starting the fire." (Rupe was found guilty on December 1, 1971, of the misdemeanor of obstructing a fireman.)

Galen Keller had been building a special file on the fire which, she believed, was the key to the shootings because it provided the pretext for calling the National Guard to the campus. She explained that Rupe, who had never attended the university, had admitted being present at the fire, throwing stones at the ROTC Building, burning an American flag, and helping to drag a hose away from a fireman.

"Who was he?" Arthur Krause asked.

"I don't know a lot about him," Galen said. "He grew up in Ravenna and was one of those kids the cops know. In 1970 he was living in a kind of commune in Kent, in an old house with several young people, including his girlfriend, a former model, who was also indicted by the state grand jury. It's important to know that at the end of 1970, almost a year before his trial on the charges growing out of the fire, he was convicted on a drug charge and drew a prison sentence of several years."

"Was he working for the police in May 1970?" someone asked.

"Who knows?" Galen replied. "What was most interesting about his trial was the testimony of the others about the fire." She named four witnesses for the prosecution: David Ambler, the Kent State assistant vice president for student affairs; Stephen Sivulich, director of the university's student-conduct program; Dr. Richard Dunn, Kent State vice president for business; and William Maxwell, an undercover policeman. Maxwell, wearing Levi's and a jacket, had mingled with the crowds at the ROTC Building.

"What did they say?" Robbie Stamps asked.

"Well," Galen said, "you have to believe either that they were incredibly stupid or. . . ."

"Or what?"

"Judge for yourself," Galen said. Referring to notes in her file, she told the following story.

As Helmling had testified, the Kent fire department, alerted to the possibility of trouble, had had a crew waiting at the firehouse, less than two minutes from the campus, since 4:30 P.M. The university fire department had been warned about the old ROTC Building and other campus buildings as early as 7 P.M., and the campus police had been ordered to don riot gear at 7:40 P.M. —about the time the assault on the building began.

During the entire time of the assault, Sivulich and Maxwell were present, the former reporting frequently by telephone to Vice President Matson, the latter in disguise and mingling with the demonstrators. Sivulich arrived on the Commons at 7:25 P.M., at a time when no more than twenty-five to thirty-five people were present, and Maxwell arrived about fifteen minutes later, when the crowd had begun to increase. Their superiors in the Administration Building, no more than two hundred yards from the Commons, were informed by Sivulich of the details of what the crowd was doing, but they did nothing to dispatch either campus police or firemen as bumbling attempts were made to ignite the building by throwing burning newspapers and railroad flares at it. (The building didn't begin to smolder until 8:30 P.M.)

At 8:40 P.M. Sivulich—who couldn't understand the administration's lack of response—ran to the office and was then told to call the city fire department. When the firemen arrived at 9:05 P.M., they saw no campus police on the scene. For some reason, despite all the warnings from Sivulich, no one had sent to the ROTC Building the thirty-odd campus police officers, who had been waiting, prepared for duty with riot gear and tear gas, since 7:45 P.M. Nor were any members of the city police force in evidence. Sixty sheriff's deputies had been available for duty since 8 P.M.; two of them were observed watching the attack from a safe distance.

"Sounds like another Reichstag fire," Arthur Krause commented.

"You mean to say," Robbie Stamps said, *"they let the building burn?"*

"I always thought they were glad to see it go," John Cleary said. "It was a temporary building put up after World War II, and they were planning to tear it down."

"Perfect!" Alan Canfora said. "They burn the building to make everyone hate us even more and bring in the Guard."

"They let the building burn?" Robbie said again. He seemed shaken at the thought. "Why haven't you told them? The jury ought to know it was a put-up job."

A lot of the other clients told me I had made a mistake in keeping this from the jury. My response was that it was a task for an investigating group such as the Scranton Commission, not a job for lawyers who were trying to win a civil suit. Even if it turned out that everything from the Friday night trashing (which the Kent police could have halted by using the tear gas at their disposal) to the fire had been carefully stage-managed, this had no bearing on the issues of our case. Our complaint was not that the fire had been staged but that the Guard had used excessive force and violated civil rights.

This is not to say that I did not think about the suspicious origin of the fire in the still small hours of the morning; it was certainly another hint of the hidden forces we were opposing in the courtroom.*

David Amsel, a Kent shoe-store owner, was brought on by Brooke Alloway to show the merchants' need for protection. He described the damage done to his store, yet he also admitted that several students had helped him clean up, that the damage had been covered by insurance, and that business on Saturday had been excellent.

White-haired Roy Thompson had moved to Kent and joined its police force in 1943, when he was discharged from military service. He had taken over the department in 1961 and retired ten years later, in the spring of 1971, a year after the shootings, to become a probation officer. Like many members of Troop G, Thompson had grown up in West Virginia. His bugaboo was Communism; he believed it sought to undermine police departments as the first line of the nation's defense. He was so popular with townspeople that his attempt to resign in 1969 was forestalled by a petition.

He stayed on, believing that Communists were subverting the Kent State campus, and expecting trouble. He could not understand why Jerry Rubin had been permitted to speak there in mid-April, and was apprehensive when the four Kent State SDS leaders were released from jail on April 30.

On Friday night, when the trouble began with youths stopping cars on Water Street, the chief panicked and closed all the bars, driving hundreds of persons into the streets and worsening the situation. Thompson was the person who was heard to say, on the tape of the May 3 press conference, that he would be right there with the Guard and would shoot if necessary.

The former police chief, who looked older now than his sixty-four years and had some difficulty recalling details, testified that his force had jurisdiction over the Kent State campus, that his men had been called there many times

---

*After Hemling and the other firemen had been called away following their 9:05 arrival, campus police surrounded the building, which, according to a photograph taken at the time, was *not* burning. Was Hemling's testimony that the fire was not out mistaken? If so, how was a building guarded by police set on fire?

during student demonstrations, and that his twenty-two-man force had been augmented on Friday and Saturday nights by fifty to sixty police from neighboring towns and by deputy sheriffs.

According to Thompson, the Kent City Police Department had tear-gas grenades and gas masks. Ahern had said that he had never seen tear gas fail to disperse rioters. Why then had gas not been used downtown on Friday night? When it was too late to prevent the fire, the campus police had appeared from their nearby hiding place and easily routed the crowd on the Commons with tear gas. Why were events allowed to evolve when the means to curtail them were at hand?

The defense thought it could use Thompson to shift the blame for banning assemblies away from Rhodes and Canterbury. Thanks to the "evidence hole" rule, they had already shown the jury that all assemblies (contrary to the actual words of the Matson-Frisina letter) had been banned by the university. Now, for good measure, Fulton sought to have Thompson put the blame for the ban on Mayor Satrom by having Thompson claim that a Kent ordinance (that under the "evidence hole" rule the jury could not hear read) gave Mayor Satrom the power to ban assemblies.

To Fulton's surprise, however, for the first time in the trial his stratagem didn't work. For once I was able to show the jury the dice in Big Julie's hat.

Thompson testified that Mayor Satrom had banned all assemblies under a city ordinance, No. 10140, passed in 1968. In reality the ordinance said nothing about banning assemblies; it merely permitted the mayor, during a civil emergency, to close liquor stores and bars and prevent the sale of gasoline and firearms. When I asked Thompson to find that part of the ordinance that referred to banning assemblies, Fulton jumped up and invoked the "evidence hole" rule.

When Judge Young refused, for the first time in the trial, to go along with this, Fulton became angry and insisted that only the Court could interpret the ordinance.

Fulton then tried to obscure the issue by claiming that Thompson had never said that the mayor could ban assemblies, but I had caught Fulton with his documents down. "Did you say," I asked Thompson, "just a few moments ago, and I am quoting, sir—tell me if I wrote it down wrong—'The mayor wouldn't allow assemblies for both the City of Kent and Kent State University'?"

"I should have said unlawful assemblies," Thompson said.

He then changed his story to say that the mayor had operated under state law.

There was no state law authorizing the banning of peaceful assemblies. No such law would be constitutional.

Thompson's testimony on the Monday morning meeting contradicted Canterbury's testimony at several points. He said the meeting had been called by Mayor Satrom and the decision to break up assemblies on campus was made by the mayor. The mayor, of course, was not a defendant.

Paul Gibson Locher, the religion editor of the *Wooster Record,* the hometown newspaper of about half the members of Company A, was a slender young man who in 1970 was a freshman at Ashland College, a small institution in the Wooster area. It was never clear what he was doing on the Kent State campus on May 3 and 4. He told Charlie Brown, who examined him, that he had been working for the Ashland daily paper and that his intention had been to write about the events at Kent State. But he admitted to me that he had never published anything about that weekend.

He arrived at Kent State at 7 P.M. Sunday and witnessed everything that occurred up to the shooting. What Charlie Brown was interested in was Locher's testimony that after the dispersal he had seen students passing out rocks from buckets and that more than a hundred rocks had been thrown at the guardsmen on the practice field.

Locher gave a graphic description of five hundred shouting students charging up the hill after the guardsmen and showering them with rocks.

Donald E. Manly, Jr., a big man with a bold no-nonsense face, was a high-ranking officer of the Ohio Highway Patrol in 1970, a major in charge of one of the state's three zones. He testified that he had mobilized 91 men and a helicopter for duty at Kent State Saturday night. Thus, with the 22-man Kent police force augmented (as Chief Thompson had testified) by 50 to 60 out-of-town police and sheriff's deputies, a total of at least 163 nonmilitary law-enforcement personnel had been available in Kent on Saturday, in addition to the more than 800 National Guard troops who were dispatched there.

Major Manly thought the students the most vicious and aggressive people he had ever seen. He described how his men and some guardsmen had "made a sweep of the library on Saturday night," closing it and doubtless driving away a number of students engaged in such threatening activities as reading Chaucer.

Fulton had used Thompson to pin the dispersal decision on the mayor. Manly's job was to pin it on the university (via the Matson-Frisina letter) and to support Canterbury's position that everyone present at the Monday morning meeting had agreed to the dispersal. Manly said the main subjects discussed at the meeting were the law-enforcement difficulties arising from the different curfew times in town and on the campus and the noon rally "in defiance of the proclamation put out by Dean Matson."

When it came to specifying the contributions of the different participants to the dispersal decision, all Manly could say was that "quite a few people had input . . . everybody was of a consensus." He was unable to testify as to what anybody had actually said.

Like everyone else in the firehouse Monday morning, Manly assumed that it was General Canterbury's prerogative to chair the meeting—prima facie evidence that the Guard was not just assisting the civil authority but had taken charge.

Under cross-examination Manly admitted that no one knew whether the noon rally would be violent or peaceful when the decision was made to disperse it. He also admitted that there was no rock throwing before the jeep moved out.

In his cross-examination of Manly, Blakemore brought out one interesting fact. "I believe you indicated earlier," Blakemore said, "that General Canterbury gave you an order. When you were on campus, as you were in May 1970, did you consider yourself to be subservient to the National Guard at that particular time?"

"I was supplemental to the Guard."

"Did you consider your forces and the Guard subservient to the direction of the mayor?"

"No, sir."

We had heard Chief Thompson assign responsibility for the dispersal of the noon rally to Mayor Satrom and his proclamation. Now the defense put the former mayor himself on the stand.

LeRoy Satrom was a tall, thin, slow-speaking North Dakotan who had come to Kent in 1956 to serve as city engineer after receiving a degree from Case Western Reserve. Satrom, who looked like an older, drier version of actor Ben Gazzara, was the first full-time mayor the city had ever had; his term began on January 1, 1970. When the disturbances started on the night of Friday, May 1, Satrom was in a motel in Aurora, twelve miles north, playing poker with a bunch of Portage County politicians (including Seabury Ford, who was later appointed by Rhodes to head the special state grand jury).

Satrom left the game shortly after 11 P.M. when he got a call informing him of the disturbances on North Water Street. He sped through the rain to Kent and soon found himself helping a policeman ferry young rioters to the jail. The new mayor had never before been confronted with anything of this sort. He knew the university well; two of his sons had graduated from Kent State, and a third attended the university's high school, where student teachers practiced.

He knew there had been disturbances at Ohio State University in Columbus; his son Tom, a medical student there, was home for the weekend to avoid the tear-gassing. Tom had told his father that events there had gotten out of hand, that police and national guardsmen were all over the campus. No doubt Satrom had his son's experiences in mind as Chief Thompson pressured him to call for outside reinforcements.

Satrom telephoned the Ohio Highway Patrol to obtain assistance. They sounded reluctant, so he got in touch with John McElroy at the governor's office to discuss sending in the Guard. McElroy telephoned General Del Corso, who sent a young officer, Lieutenant Charles Barnett, to assess the situation.

Barnett arrived at 3 A.M. Saturday and spent most of that day with the mayor, telling him that he had until 5 P.M. to decide whether he wanted the Guard or not.

Saturday passed without incident but with rumors galore. Mayor Satrom hesitated until the last minute and finally requested the Guard at 5:27 P.M. The request was formalized when he put his signature on a letter that had been typed on his official letterhead by Major William R. Shimp, a Guard legal officer.

THE CITY OF KENT, OHIO

LeRoy M. Satrom
Mayor   Progress in the Seventies

May 2, 1970

Commander of Troops
Ohio National Guard
Kent, Ohio

I, LeRoy M. Satrom, Mayor of the City of Kent, Ohio, pursuant to the power invested in me as the chief magisterial officer of this City do hereby request the assistance of the Ohio National Guard to assist the Police Department and other local law-enforcement agencies in restoring law and order in the City of Kent and particularly in the area of Kent State University and its environs.

Local law-enforcement agencies can no longer cope with the situation and I instruct you to provide the necessary assistance to restore peace and order to our community.

In accordance with Section 5923.23 of the Revised Code of Ohio, I leave the mode and means of execution to your direction.

Sincerely,

LeRoy M. Satrom
Mayor

Section 5923.23 is the statute authorizing use of the Guard in aid to civil authorities.

At 5:27 P.M. there existed no situation in Kent that the local law-enforcement agencies could not cope with. Fifteen of Friday's rioters were in jail, and nothing had happened for sixteen hours. Yet the mayor, elected by the people of Kent, had just taken a back seat to the National Guard, leaving the "mode and means of execution" to its direction. In retrospect, the use of the word "execution" is ironic.

When he appeared on the stand on Monday afternoon, August 11, 1975, Satrom had been out of office almost three years and was engaged in a private engineering practice. He proved an unsatisfactory witness. Like Major Manly, he was unable to affirm that any one individual had said anything about dispersing the rally. He claimed to recall the pros and cons, but he could not recollect who was con. His evasions exasperated even Judge Young.

One of the persons who former mayor Satrom said had attended the Monday morning meeting on behalf of the university was Chester Williams. As it turned out, Williams had not been at the meeting.

Williams, a well-built man of about forty with gray crew-cut hair and the rough, self-confident demeanor of a football coach, had made a career of Kent State University. He graduated from the school in 1957 and then occupied various administrative positions. In May 1970 his title was director of security; his responsibility for fire prevention, environmental health, and parking and traffic included supervision of the campus police, whose head, Donald Schwartzmiller, reported to him.

Because of his concern with fire prevention and security, Williams played a key role in the events that led to the introduction of the National Guard on the Kent State campus. Williams had not expected trouble that weekend. Unlike Kent's police chief, who had even been apprehensive that empty pop bottles might be used as containers for molotov cocktails, Williams had left the city Friday night to spend a weekend in Dayton with his family.

Summoned by Schwartzmiller, Williams returned to Kent in the early morning hours of Saturday and spent a good part of the day making plans to avert further trouble. Early Saturday morning he and Vice President Matson obtained a meaningless injunction that sought to bar damage on the campus. A few hours later they got Mayor Satrom to allow students the freedom of the campus until 1 A.M. (an exemption from the 8 P.M. town curfew). To keep the students happy while confined to the campus, they arranged for the cafeterias to remain open that night and scheduled dances and movies.

Williams told the Scranton Commission he had been informed by city hall that if the Guard came, it would not operate on the college campus. The university, according to Williams, did not want the National Guard. Its own contingency plans involved calling in the Ohio Highway Patrol, which had made the arrests during the Music and Speech Building occupation in 1969.* As it turned out, the Guard arrived in Kent more than an hour before the highway patrolmen, who had refused to come until actual lawbreaking had occurred. (With the ROTC Building ablaze, Williams agreed to bringing the Guard on the campus.) He and Schwartzmiller met the guardsmen at the corner of Lincoln and Main, provided them with maps of the campus, and escorted them to the ROTC Building.

Fulton brought out that Williams had been at the ROTC Building ruins with Schwartzmiller when the guardsmen moved out against the students on Monday. Therefore I asked him whether he had ever requested that national guardsmen disperse the rally.

"No, sir," Williams replied.

The defense's one "suprise" was a tall, good-looking young lady named Joy Bishop. We knew who she was and had known about her for months; the surprise was that she was a witness for the defense after what she had told us.

Early in the year our staff had found several photographs showing a man and two women standing on the roof of Johnson Hall. In the background of the photos they loomed against the sky as the guardsmen wheeled and fired at the top of the hill. It was obvious that they had had a superb view of the events leading to the shooting, so we tried to find out who they were—a difficult task, for their images were small and unclear.

Sometime in May, through a stroke of luck, Professor Jerry Lewis learned that one of the three people on the roof was a teacher of retarded children in Canton who had graduated from Kent State in 1972. Mrs. Bishop sounded as though she would make a good witness, and Lewis, Bob Kelner, and Engdahl had gone to see her. Joy Bishop (her name was Joy Hubbard in 1970) had indeed seen the shooting, and she said that it was preceded by neither a barrage of rocks nor a rush of students. Impressed with both her story and her demeanor, Bob put her on our list of prospective witnesses, but when he called her back, she hesitated to commit herself. We learned why on Monday, August 11, when her name appeared on a list of defense witnesses scheduled for Tuesday.

*The KSU newspaper, the *Kent Stater*, reported that the students had been entrapped by two *agents provocateurs.*

We knew that in 1973 Mrs. Bishop had told a Justice Department official that she had witnessed the Terry Norman incident from the roof, and we assumed the defense was going to try to use her story to show that a nonmilitary shot had precipitated the shootings. Impulsively, Engdahl telephoned her at her hotel to caution her to be careful what she said lest she be embarrassed by our cross-examination.

To understand the story that Joy Bishop, with a great deal of self-assurance, told Burt Fulton and the jury on August 12, some knowledge of the shape and orientation of Johnson Hall is essential. The building consists of two wings set at a right angle. One wing lies in the same direction as the long dimension of Taylor Hall, that is, it points to the northeast. It is at the end of this wing that Johnson Hall comes closest to Taylor Hall. (Between the two buildings is a 40-yard gap through which the guardsmen marched on their way from the Commons down Blanket Hill.) The other wing lies southeasterly, in the direction of another dormitory, Lake Hall.

The narrow end of the northeast wing overlooks the side of Taylor Hall that faces the Commons. The southeast wing overlooks the Pagoda and Blanket Hill. A person standing in the middle of this wing could see directly across the Pagoda and the greensward in front of Taylor Hall, toward the Prentice Hall parking lot.

Fulton did not ask Mrs. Bishop on which wing she was standing when she made the observations he asked her about. He asked her only in which direction she was facing. She replied that she was facing southeast, which meant she was facing not the Pagoda but Lake Hall.

Fulton showed her the Howard Ruffner photograph of the guardsmen (with Pryor's pistol raised), and she identified herself, Pat Frank, and Bruce Phillips on the roof of Johnson Hall.

"Now, from that position you have described, were you able to have observation of what was taking place that day?"

"In part," she replied.

From the photograph (invisible, of course, to the jury) it is clear that she was standing on the southeast wing of Johnson Hall and that she was facing not southeast, as she had said, but northeast.

Prior to the firing by the guardsmen, she said, she saw "a male dressed in a gold, yellowish-gold sportcoat come to the corner of Johnson Hall from the Commons area, from that general area, come to the corner of the building. He had a briefcase in his left hand, he stood at the corner very briefly, pulled a gun from his briefcase, and fired one shot into the air."

"What was the next thing you heard or observed?"

"I then saw this individual leave the same way he had come."

"How much time elapsed between the time you heard the first shot you had described and the shots from the guardsmen's rifles which you have described?"

"From two to five seconds."

There were a number of flaws in her story. They involved the position from which she had observed the gold-coated civilian and her claim to have watched other events simultaneously from a different location.

Position: She had told the Justice Department that the gold-coated civilian was standing just in front of the corner of the northeast wing of Johnson Hall, near the Commons. A man at this location could indeed be seen by someone standing near the end of the roof of the northeast wing. But photographs taken before and during the shooting, including the very photograph in which she had identified her position for Fulton, showed Mrs. Bishop standing in the middle of the southeast wing, a position from which the man in the gold coat would have been unobservable.

Simultaneous events: Mrs. Bishop had told Dave Engdahl and Jerry Lewis that she had watched the guardsmen approach the top of the hill, turn, and fire—a sequence of events that must have taken at least thirty seconds. She also claimed to have seen the gold-coated civilian approach Johnson Hall, open his briefcase, fire, and leave two to five seconds before the guardsmen opened fire. She could not have made both observations. If she had been watching the civilian just before the shootings, she could not, from that vantage point at the end of the northeast wing, have seen the guardsmen approach the hilltop, turn, and fire. On the other hand, if she had been watching the guardsmen, she would not have noticed the civilian.

However, she could have watched the guardsmen climb the hill and fire *and* the Terry Norman incident if the two events had taken place not five seconds apart but—as previous testimony had established—several minutes apart. If, as had already been shown, the Terry Norman business had occurred several minutes after the shootings, she would have had plenty of time to go from the southeast wing to the northeast wing.

I expected it would be easy to discredit her story even if I couldn't show the photographs to the jury, and I attempted to do so by getting her to indicate her position on the map of the campus. No photograph showed her on the northeast wing, and she readily agreed, looking at the photos that I showed her, to having been on the southeast wing.

I established that she had watched the guardsmen for at least several seconds before the shooting, during which time they reached the hilltop and stopped, Pryor drew his pistol and pointed it, and the guardsmen turned.

Mrs. Bishop insisted that she had watched the man in the gold coat from the northeast wing. Reminding her that she had testified that five seconds had elapsed between her mysterious man's shot and the first of the guardsmen's shots, I asked her how she had gotten from the northeast wing to the southeast wing in time to have watched the guardsmen arrive at the top of the hill before they began shooting.

Mrs. Bishop then claimed that she was on the northeast wing when the guardsmen's shooting commenced. Yet this not only contradicted her earlier testimony of having been on the southeast wing at the time, it was belied by the photographs taken when the shooting began, which showed her on the southeast wing.

When I asked her to explain this, she said she had moved back and forth from one position to another.

"Did you walk or run?"

"Walked."

I showed her that the two positions, from the middle of the southeast wing to the end of the northeast, were about 250 feet apart.

"And did you keep going back and forth at approximately 250 feet, or did you just make one trip?"

"No, I made several trips. I may have run," Joy Bishop said. "I may have walked. I don't recall specifically what my gait was." Nor could she recall how many trips back and forth she had made.

As I hammered away at the inconsistencies in her story, Fulton objected that the photographs showed her standing at the end of the northeast wing. (Here I realized that Fulton had made a mistake; apparently he didn't know what the photographs really showed.)

"He can cross-examine all day about the pictures," Fulton told Judge Young. "I think they show something entirely different than what Mr. Kelner says. He can question about where she was, but the question about where she is in the picture speaks for itself, and we can argue about that to the jury."

"That's right," Judge Young agreed, "and I am going to sustain the objection to the question."

Mrs. Bishop admitted that she had never said anything about a man in a gold coat firing a shot before the guardsmen's shooting to either of her two companions on the roof, nor to anyone else until she was interviewed by a lawyer representing the guardsmen at the time the Justice Department was reopening its investigation in August 1973.

24

The Judge Makes
a Suggestion

——

That Tuesday night, at home, Fred Mandel received some disturbing news on the telephone. A stranger's voice asked him if he was one of the lawyers for the plaintiffs in the Kent State case. Mandel said he was and asked the name of the caller. The man refused to say. "I am afraid," he said, "like other people."

The caller explained that he was a worker at the Ford plant in Walton Hills, where juror Douglas Watts was employed. (Watts was an alternate who early in the trial had replaced Mrs. Jakaitis when she became ill.) The caller told Mandel that Watts, while an alternate juror, had said that the students got what they deserved and that Watts had continued talking in that vein. Recently Watts had said that pictures he had seen showed that the people who were shot were rabble-rousers and that he wouldn't give them one dime.

The caller told Mandel that when one of his listeners asked Watts how, as a juror, he could talk about the case, Watts had laughed the question off.

On Wednesday morning I told Fulton that we had something serious to tell the judge.

When Young entered his office in his gray business suit, Mandel told him about the telephone call, and I added that we were "deeply concerned about the presence of this juror on this panel" and felt that the matter required "additional inquiry by the Court."

"Well," Judge Young said, "I am going to find out . . . what do the defendants say to this?"

Brown replied that "it has no weight at all, as far as I am concerned."

The judge remarked that usually he didn't pay much attention to anonymous phone calls. "However," he added, "it appears to me that the nature of this matter is so extremely serious that the least that I can do is to get Mr. Watts in, have him told what the anonymous statement is, and ask him what he says about it.

"If he denies it, why then I am going to allow him to remain seated, because I certainly am not going to disqualify a man on anonymous statements that he denies. But if he admits it, then of course we don't really have any choice except to excuse him."

It was usual in such cases to question the juror in front of the lawyers; but Fulton and Brown said they preferred not to watch. "I don't want to be present," Fulton said. "Let Mr. Kelner be present." He and Brown left, presenting the rest of us with a problem.

It was our duty to remain, for a judge was not supposed to talk to a juror alone any more than we were. But for counsel for just one of the parties to be with the judge and the juror wasn't right either. While I conferred with our staff, the judge went into the other office and talked with his law clerks. When he returned, he told us he had decided that no lawyer should be present. He assured me, however, that his conversation with the juror would be transcribed for the record.

The record, which we received the following day, revealed what had passed between juror Watts and the judge.

When everyone had left the room except for Judge Young and a court reporter, Watts entered and was told to sit down. "I am awfully troubled," Judge Young told him, "because of information that has just come to my ears that I want to discuss with you.

"One of the attorneys got a phone call from a man who said he was one of your fellow employees at the Ford Motors plant—I believe that's where you work?"

Watts nodded.

"And he says that you have discussed this case with him and with other fellow workers and that you have expressed opinions that plaintiffs were troublemakers and were bad and the evidence shows that and that you don't propose to decide in their favor.

"Now, I don't like to act on anonymous phone calls, but because of the fact that—this type of matter is a very sensitive one, this is a case in which emotions and opinions are running high and have at all times, we have to be much more careful than I would if this were an ordinary automobile collision case. What about it?"

"Well," Watts said, "I will admit I talked to one fellow up at the shop, he always talks to me. But outside of that one fellow, I don't discuss it. But I will admit—I didn't hide nothing as far as my feelings are concerned to the man."

"Well, under the circumstance," Judge Young said, "I am sure, I hope you will understand, I think I am going to have to excuse you from further consideration of the case because the rules, the law is very rigid about this, and it is just as I explained to you and have explained to you repeatedly, that you may not talk with anybody, not even your own family, about any phase of this case on which you are sitting as a juror, even though a juror may do it in the best of good faith. . . . So I am going to have to excuse you as a juror."

"You said they called the plaintiffs?" Watts asked.

"Yes."

"They did," Watts said.

"You better be careful who you think your pals are," Judge Young told him.

When Judge Young told us he had dismissed Watts, Fulton tried to persuade him to release the story to the press. This, of course, would have resulted in the other jurors' learning what Watts thought of the plaintiffs. Fortunately, Judge Young disagreed. Without revealing the nature of Watts' opinions, he merely told the jurors that Watts had been dismissed for violating his instructions and discussing the case with others.

The judge told us that the matter had troubled him a great deal. If Watts had denied the allegation and remained on the jury, he would have been in a difficult position "because it is improper for a Court, for anybody, to talk with a juror alone about anything in connection with the case.

"I will tell you, I went into that conference with this man feeling I was on the horns of a dilemma."

I refrained from pointing out who was responsible for his dilemma, but I requested that he ask the jury, "either individually or collectively, in the absence of the press, as to whether [Watts] has expressed opinions to them, and if so, that the jurors should ignore whatever opinions he may have expressed to them."

"Absolutely not," Brown said.

"No, no," Judge Young said.

Brown said that I was presuming that none of the jurors had followed the standing instructions to report anything any juror said about the case.

Watts was replaced by alternate Mary L. Blazina, a machinist's wife from Lorain whose brother had graduated from Kent State in 1970. A sure enemy had been replaced by a juror who could possibly be fair and unbiased.

When I read the record of the interrogation of Watts, I was astonished to see that instead of fining or reprimanding the juror, the judge sounded apologetic about dismissing him. His cautioning Watts to "be careful who you think your pals are" was, I thought, going too far. Yet there was more to come.

Lonnie Hinton and Russell Repp, the Company A guardsmen we had not bothered to call, both testified that they were terrified of the students. Hinton, untrained and nearly blind without his glasses, had fired one shot in the air. Repp's only shot, he said, plunged into the rising ground ahead of him, for he had been on the reverse slope of Blanket Hill when he pulled the trigger. Repp had had at least six tear-gas canisters in his bandolier—a refutation of any defense contention that the guardsmen were out of gas when they fired their weapons.

Dr. Norman Rich, a surgeon at Walter Reed Hospital in Washington, appearing in the courtroom on a videotape deposition that was played on two television sets for the jurors and the judge, gave his opinion that the entry and exit wounds, as shown in photographs taken of Scott MacKenzie in the Akron hospital, were too small to have been made by bullets from either an M-1 or a .45 automatic. This testimony supported the defense contention that a non-military weapon had panicked the Guard into shooting.

The following day the defense put five men on the stand: John Brambeck, Dennis Breckenridge, Arthur Reedy, Henry Dumbrowski, and Lieutenant Robert Maxwell. Brambeck, Reedy, and Dumbrowski were offered for purposes of supporting the nonmilitary shot theory; guardsman Dennis Breckenridge was put on the stand to testify that he had fainted from terror; and Maxwell had information on National Guard civil disturbance training.

With Dumbrowski, who had tape-recorded the test firing of some weapons, the defense hoped to refute our tape and sound expert, Scott Robinson. With Maxwell they planned to show that the guardsmen on the Kent State University campus had been adequately trained and that the OPLAN corresponded with Army rules.

As a unique forum for determining the truth, a trial jury does not have to accept the findings of any other body concerning any fact at issue. If every previous investigative body from the FBI to the federal grand jury, including the National Guard itself, had found no evidence of a sniper or the firing of a nonmilitary weapon, the defense still did not have to ignore the possibility. Thus the defense had elicited from a number of guardsmen the testimony that a low-caliber shot had been heard before the firing began, and then they had put Joy Bishop on the stand to describe the man in the gold coat.

John Brambeck, a short, stocky surveyor from Medina who had been supervising the installation of a new steam utility terminal on the Kent State campus on May 4, claimed to have heard a single low-caliber shot from the vicinity of Lake Hall or the gym before the guardsmen's volley, and to have seen a student carrying a small "16-inch Thompson Contender" rifle after the shooting.

Brambeck, a gun collector, had been a thousand feet from Blanket Hill at the time, on a roadway on the far side of the gym, and his view of the area of hostilities had been restricted to the foot of the hill near the practice field. This limited view did not prevent him from testifying that he had seen three hundred to five hundred students charge up the hill after the guardsmen.

Arthur Lewis Reedy, a dark-haired, rosy-cheeked Ohio highway patrolman, testified that on May 4, while standing outside his patrol car at an intersection three thousand feet from the Commons area, he heard "what appeared to be a shot, a noise normally associated with a low-caliber weapon" before hearing a volley, "which I normally associate with large-caliber weapons."

Henry Dumbrowski, a serious-looking, gray-haired gentleman who worked for the Ohio attorney general in a Bureau of Criminal Identification laboratory at Kent State, was called to give expert testimony about a tape recording of shots fired by different weapons at an outdoor firing range on Saturday, July 26, 1975.

However, the recording was excluded because the defense, contrary to the rules set at the beginning of the trial, had not invited us to take part in the test firings.

Dumbrowski had passed me a note suggesting that I ask him about "tunneling effects." I wasn't sure exactly what he had in mind, but I used my cross-examination to find out.

It turned out that he had investigated a number of physical aspects of the shootings. He had determined, he testified, that the bullet that penetrated the modern sculpture near where Cleary had been standing, 90 feet from the guardsmen, had entered from the direction of the corner of Taylor Hall. He had also found four to six tunnels in the hill, where M-1 bullets had apparently entered the ground and then exited, indicating that shots fired into the ground could have continued on to inflict damage. The inference was that guardsmen who shot into the ground could have been among those who maimed or killed students.

With guardsman Dennis Breckenridge, we were able to keep out as prejudicial any testimony that he had fainted; and although he depicted graphically the vicious, charging students, he gave us one valuable piece of testimony.

"When had you locked and loaded your weapon before the shooting took place?" I asked him.

"When I started roving patrol."

"That would have been when?"

"That would be Monday morning."

"Who ordered you to lock and load?"

"It is just procedure, sir, standard procedure," Breckenridge replied.

Lieutenant Colonel Robert D. Maxwell presented an impressive collection of Army and Ohio Guard documents to show that the 107th Cavalry and the 145th Infantry had had adequate civil disturbance training.

However, under cross-examination Maxwell had to admit that he could not be certain that documents dated one week or six weeks before the shooting had in fact been received by the Guard units before the fatal weekend at Kent State —or, if they had been received, that there had been sufficient time to use them for training.

The final witnesses for the defense were two lieutenants, Ralph Tucker and Dwight Cline, both of whom testified on Monday morning, August 18.

We knew that Lieutenant Tucker had accompanied General Canterbury on May 4 as liaison, carrying a radio over which, at one point, he received a report that a sniper was on the roof of Johnson Hall. (The post-shooting investigation revealed that such reports had been based on sightings of persons such as Joy Bishop and her companions and a photographer using a long telescopic lens.) We were able to prevent the introduction of testimony on such sniper reports as hearsay, and Tucker was confined to describing the student menace.

First Lieutenant Dwight Cline, the executive officer of Company A, had been on the other end of the line, toward Lake Hall, as the guardsmen left the practice field. He had led his men up the hill, walking backward in order to watch them. He said that rounds fired by Troop G to his left had kicked up dirt between his men and the practice field, causing some of his men to wheel and fire their rifles in the air.

When Cline stepped down from the stand, the guardsmen's defense ended its case by playing six minutes of videotape selections from a news broadcast that had followed the shootings and featured interviews with persons who thought the guardsmen had been frightened and provoked into firing.

The defense of the guardsmen was as significant for what it excluded as for what it included. The defense could have tried to use former police chief Thompson or others to refute Delaney's testimony regarding what Rhodes had said at the firehouse meeting. They did not do this, *nor did they introduce a single military or civil expert to support the crowd control actions of the Guard on May 4.*

In defense of former Kent State president Robert White, Blakemore called the chairman of the university's Board of Trustees and White himself.

Robert C. Dix was serving his thirtieth year on the board, the body appointed by the governor to oversee the running of the university. He had been chairman since 1963. Dix was publisher of the *Kent-Ravenna Record Courier,* a newspaper that had printed many of the vituperative letters that followed the shootings. He also owned three radio stations and a television station.

Curiously, the Kent State University Board of Trustees was heavily weighted with newspaper executives. Four of the nine members were in the business: Dix; Clayton Horn, executive editor of the *Canton Repository;* Donald C. Rowley of Rowley Publications; and Robert H. Stopher, associate editorial page editor of the *Akron Beacon Journal.*

It was Dix's *Record Courier* that had featured, on Saturday, May 2, Nixon's "bums" talk at the Pentagon. Stopher's *Beacon Journal* had won a Pulitzer prize for its May 24, 1970, supplement on the shootings. Dix's paper had stirred the students up; Stopher's had gained a reputation by dissecting the tragedy that followed. One could make a case that the disturbances at Kent State presented some of the university's trustees with a conflict of interest.

Dix testified that he spoke to White twice on Sunday, telling him that people were worried that the university might be closed and urging him "to cooperate with the governor and the civil authorities and the Guard in keeping the university open."

That statement raises the question, Who wanted the university closed? The only person who suggested that it be closed, according to testimony at the trial, was Portage County Prosecutor Ronald Kane, and that was because he feared a collision between the students and the Guard. Certainly no student wanted the university closed. At the Sunday press conference Governor Rhodes asserted that dangerous agitators wanted it closed, but neither he nor anyone else had any evidence to support this statement.

White's testimony proved to be abortive. His lawyer wanted to use some doodles that White had made during the Monday morning meeting as evidence that he had opposed dispersing the noon rally. The Judge would not admit this material as evidence.

Part Four

SUMMING UP AN
AMERICAN TRAGEDY

25

Rebuttal

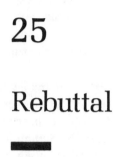

We had three issues to rebut: the nature of Scott MacKenzie's wound, Joy Bishop's story of the man in the gold coat, and John Brambeck's story of the "Thompson Contender" rifle.

As soon as Robert White had finished testifying, I handed the judge a list of our rebuttal witnesses. He had to have this before he could let us see the charge he had prepared for the jury, to make sure that we did not tailor our rebuttal to some element contained in the charge.

The rebuttal witnesses on our list were:

1. Re: Scott MacKenzie's wound—Dr. Milton Helpern, legendary medical examiner of New York City, and Scott MacKenzie.

2. Re: Joy Bishop—Three persons who had been with her on May 4, two of whom had stood beside her on the roof.

3. Re: John Brambeck—Colonel Thomas McNeal, who had told us that a "Thompson Contender" rifle did not exist in 1970, and Henry Dumbrowski, whose laboratory was in the building to which Brambeck said the weapon was being taken, and whose log might show any delivery of weapons on May 4.

We then moved to discontinue the cases against three more of the Company A guardsmen: Lonnie Hinton, who without his glasses could not count my fingers; James Brown, who had worn his gas mask over his glasses; and Ronnie Myers, who after leaving the practice field had not seen any rocks thrown.

Dr. Helpern explained how a high-velocity military projectile would produce a wound like Scott MacKenzie's. The further it traveled, he said, the more stable its trajectory; after going more than 500 feet, it would be expected to make a small, clean hole where it entered soft tissue. He explained that the exit hole would similarly be smaller than expected because of the collapse of tissue, and that the absence of bullet particles in Scott's neck and mouth resulted from the fact that the bullet was jacketed with hard metal, a characteristic of large-caliber projectiles.

His presentation was handicapped to some extent by the judge's refusal to allow him to say anything about the wounds of eleven of the other victims. The other wounds—all but Russell's—were conceded by all to have been produced by M-1 bullets, and Helpern's conclusions before the Scranton Commission had been supported by comparisons of the MacKenzie entrance and exit wounds with the others. The judge's ruling was based on his holding a strict view that rebuttal had to be limited to the exact testimony it was rebutting. As Dr. Rich had mentioned only MacKenzie's wound, Dr. Helpern was precluded from comparing MacKenzie's wound with the others.

We decided not to bother rebutting Brambeck's story about the "Thompson Contender" rifle. This meant that only three witnesses remained, all in connection with Joy Bishop's man in the gold coat.

With Professor Jerry Lewis' help, we found the two people who had stood with Joy Bishop on the roof of Johnson Hall. They were Pat Rivera (formerly Pat Frank), who had been Joy's roommate and was now a Cleveland schoolteacher, and Bruce Phillips, a salesman in Columbus.

Pat and Bruce had told us that none of them had seen anyone fire a pistol before the guardsmen opened fire and that all of them, *five minutes after the shooting,* had seen Terry Norman brandishing a pistol without firing it. At that time, they said, they had been standing on the northeast wing of Johnson Hall, where they had gone after witnessing the guardsmen's volley from the southeast wing, as depicted in the photographs.

However, the judge so restricted the rebuttal process that we were unable to get this information across to the jury. He confined us to questions about what Pat and Bruce saw *before* the shootings, on the grounds that Joy had not testified on anything that happened *after* the shootings. When I objected that this prevented us from demonstrating one of the fallacies of Joy's story, the judge told me I should have brought it up when I was cross-examining her. In fact, however, he had prevented me from questioning Joy about the Terry Norman incident.

Consequently the jury could hear only that neither Bruce nor Pat, who had stood next to Joy Bishop the entire time, had seen anyone fire a pistol before the shootings. Furthermore, they heard Fulton tell me that my contention that

Joy had confused an incident that occurred after the shooting with one that had occurred before was "hogwash," and they heard the judge threaten me with contempt when I tried to ask Pat Rivera whether she had seen any civilian with a pistol five minutes after the shootings.

We finished our rebuttal Wednesday morning with Bill Gerstenlager, Bruce Phillips' roommate, who had been standing in front of Johnson Hall and who denied having seen the man in the gold coat before the shootings. We spent the rest of the day going over the charge to the jury with the judge, but not before we had been confronted with a difficult situation.

26

"Blood on My Hands"

Wednesday morning all the lawyers were summoned to Judge Young's chambers, where we found United States Marshal Robert Wagner and United States Attorney Frederick M. Coleman.

Judge Young told us that serious criminal matters were now involved. He lectured us on the need for secrecy, admonished us that, contrary to his instructions, someone had given a copy of the proposed charge to a newsman, and then he got to the heart of the matter.

"I find that at least one of the jurors has been approached on several occasions," Judge Young said, "and threatened and actually physically assaulted in connection with the threats; threats have been made on his family, if he doesn't bring in a verdict in a certain way."

His concern, he explained, was the possible damage to the integrity of the jury and the trial itself. The problem, he said, could not be solved by excusing one juror. "If these people are really serious," he said, "then they will shift their attention to some of the other jurors. We have no way of knowing that they have put out some feelers to the other jurors, but the other jurors may have not attached any significance to the preliminary approaches. This juror didn't pay attention the first time, it was only when repeated attempts were made and physical assaults were made on him that he thought there was something serious here and reported it to the authorities."

Judge Young said he thought he would have to sequester the jurors, and he asked our opinions.

A few evenings before this, the doorman of the Chesterfield had handed me a telephone message that read, "Lay off the defendants or we will get you." The doorman told me that he had given the message to the police, who wished to see me about it. I did not take the threat seriously, and I declined the police offer of protection.

The following morning I casually mentioned the matter to Chris Jindra, who was covering the trial for the *Cleveland Plain Dealer.* Since I had not taken the matter seriously, I was surprised to find it reported in the newspaper the next day. Now, in his chambers, Judge Young referred to the newspaper account of the threat to me and said that before learning of the threat to the juror he had planned to call Mr. Coleman to obtain protection for me.

I asked the judge for the details of the assault on the juror.

"The assault consisted of a person who approached this juror and made three approaches to him; on one of these approaches he grabbed the juror and pushed him back against the wall and told him that he better not find his verdict the wrong way from the way he wanted it to be found."

There apparently was no corroboration, Coleman added, just the juror's story.

I then raised the point that it was likely that the juror had been swayed by the threat, either to submit to it or to react against it. Whether he was for me or against me, I said, I wanted him off the jury.

"The thing I am concerned with," Judge Young said, "is what we are going to do to protect the rest of the jury."

Brown said he would be opposed to sequestration unless the threat to the juror had been serious. The judge explained that it had been. "If a fellow says he is going to kill somebody," he said. "There's at least one person dead because I didn't take such a threat as seriously as that."

"Was this a death threat to this juror?" Brown asked.

"Yes," Judge Young replied.

"I did not know that," Brown said.

"Isn't it?" Judge Young asked the marshal.

"Threatened to blow up his house," Wagner replied.

Judge Young said that the problem of the threatened juror could be resolved by discharging him, which he ought to do, but that the only way to protect the rest of the jurors was by sequestration.

I asked the judge whether he intended to discuss the threats with the jury.

The judge said he would in order to prevent their having uncharitable thoughts about the reason for the sequestration.

I told him that I was against that because whoever had threatened the juror might have calculated on creating a situation in which, out of resentment, the jury might vote against the party the threatener was pretending to help. One could easily imagine, I said, that the inconvenience of being sequestered would instill "something more powerful than any ten witnesses that testified in this case."

Brown and Fulton argued for full candor. The judge "doesn't have to overemphasize the threats," Brown said. "I would play it down, frankly, if I were the Court."

"I am going to," Judge Young said.

I suggested that the judge simply say they were being sequestered at the Court's discretion. Discussion of the threats, I said, would magnify them. "It may cause fears of retribution concerning their verdict after they go home . . . after they are discharged.

"I say this is going to infect this jury with an intangible factor that either side can't measure." A mistrial, I feared, was becoming a real possibility.

I was alone in opposing the judge on this issue. Everyone else sided with him, even Engdahl, and Fulton went so far as to imply that my giving the story about the threat to myself to the newspaper had inspired the threat to the juror.

"I am going to sequester this jury," Judge Young said, "and I am going to tell the jury exactly why I am sequestering them. And I am going to let the chips fall where they may."

He promised to replace the threatened juror with an alternate, "for the sake of the integrity of the record," as soon as the jury left the courtroom to deliberate, but Fulton got him to reconsider the matter by arguing that it was unfair to penalize a juror for dutifully reporting a threat.

"Sorry we have been so late in getting started," Judge Young told the jurors after we entered the courtroom. "At this point I find it necessary to do something that I have never done before in something more than twenty-three years on the bench. I must have the courtroom cleared." Everyone was sent out, even the parties to the suit. When only the jurors and the lawyers were left, the judge stepped down from the bench, stood before the jurors, and gave a speech.

I looked at the courtroom doors, which had glass panels in them. I could see the reporters looking into the courtroom, hoping to pick up a good story.

The judge addressed the jury as though he were delivering a summation. "I am very much troubled and disturbed by information that has come to my ears that threats have been made to at least one of your number in an attempt to influence your decision in this case.

"I was brought up in an old school that threats of the type that were made are not to be ignored and not to be taken lightly.

"There have been times when I have ignored such threats, and I have blood on my hands, and it is not easy to carry blood on your hands for ignoring this, and I don't propose to have it happen again if I can avoid it."

Blood on his hands! This was his way of playing down the threat! The fear he was dinning into the jury was exactly what I had warned him against. Once again the judge had gone too far.

He cautioned the jurors about the necessity of keeping what he said in strictest confidence, and he added that "with tremendous reluctance, I am going to arrange, when you come back tomorrow, for you to bring clothing and things so that you can stay and be under the protection of the marshals and stay together until this case is finally concluded. . . .

"I am sorry about this, but as I say, threats have been made on the life of one of your members, and I have no assurance that we can solve it simply by getting rid of that one.

"Maybe some of you others have been threatened and have passed it off or have not even realized, perhaps, it was a threat."

He said he had thought he would never have to sequester a jury, even though it was frequently done in important criminal trials, because he regarded it as an insult to the jurors' integrity.

"I am not now dealing with a matter of your integrity, which I have no doubts about whatever. But I am dealing with threats. . . . And it is your safety with which I am concerned." He explained that the reason he was not sequestering them immediately was to keep up an appearance of normality in the hope of catching whoever had been threatening the juror. "I think that the threateners," he said, "will not change their tactics. They will continue to concentrate where they have been concentrating.

"As to one of your members, at least, we can provide and will provide around-the-clock protection and surveillance."

The jurors' mood could be gathered from the questions they put to the judge.

"What happens between now and the time we return tomorrow?" one asked. "Will there be protection provided, or do we have to go on our own?"

Judge Young explained that as long as they kept the matter quiet, the only person who required protection was the threatened juror. When another juror asked about the possibility of having visits from family members, the judge pointed out that the threateners could try to get at the jurors through their families, expecting them to pass on the threats during their visits.

Still another juror worried about preventing a teenage daughter from talking about the sequestration, and the judge explained that it was necessary to control her only until they were actually sequestered. "Once you are here so that people can't get at you," he said, "there is no point to their making threats to your family."

"Once we are sequestered," one juror asked, "will our families be protected?"

Judge Young said it would be impossible to keep them all under twenty-four-hour guard. "The marshals' service will give your families their telephone number," he explained, "so that, if they get jittery or anything, they can call and someone from the marshals' service will respond."

Mrs. Blanche Layman, the next alternate in line, asked what she should do, and Judge Young replied that the alternates were in the same boat as the jury. "You better come prepared," Judge Young said, "the alternates better come prepared for a day or so. . . .

"So you probably should prepare yourself as the rest of the jurors, because I hope Jove's thunderbolt will not strike any of you between now and then. That's what alternates are for," he added. "It's like an insurance policy, you never want to use it, but you don't want to be without it.

"Like the Burma Shave ad said, 'Remember, even though you are insured, they don't pay you but your widow.' "

I could hardly contain myself. The judge was reminding the jurors that any one of them might die at any minute, to be replaced by an alternate. He had told them that their families were possible targets and that they could not be protected. And he had wavered on dismissing the threatened juror.

Watching the judge, I began to suspect that he was going to leave the threatened juror on the jury. Were he to do so, I believed, the jury would be compromised beyond repair.

27

Flattery Gets Me Nowhere

Before our rebuttal the judge had given each team of lawyers three copies of his charge to the jury. He had been working on it for weeks, getting to his office at seven in the morning.

We were very concerned about what the charge might hold. It would be as important in determining the outcome of the case as everything that had gone before, for in it the judge would be giving to the jury the law as it applied to the case. His interpretation of the laws concerning the right of assembly, rioting, and the use of excessive force would provide standards against which the jurors would measure our case. It could determine whether we won or lost.

The charge ran to seventy-seven pages because of the large number of defendants and the different claims made against them, and it consisted of five parts: an introduction, a description of the plaintiffs' allegations, a description of the defendants' defenses, explanations of the issues against the different defendants, and a conclusion.

The introduction dealt with the duties of the jurors, gave an outline of what the cases were all about, and discussed the nature of evidence; it listed the plaintiffs and the twenty-nine defendants, who were divided into five classes: Rhodes; Del Corso; White; the nine officers; and the remaining seventeen enlisted guardsmen (we had voluntarily dropped the charges against the other fifteen).

The section that covered the plaintiffs' allegations described the violations of civil rights (federal suit) and the claims of wrongful death and assault and battery (state suit).

The two types of defense were: (1) a standard defense denying that the injuries or deaths had anything to do with civil rights violations; and (2) affirmative defenses of (a) executive immunity, (b) self-defense, and (c) "contributory negligence." (An affirmative defense is one that has to be proved by the defendants.)

In the fourth section of the charge the judge got down to brass tacks, explaining the claims against each of the five classes of defendants and exactly how the jury was to go about deciding for or against them.

The final section of the charge contained a number of caveats, the dos and don'ts of proper jury behavior.

We believed that the charge was biased in favor of the defendants in two respects: its handling of the dispersal issue and its failure to make clear that contributory negligence was not a defense against the federal civil rights claims. The charge emphasized not the First Amendment right to assemble peaceably but the conditions under which assemblies could be dispersed. This meant that anyone who for any reason had remained on the Commons after the dispersal order, even in order to cross it on the way to a classroom, became contributorily negligent and was fair game for the trigger-happy guardsmen.

It was bad enough that the plaintiffs' failure to leave the Commons area once the dispersal order was read could be considered contributory negligence. What made the situation worse was that the charge failed to show that contributory negligence was a defense only against the claims under the state law.* A juror following the judge's instructions and finding the plaintiffs contributorily negligent for having remained on the Commons would then find for the defendants, even with regard to the federal claims, under the mistaken notion that contributory negligence was a defense in a federal civil rights suit. It was the judge's duty to make it clear to the jury that contributory negligence did not enter into the claims under federal law, and he had not done so.

Mulling this over, we concluded that the best solution would be for us to remove contributory negligence from the charge completely by dropping our claims under state law. With the state claims out, the judge would have to omit all the language about the plaintiffs attending a forbidden rally, not excercising proper care, and so on. The charge would then be greatly simplified.

Our team prepared an edited version of the charge, making a number of changes we thought necessary. (Among other things, we found that Judge Young had knocked out the martial law issue by again misstating one of our

*Contributory negligence, while a defense against our claims of negligence under state law, was irrelevant to our federal suit because we could not claim negligence under the federal Civil Rights Act.

principal claims against Governor Rhodes. He repeated the error he had made during the trial, saying that we disputed Rhodes' right to send the Guard to Kent rather than that we disputed the procedure he had followed.)

Engdahl moved the discontinuance of our state claims, pointing out that throughout the trial we had argued the case as a civil rights case in virtual disregard of the state law claim. He added that it would be a dismissal with prejudice, which meant that the state claims could never again be brought against the defendants.

Judge Young said that he would have to decide on the dismissal only if the defendants did not agree to it. When Brown and Fulton did not agree to it, he ruled against it. Among other things, he said that he thought we had a better case under state law than we had under federal law. He also wanted the jury, he said, to consider all possible claims under all possible laws so that it could be said that, once and for all, all important issues arising out of the shooting had been considered.

Our experience had taught us that the judge did not take kindly to any criticism that challenged his legal acumen. We decided to be as tactful and as positive as possible in making our suggestions.

"The charge is not only fair with all the complexities," I said, "I am the last one to indulge in flattery, but I thought it was the most intricately and beautifully constructed charge that I have ever seen in any case that ever rivaled the complexities of this case.

"We are seeking to have a *simplified approach* for a jury so that this case should not end in a dud, like a firecracker that didn't go off," I said, adding that I had seen long cases end in mistrials, particularly where there were "a large number of alternative verdicts available."

The judge denied all suggestions by both sides. Flattery had gotten me nowhere. In retrospect, I see that I erred; I should have called the charge, for the record, a monstrosity that no jury could apply intelligently.

After four hours of discussion the charge remained intact except for the correction of a couple of typographical errors and the insertion, at David Engdahl's request, of some Ohio statutes on the right of peaceful assembly.

28

The Final Say

───

The judge allotted two hours and forty-five minutes to each side for summations. The plaintiffs' portion was to be divided into two parts, an opening and a rebuttal; the whole of the defendants' summation would come in between.

There were various strategies that we could use. As our opening would be followed by the defendants but our rebuttal would not, we could save most of our presentation for the rebuttal, when it would remain unanswered. On the other hand, the judge could object that too short an opening would be unfair to the other side. He suggested that we take at least forty-five minutes for the opening.

Fulton pointed out that the defense had available a counter strategy, which was to "squat" and say nothing at all. This would deprive us of our rebuttal. I had never heard of the device, but Judge Young assured me that it was common in Ohio. The message was plain: make a fair opening, hang out your case so that we may answer it, or you'll be left high and dry.

Galen Keller and Steven Keller had pored over the transcripts in order to prepare summaries of the testimony on certain subjects. We selected the most significant photographs and made lists of what witnesses had said about rock throwing or the sound of the first shot. I had the numbers of the transcript pages on which guardsmen Herschler, Thomas, Cline, and Farris had denied that the students were rushing them at the time of the shooting, and I could quote seventeen guardsmen who had denied that their lives were in danger on Blanket Hill. I had a list of the nine guardsmen whose vision had been impaired and the testimony of Canterbury, Fassinger, and Jones, the three highest-ranking officers at Kent State on May 4, describing the firing as indiscriminate. I had all the information I needed to remind the jurors of the evidence that showed that the shooting was unjustified and to show the contributions made by Governor Rhodes and General Del Corso.

Best of all, during the summation I would at last be free of the judge's "evidence hole" rule. For the first time since the trial began, I could read any document that was in evidence, show the jury any photograph, and tell them what those exhibits meant.

At last the jury would hear that the Matson-Frisina letter says that the governor and the National Guard were in control of the Kent State campus. They would be shown the Beverly Knowles photograph of the practice field and be given an explanation of the significance of the absence of students for 200 feet and more in each direction. They would see the Joe Lewis photograph, showing no students approaching the Troop G guardsmen; the Darnell and Ruffner photographs, indicating that the guardsmen had stepped back toward the parking lot; and the photographs that showed that Joy Bishop and her companions had not been where she said they were when the shooting began.

In the past I had won many cases on the strength of my summation, and I had confidence in my ability.

Summation, in my opinion, is a 20 percent factor in influencing a jury one way or the other. In a close case it provides the difference between winning and losing. The trial lawyer can score or flop, depending on the chemistry he generates. If the jury is not too far gone in its prejudice, its thinking can be reversed.

The summation of this case had to be a moving plea for justice in a historic cause and a counterattack against our opponents' appeal to the prejudices of the jurors: their blind respect for authority, their identification with the guardsmen, and their disdain for out-of-state lawyers.

My decision to handle the summation alone was to leave permanent rifts within our trial team, but my conscience was clear. I had had far more experience than the rest of our lawyers. I also felt challenged to do my best in this hostile mid-American atmosphere.

I arranged various exhibits and the key photographs in a line near the jury box so that I would not have to fumble to find what I needed as I spoke. My outline was mounted on a lectern in large letters visible to me from as far as ten feet away.

I am an ad lib speaker. I rarely read anything to a jury that is longer than a few seconds. Extended reading bores a jury. One or two words in my outline would suggest an entire line of discussion that I wanted to cover. I could walk about and glance at it from a distance to keep myself on the track without pausing or fumbling with notes.

I believe in moving about; this holds the jury's attention. The tone of my voice may fall to a whisper or rise to a shout as I try to fit my mood to the subject I am discussing. Juries respond to logic and reason mixed with honest emotion, but one must be careful: The lawyer who would persuade must truly feel what he is saying.

Of all the cases I had tried, none matched this one for me. So much was at stake. Not only the money damages, but the freedom to say what we think; the faith of our children in our system of justice; the right to protest without facing bullets.

Just before I rose to speak I said a silent prayer, "God, let me be good."

The courtroom was crowded with the plaintiffs, their families, many of the defendant guardsmen, Guard officers, reporters, and spectators. I sensed an electric tension in the air.

Looking at the twelve faces before me, I saw that I had their attention. This was a good start. Perhaps some of them have not made up their minds, I thought. If only I can persuade the fence sitters, I can get them to work on the others when they deliberate.

We had the facts on our side; my problem now was to overcome the prejudices lurking among the jurors.

I hoped that the jury, in fourteen weeks, had come to know me and at least to respect me as an individual. I hoped their sense of fairness would impel them to realize that we were the underdogs in an unfair trial, that we had used restraint and maintained our dignity in the face of many provocations and unfair rulings of the court.

I felt I was in top form, speaking in high, ringing tones, taking the jury into my confidence, lowering my voice as I read from a document as if imparting a secret, then shifting to a scolding note, "You don't shoot!" (You warn, you threaten, you use butt strokes, you use bayonets.) The Ohio National Guard, I told the jury, might be a wonderful institution. Governor Rhodes might be a splendid governor. But the National Guard was poorly run, and Governor Rhodes had goofed.

I had decided to go almost two hours in my opening, outlining our entire case and preventing a squat. I discussed the Friday night disturbances in the context of too many bars and liquor licenses in Kent. "Oh, everything sounded like there had never been a single bit of problem before Friday, May 1, that night.

"Who smashed the windows? Perhaps there were some students there, I don't know. They didn't tell us. Does any one of you know if there were students who smashed windows? . . .

"Nobody tells us. We don't know. We don't know if the Chosen Few [a motorcycle gang] started a bonfire in the street. We don't know that. It is thrown at you as a diversionary tactic because these are very skillful lawyers, they don't come any better. I have had my hands full with them, I can tell you. They are good. They know how to get the eyes of the jury off the ball.

"But I suggest they won't accomplish it because there wasn't a single one of these thirteen kids, the four dead and the nine injured, who were shown to be implicated on May 1 in the City of Kent. . . ."

Bob Kelner, watching the jury closely, noticed that Mrs. Heckman involuntarily nodded in agreement when I said that not one of the thirteen kids had been implicated in the trashing on May 1.

Bob was astounded. If Mrs. Roberta Heckman, the dark-haired, stern-faced lady from Avon whose husband, we had learned, was a member of the VFW, was agreeing with us, we were carrying the jury.

"I will not condone anybody, my kids or anybody else's kids—forgive me for my use of the word 'kid,' I don't mean any disrespect to anybody—breaking a window, breaking the law, because I am a strong believer . . . that we shall have law and order in America, and I mean for everybody, not just for some, not just students—guardsmen, everybody else, everybody equal under the law, and we have seen the highest persons in this nation come before the bar of justice and that can go for a judge, for a governor, that can go for a president."

The courtroom was silent except for my voice. Even the judge was listening intently.

Among the appeals to the jury I wove photographs that showed the gathering at noon to have been peaceful (young women seated on the grass with books). I read the Matson-Frisina letter and the part of the OPLAN that authorized shooting as a last resort to disperse a crowd, contrasting it with the strictures against deadly force in the Army field manual. I quoted Michael Delaney's unrefuted testimony on the secret May 3 meeting and Rhodes' press conference speech, emphasizing his recommendation that "the National Guard should use whatever force was necessary."

"And what can 'whatever force was necessary,' what can that be but a green light to those who have the weapons, the loaded weapons?" I reminded the jury that the governor claimed not to have known, not to have tried to find out, whether the guardsmen's weapons were loaded." And he did not want to see any two students walking together. . . . This is unheard of in American law, in every community in this country." I reminded them of Sergeant Delaney's testimony that Governor Rhodes was the commander of the troops, and I read from the record Alloway's question and Delaney's answer.

" 'Question: Did you hear Governor Rhodes issue any orders as commander of the troops?'

" 'Answer: That the Guard were to use any necessary force to disperse any meetings, any gathering of students.'

" 'Question: Mr. Delaney, to whom did he issue such an order?'

" 'Answer: It was to the Guard representatives present at the meeting and to the meeting in general.' "

I quoted from the governor's public speech smearing the students as brownshirts, Communists, and worse, and I asked if any of the thirteen students, whether putting himself or herself through school or being helped by parents, was trying to destroy higher education or in any way fitted the governor's rhetoric.

"This is calling for publicity. . . . The next quote, 'We will apply whatever degree of force is necessary.' This is the fourth time talking about force. . . . Some of these guys in the National Guard are a little trigger-happy, a little itchy on the trigger, and this is the commander-in-chief talking in the presence of the National Guard officers. The word filters down the ranks, 'we will apply whatever degree of force is necessary to provide protection for the lives of our citizens and his property.'

"Irresponsible, I say irresponsible. It is thoughtless. It is reckless. . . . He drew no distinction between peaceful and nonpeaceful, which we say is against the law, because we say it was a peaceful assembly the next day. . . . The governor . . . pushes the button and they go."

I quoted Chief Thompson's remark about shooting if necessary. "Why didn't the governor," I asked, "why didn't General Del Corso, who was there, say, 'Hey, you are going too far, we don't want any shooting around here.' That was not repudiated by anybody there. Listen to the tape. I don't care if it was Thompson, I don't care if it was Del Corso."

I recounted the subsequent events up to the time of the shooting: the Matson-Frisina letter, the horrors of Sunday night, the Monday morning meeting, and the differences in the testimony of General Canterbury and the Kent State officials, Then I returned to the OPLAN and the Army rules of engagement, reminded the jury of Colonel King's testimony on the use of the rifle butt and bayonet and James Ahern's testimony on keeping cool, and pointed out that the defense had produced not a single expert to refute them. I reserved the rest of our ammunition for the rebuttal.

29

"Fine American Human Beings"

The defense didn't dare squat after my opening. Alloway argued, predictably, that Governor Rhodes was being sued for having performed his duty, and he warned the jury that if a judgment were made against Rhodes, future governors would fear to take the measures necessary to restore order in emergencies. Blakemore argued that Robert White had been a small oak tree caught in an avalanche of history, and he enumerated fifteen decisions made over the weekend, in none of which the former Kent State University president had had a voice.

Fulton and Brown each took about twenty-five minutes for their summations. Their arguments were pretty much of a piece, aimed at discrediting the plaintiffs rather than asserting defenses. Fulton began by reminding the jurors of the differences between what the plaintiffs' lawyers had said they were going to prove and what they had actually proven. He was correct in pointing out that we had not shown directly that there had been an order to shoot, but I thought his other arguments were fallacious. He argued, for example, that testimony that local law-enforcement people in Kent had requested the Guard refuted our claim that Rhodes had superseded local law enforcement (as if a request for assistance were the same as agreeing to an illegal takeover by the Guard of local law enforcement).

Fulton emphasized that most of the thirteen plaintiffs and plaintiffs' decedent children had been present at one or more of the disturbances during the weekend. He argued tearfully that the guardsmen from Company A, not having fired into the parking lot, should be dismissed, and that the differences in the stories of those from Troop G, who had fired at students, proved that they were not involved in a coverup conspiracy.

"You have heard McGee and Morris and Perkins and Shafer and Zoller, and I am going to ask you to reflect on the testimony and ask yourselves, Did these men lie? Did those men refuse to talk to the Ohio Highway Patrol? Did those men refuse to talk to the FBI? Were those men instrumental in a coverup? . . .

"In concluding, I want you . . . just to remember a few facts about these individuals.

"Canfora admittedly attended a number of SDS meetings, downtown on Friday, at the ROTC Building on Saturday, and there on Monday, and refused to talk to the FBI. . . .

"Even Dean Kahler, poor Dean, he was there on Sunday, and his pictures are there. We have pictures of him in the crowd, the young man who apparently was agitated into doing things by people, by others, to vent his frustration, and he honestly said that was what he was doing, in anger, venting his frustration, throwing rocks.

"And MacKenzie, who was there Saturday when the ROTC Building burned, and Sunday at the president's house, and at Lincoln and Main, there on Monday on the Commons by his admission, if not by his picture.

"And Russell, whose picture was shown Sunday night at Lincoln and Main, and Cleary, who was there at the Saturday burning of the ROTC Building and who on Monday stated he recalls the taunting of the Guard.

"Mr. Stamps . . . by his own admission . . . in the area of the Commons . . . I believe he stated that he felt the rally was illegal but was still there when those shots were fired.

"And Wrentmore, whose photo was shown on TV and admitted that the Guard was provoked."

The National Guard and Army principles of crowd control, Fulton argued, authorized dispersal of the noon assembly on the basis of prior disturbances. He asserted that the guardsmen had been well trained and that the person with the pistol seen by Joy Bishop could not have been Terry Norman.

Charlie Brown elaborated on Fulton's candid guardsmen argument, claiming that the guardsmen had provided "the plaintiffs with the ammunition for their lawsuit because they are honest, honorable men." How could they be termed conspirators, he asked, when they had been in Kent only because ordered, at the request of local law-enforcement officials? He added that it was ironic that the guardsmen were being sued when those who had asked for their help—the mayor, the chief of police, the sheriff, the prosecutor—were not.

"These men, who were doing what they were asked to do and ordered to do as good, fine American human beings, have been sued."

Brown asserted that each guardsman had received sixteen hours of riot training, that all the plaintiffs had attended SDS meetings, and that the noon rally was a mob. To illustrate the way a mob was to be treated, he quoted from Clarence Darrow's summation of a case in which he defended a black man who had fired into a mob attacking his home in a white neighborhood. He claimed that plaintiffs' counsel had long known about Joy Bishop's story of the man in the yellow coat and that MacKenzie had been struck by a low-caliber bullet.

"These guardsmen were in fear of their lives on that hill on May 4, 1970. You have heard them say what happened.

"What were they afraid of? That they were going to be overrun, their weapons taken from them, the crowd was coming in, they were out of tear gas. My goodness, we shot almost 180 rounds of tear gas, more than ever had been used before anywhere, and that crowd kept coming. Peaceable?

"First Amendment? Don't insult my intelligence. You have a First Amendment right to charge yelling, 'Kill the pigs—sieg heil.' First Amendment? That's worse than saying you have got the right to go into a crowded theatre and yell 'Fire.' "

In my rebuttal I reminded the jurors of the peaceful nature of the noon assembly before the jeep went out, as described by Chaplain Simons and others. I recounted the testimony concerning the guardsmen's lack of training and proper equipment. I gave them the first close look at the photographs of the shooting guardsmen, photographs in which no student could be seen nearer than Joe Lewis, who was 60 feet away. "Look at Troop G over here," I said. "Captain Srp is wandering down the field there somewhere. Captain Srp, who had no control over his men."

I showed them where Joy Bishop was standing, went over all the antisniper evidence and testimony, the Strubbe tape and the Abell film, and described the roles of the officers in the field—Canterbury, Jones, Fassinger—and of the captains, the lieutenants, and the enlisted men.

Sergeant Pryor, "older, thoroughly experienced, a leader of men in Troop G. What did he do? He had the temerity to say he didn't fire a weapon. Three eyewitnesses said they saw him fire the weapon. One of them said he saw the shells popping out, and each time the sound of the gun with the recoil. Each one, like that, like that, and like that.

"And for eleven seconds, if this man had not fired, if he had not fired, what was he doing as a leader of the men who were firing, standing there until some officer comes over to him and yells, 'Help me, put that damn gun down'—I think that was the word he said—'and help me get these guys to stop firing.'

"There was a fury and there was a rage.

"This is not a criminal case, ladies and gentlemen. We only need to show their responsibility by a fair preponderance of the evidence. It is not like a criminal case where you have to prove guilt beyond a reasonable doubt. Nobody is going to jail.

"We want responsibility fixed. Take the fact that thirteen seconds go by, sixty-seven shots, by actual count. When I go like this, let's just pause and be silent for thirteen seconds and see what those officers and what Pryor could have done to stop this bloodletting while students were running away from the very first shot, which is what the testimony was, and they kept shooting and shooting. Why? Why? Why?

"Starting now for thirteen seconds."

As I slapped the lectern with my hand, the silent thirteen-second countdown began. I watched the second hand of my watch, glancing from time to time at the jury. The courtroom was deathly silent. During this thirteen-second re-creation, I hoped the jurors could envision the sight and sounds of a firing squad indiscriminately shooting unarmed persons, the sickening sight of Jeffrey Miller's brain and bone fragments flying through the air (as Captain Snyder had testified), and other young lives snuffed out or bodies smashed.

"Thirteen seconds," I resumed, "an eternity of time . . . to stop them from shooting so a boy flinging himself on the ground like a Dean Kahler won't be shot in the back, or a girl like Allison Krause could have had her life saved. Perhaps if she was a menace to someone she could have been bayoneted and maybe could have recovered. Anything could have happened. Nobody did anything for an eternity of time.

"Identify with these people, not for any sympathy, we don't want it that way. We come in dignity before you, and we say to you, ladies and gentlemen, this case is perhaps one of the most important things you will ever do for your country for the rest of your lives. We have selected the guardsmen who did the firing in our best judgment, every single one of them fired, every single one of them fired, and I don't have the time to run through all of them, but . . . I will just read off this list very fast.

"Flesher, fourteen years in the National Guard. . . . Threw rocks at the students, fired three times. Didn't feel his life was in danger. Now, he could only fire to protect his life. . . . Before he fired he couldn't believe there was firing, and then he goes ahead and fires.

"Thomas fired once in the air. Heard an order to fire overhead. He saw no necessity to shoot but shot anyway. At page 2079 he said that students were actually retreating at the time of the shooting but he keeps on shooting. . . .

"Farris testified that there wasn't a single rock thrown from the time they left the practice field down over 250 to 300 feet away and for the last three minutes. . . . Farris, whom we voluntarily dismissed in our attempt to segregate those who were innocent from those who were not. . . .

"Captain Snyder . . . this is one of the most shocking incidents in over thirty years of experience I have ever seen in the courtroom, he admits that on the body of a dead boy, Jeffrey Miller, he plants a gun. . . .

"How low can you go? How low can you go? And this is the way it went.

"There was no defense, they invented a defense, and the first flood of reports that went to the public made this group of students look like the worst bunch of criminals, until there came a time, after five years of struggle, when six ladies and six gentlemen gave up their summers, a great sacrifice to you, all of you, I know that, but said there are principles in America that are deserving of careful consideration and treatment by you as citizens.

"All of you undertook the responsibility, none of us dreamed this was going to be this long and this hard. We can only say from the bottom of our hearts that we are so grateful to you.

"We plead with you, call it on the evidence, be proud of the result you come in with. There was never any explanation for shooting down these youngsters at these tremendous distances, not one of them who had a rock in his hand at the time, not one of them constituting any kind of a threat to the safety or life of any of the defendants.

"And the defendants have the burden of proving a genuine fear, not just an empty fear where they say they feared for their lives. This is something you must take into consideration. Be proud of the job you do. . . .

"Try to understand what you do in America and what you do on this case is going to ring out all over the world, and we pray it will be a very sharp, loud, and clear message that this jury says 'No' loudly, and I am hoping it will be unanimous. I am hoping you will say loudly and clearly, 'We called it the way the evidence showed. There was no justification for what happened,' and let the world know that this tremendous effort that you have poured in on this case was well spent for the purpose of sustaining the principle of law and the constitutions of the State of Ohio and the United States. And may it be a very, very strong showing that the rule of law and order is truly alive and remains and will remain alive in America, so help us God, because we need it. Thank you very much."

When I finished speaking, the court session was recessed.

An emotional scene followed in the plaintiffs' meeting room. Some of the parents were in tears.

The parents, victims, and even some of the lawyers kissed me on the cheek.

There was an atmosphere of exhilaration and optimism now that our side of the case had been explained and the photographs and documents had finally been shown to the jury.

I was grateful for the reception, but I repeated the old cliché of trial lawyers, cautioning our clients, "You never can tell what a jury will do." Most of the parents felt that it would be hard for the jury to vote against us now, but some of their children, the shooting victims, were less confident.

Tom Grace, who had just returned from Ireland, thought I had gone too far in praising the Guard as a fine institution. But Joe Lewis was optimistic. He thought that only one of the jurors, Richard Williams, appeared to be unsympathetic. He expected Mrs. Dotterer, the Mennonite lady, to vote in favor of the plaintiffs, as well as Mrs. Gaskella and the two blacks, Hunt and Collins. That made four; if half of the other seven favored the plaintiffs, that would give them seven jurors for a start. The seven would have to persuade just two more to reach a verdict.

Mrs. Schroeder did not like the looks of the men on the jury. To her they appeared cold and stony-faced. She had faith, however, that they would take seriously their oaths to weigh the case on the evidence they had heard in court. She also prayed.

Doris Krause expected a favorable verdict because, in spite of everything the defense had tried, the evidence had been overwhelming. Arthur Krause was more guardedly optimistic. He feared that the great length of the trial had exasperated some of the jurors to the point where they would not want to take the further time necessary to consider the evidence carefully.

The Scheuers took heart from my summation. After all, Mrs. Scheuer reflected, the jurors were Ohioans like herself. They could not be so different as to deny what they had seen and heard in the courtroom.

Robbie Stamps thought I had done the best that could be done by way of arousing the jurors' sympathies, but he found himself remembering how they had laughed when Fassinger had testified that the protesters on campus were not nice people.

That afternoon the fourteen men and women of the jury were escorted by U.S. marshals to the nearby Cleveland Sheraton. They strolled there in the hot afternoon sun, carrying battered suitcases and plastic overnight bags. Sequestered from the world, they had dinner, chummed for a while in a fourth-floor suite, and then went to bed.

Part Five

VERDICT

30

"The Gratitude of All the People"

—

Friday morning the twelve jurors and two alternates returned half an hour earlier than usual to hear the judge's charge and to begin their deliberations.

As Judge Young drawled through the lengthy document, Alan Canfora listened attentively, trying laboriously to follow it. The more he heard, the less he liked. It didn't sound like the same case; the judge was telling the jurors that he and the others on the Commons had had no right to remain there once they had been told to leave.

The Scheuers didn't like the sound of the charge either. They listened to the judge's thin, sandy voice and glared at him as he paused to sip from a glass of water. They hadn't had any use for him since, at the outset, he had addressed Rhodes as "Your Excellency."

Arthur Krause found himself remembering the judge's admonishing him for having attended the "so-called memorial rally." He believed the judge had been against them even before the trial started. The jury, he decided, was being befuddled and manipulated.

John Adams, seated in the back of the courtroom, was wondering how much strength the jurors possessed. He had long since discounted the judge, who had curried favor with Governor Rhodes. Had the jury discounted the judge too?

I wondered whether Blanche Layman, the third alternate, would prove a better juror for our side than the threatened juror, whoever he was.

The charge is a monstrosity, one of the lawyers told himself; it is representative of so many things the judge has done—ingenious, plausible, and wrong. He had long been puzzled by the judge's behavior, seemingly so unrelated to his acknowledgment at the pre-trial conferences of the great constitutional issues involved. Then it occurred to him that when Judge Young spoke of the Constitution he really meant the powers that be; that the judge heard no bugles and saw no stars and stripes in the camp of the plaintiffs.

Before he sent the jury out, the judge called the lawyers to the bench to ask whether they had further specific suggestions regarding the charge. Neither side could add to their criticisms of the preceding day.

I was counting on the jurors' seeing through the instructions as, I hoped, they had seen through the judge's exclusion of vital evidence. I hoped they would have the intelligence to realize that we were the underdogs and would study the documents and photographs carefully in the jury room.

However, what was bothering me most was that the judge had not yet discharged the threatened juror and replaced him with Mrs. Layman. I had expected him to do so when the jurors filed in that morning. When he didn't do it then, I expected him to do it at the conclusion of his charge. Was it an oversight? I couldn't believe that Judge Young meant to keep the juror. It was bad enough that the judge had not tried to learn how much the jury had been affected by the threat; that he would retain the threatened juror, whose mind would be preoccupied with worry about what might happen to his family, was unthinkable.

At the bench I reminded the judge that he had deferred his decision on dismissing the juror. "I take it as of now," I asked, "you have elected not to excuse that juror?"

"I am electing not to excuse that juror," Judge Young replied.

I inquired whether the judge knew something we didn't know regarding the juror's ability "to fulfill his duties as a juror in deciding the case untrammeled by any further threats, or any other details that we had not been provided with."

The judge said he knew nothing more than he had known two days before and that his decision was based on the consideration that the man had done the right thing. He had adopted Fulton's reasoning.

The bench conference completed, the judge turned again to the jury, dismissed the two remaining alternates, Mrs. Layman and Richard Hunt, and gave the twelve remaining members of the panel further instructions.

He told them he would never be more than a couple of minutes away. "From now on until your verdict is returned, you people are in charge of the show."

John Adams came forward and led a prayer that the jurors' minds and hearts be open "for the free flow of information and truth." Silently I joined the prayer.

All lawyers live with the possibility of jury prejudice; it is something we confront in every case. The alternative is to waive the jury and to have a judge decide, and this leads to an even more hazardous crap game. The vast majority of judges are fair and objective. But the small percentage who have inherent biases lead most trial lawyers to prefer juries as the lesser evil.

It is believed that, unless the prejudice among the jurors is too deep and too fixed, the unbiased jurors may shame the biased ones into deciding the case on the evidence.

The twelve jurors left the courtroom, carrying with them a grave responsibility to the thirteen plaintiffs, to the twenty-nine defendants, and to their country's Constitution and its laws.

The jury had thirteen forms to complete, one for each plaintiff. At the top of each form were two boxes, one to be checked if the jurors found in favor of the plaintiff against all the defendants, the second if the jurors found in favor of all the defendants against the plaintiff. Below the two boxes on each form was a list of the twenty-nine defendants, who could be voted on separately in the event the jury did not decide to vote for or against the defendants as a whole. This gave the jury the opportunity to find against Rhodes, for example, to the exclusion of the other defendants, or to pick out any individual it found culpable; on the Joe Lewis form the jury might find against Shafer, who admitted shooting him, to the exclusion of the other defendants.

With thirteen forms and twenty-nine defendants, the maximum possible number of separate verdicts was astronomical.

The court recessed. It was 11:30 A.M., Friday, August 21, 1975, ninety-four days after the trial had begun.

When we got together in our anteroom, Robbie Stamps got up and said, "I'm sorry, we have lost the case." He waved and headed for the door.

I went after him. "Where are you going?" I asked.

"To San Diego to see my sister Penny."

"Let him go," his father said.

"Robbie," I said, "you mustn't give up now." I tried to joke. "Won't you feel foolish in California when you hear on the radio that we won and we're all celebrating here without you?"

Robbie looked directly into my eyes. It was a look I'll never forget. "You don't *believe* that, do you, Joe?" He reached out and shook my hand.

"I do, Robbie, or I wouldn't be saying it."

"I never want to see Ohio again," Robbie said. He hurried off into the crowd.

Floyd Stamps put his hand on my shoulder. "He'll be all right," he said.

I wondered whether I could comprehend the depths from which he dredged up that assurance.

A moment before I had been elated; now I was plunged into gloom. I felt as though my own son had turned on me. How I ached to prove him wrong!

For the remainder of Friday and all day Saturday, the clients, minus Robbie Stamps, sat together in the first two rows of the courtroom, wondering what was going on behind the closed doors of the jury room. Only two of the defendants, Del Corso and Fassinger, remained, seated several rows behind. Occasionally a newspaper reporter would look into the room, sit down for a few moments, and chat with someone before leaving.

The jurors took Sunday off.

Monday morning we heard shouting and angry voices from the jury room. When the jurors were led out for lunch at noon, two of them, Mrs. Dotterer and Mrs. Klancar, were redfaced and crying. Florence Schroeder, Elaine Kahler, and Betty Lewis were alarmed at the sight, for they had assumed from the beginning that Mrs. Dotterer was sympathetic. They had been less certain of Mrs. Klancar, whose face wore a habitual frown. Occasionally Florence Schroeder had caught Mrs. Klancar's eye and felt that an understanding had passed between them; at other times she had thought that Mrs. Klancar avoided looking at her.

Doug Wrentmore was disturbed that someone in the jury room had made two ladies who, he was sure, wanted to vote for the plaintiffs, cry. What was happening? He also noticed that Richard Williams avoided his glance as they passed in the corridor. For the first time, Doug Wrentmore suspected that something might be wrong, that there was strong disagreement among the jurors. His mother remained serene, expecting the best.

I took the display of tears as a bad sign. I knew that the jurors had elected as their foreman Stanley Davis, Jr., the bespectacled, sharp-featured assistant engineer from Akron who belonged to the National Rifle Association and on whom we had gambled because his daughter attended Oberlin College. Now my antennae told me he was pushing for a verdict for the defendants. But what was going on in the jury room? What had been shouted or said to Mrs. Dotterer and Mrs. Klancar to make them burst into tears?

Monday afternoon at four, and again on Tuesday afternoon, word went out for the lawyers to assemble in the courtroom. We hurried from our offices, apartments, and hotel rooms, expecting anything—a verdict, further difficulties, a hung jury. In both instances the jurors had questions about the instructions.

Since beginning their deliberations on Friday, the jury hadn't once asked about any of the evidence or requested the reading of any part of the transcript. Yet portions of the section of the charge that told them how they were to find for or against the defendants puzzled them. This section, with its many multiple-choice contingency sequences, was more complicated than an IRS form.

The jurors found three mistakes in the seventy-seven page document, all of the same kind. In all three cases the judge had worded questions in such a way that answers to them gave paradoxical results. The error found on Monday was in the "Issue as to the Defendant James A. Rhodes."

> FIRST, (a) was the determination of the defendant Rhodes that it was necessary to call the Ohio National Guard to the City of Kent . . . a reasonable judgment . . . or (b) did this defendant order, or direct or authorize his subordinates to order, that peaceable assemblies on the campus of Kent State University be prohibited or dispersed; (c) . . . ?
>
> If your answer to all of these questions is "No," then you need to go no further, but should return a verdict in favor of the defendant James A. Rhodes.

What the jurors noticed was that a "No" answer to (a) resulted in a judgment adverse to Rhodes. But the same answer resulted in a judgment in his favor in the case of (b), (c), and (d). This meant that the instruction that "if your answer to all of these questions is 'No,' then you . . . should return a verdict in favor of the defendant James A. Rhodes" was incorrect.

The other errors were in the sections dealing with the claims against the group of nine officers and the claims against the group of seventeen enlisted guardsmen. I could not recall another case in which the jury had to correct a judge's charge.

Shortly after five the following afternoon, Wednesday, word went out that a verdict had been reached.

"Now, ladies and gentlemen," Judge Young said softly, "this has been a long and difficult trial, and it is the culmination of many years of efforts. I know that feelings are rising and rising very high. . . . There are thirteen verdicts, that will take some time to read. . . . I ask you, please, to make a final effort and keep your composure until the Court has recessed." He folded his hands and looked over at the clerk. "Mr. Clerk."

"Your Honor," the clerk said, "I understand the jury has reached a verdict. Shall I read the roll of the jury?"

While the clerk read the roll, Fred Mandel studied Judge Young's face. The judge, who had already seen the verdicts, looked pleased. Was it because of the result or because the trial was at last over and he could take a few days off?

I studied the jurors. Ellen Gaskella's eyes looked puffy. Mrs. Klancar looked even more unhappy than she had Monday afternoon.

"The clerk will read the verdicts," Judge Young said.

"The United States District Court for the Northern District of Ohio, Eastern Division, Civil No. 70-544; Arthur Krause, Administrator of the Estate of Allison Krause, deceased, Plaintiff vs. James A. Rhodes et al., Defendants.

" 'Verdict—We the Jury, on the issues joined, find in favor of the Defendants, and against the Plaintiff Arthur Krause, Administrator.'

"Should I read the signatures of the jury?" the clerk asked.

"No, that's not necessary," Judge Young said. "It is signed by what, ten members of the jury?"

Ten! I found myself thinking. Only two voted for us? Which two? Which two?

"Elaine B. Miller, Administratrix of the Estate of Jeffrey Glenn Miller, deceased, Plaintiff vs. James A. Rhodes et al., Defendants, Civil No. C 70-816.

" 'Verdict—We the Jury, on the issues joined, find in favor of all the Defendants, and against the Plaintiff Elaine B. Miller, Administratrix.'

"Sarah Scheuer, Administratrix of the Estate of Sandra Lee Scheuer, deceased, Plaintiff vs. James A. Rhodes et al., Defendants, Civil No. C 70-859.

" 'Verdict—We the Jury, on the issues joined, find in favor of all the Defendants, and against the Plaintiff Sarah Scheuer, Administratrix.' "

Arthur Krause's mouth was open. He looked incredulous.

The clerk's voice droned on.

" 'We the Jury, on the issues joined, find in favor of all the Defendants, and against the Plaintiff Louis A. Schroeder, Administrator . . . and against the Plaintiff John R. Cleary, a minor . . . and against the Plaintiff Donald Scott MacKenzie . . . Douglas Wrentmore . . . Thomas M. Grace, a minor.' "

Tom Grace got up and shouted, "It's still murder!" He raised his fist in the revolutionary salute.

" 'James D. Russell, Plaintiff . . . ' "

"Murderers!" Tom Grace shouted. A marshal headed in his direction, and Arthur Krause stood up. "Keep your hands off that boy!" he growled.

Sarah Scheuer and Florence Schroeder were sobbing.

"Alan Canfora, Plaintiff vs. James A. Rhodes et al., Defendants, Civil No. C 71-26. '. . . against the Plaintiff Alan M. Canfora. . . . ' "

"This is an outrage!" Alan Canfora exclaimed. "There is no justice!"

Judge Young warned that any further commentators would be removed by the marshal.

" ' ... and against the Plaintiff Dean Kahler ... ' " Valerie Manning, Dean's girlfriend, leaned over Dean's knees and moaned.

"Oh, my God!" Arthur Krause bellowed, lifting his eyes to the plastic covers of the fluorescent lighting. It had just sunk in: *Nobody was going to get a verdict. Not a single defendant was to be found to have done anything wrong!*

" ' ... and against the Plaintiff Joseph John Lewis, a minor ... and against the Plaintiff Robert F. Stamps et al.' Members of the jury, is this your verdict?"

John Dunphy, the hard-boiled *Akron Beacon Journal* reporter who had told me at the outset that our cause was hopeless, was crying.

"It is," Stanley Davis, Jr., replied. "Yes."

I still could not believe it.

Ellen Gaskella had not found for the defendants; neither had Roberta Heckman nor Mary Blazina. That made *three,* not two, as the judge had said. It was nine to three. Yet it was still sufficient for a verdict.

Roberta Heckman was a surprise; all the plaintiffs had been more certain of Mrs. Dotterer and the two black men.

Joe Lewis turned to his son and put his arm around his shoulders. "Maybe you are right," he said, "maybe we should move to Oregon."

Martin Scheuer and Louis Schroeder were trying to comfort their wives. Martin was angry. Elaine Kahler still couldn't believe what she had heard. Jan Wrentmore wished she had taken Doug to the Findhorn commune in Scotland.

Judge Young was congratulating the jurors. "I do not think that at any time in the history of our country since the trial of John Peter Zenger has a jury been given so hard a task as the task which was given to you.

"As I have said to the counsel in this case, the real questions in this case go to the very depths of the subject of civil government, and I know from your verdicts that you have plumbed those depths, and that was not an easy task. . . .

"You can leave with the satisfaction that you have done the task that no other body in our civil government can do . . . only a jury could rise to this occasion; and you, ladies and gentlemen, have risen to it.

"You are entitled to the gratitude not only of everyone in the courtroom, regardless of how they may be affected by your verdicts, you are entitled to the gratitude of all the people of this free land."

"What freedom?" Tom Grace shouted.

"You did the job that had to be done," Judge Young added, "that none other than the jury could do."

"This trial has been a sham in every way!" Tom Grace yelled. He walked over to the jurors as they were led from the courtroom and told them, "We don't blame you. We blame this rotten system."

"Murderers!" Valerie Manning shouted as Del Corso and Fassinger left the courtroom.

I rose. "I don't speak in anger," I told Judge Young, "I don't speak in emotion, and I don't speak because I have disgruntled clients. I speak on the overwhelming weight of the credible evidence . . . on the documentary evidence and the physical evidence which was utterly unrefuted, films, a tape recording prepared by impartial sources, government agencies. I speak on the admission of indiscriminate firing by three of the highest officers. . . .

"And I speak to the suppression of certain evidence on which we say the Court erred and erred repeatedly, and which will be reviewed by a higher court.

"I say it is a sad day in American justice." I paused while those remaining in the courtroom applauded and were silenced by the judge. After joining the judge in the request that decorum be maintained, I made a motion that the Court set the verdict aside.

"I say, sir, many errors were committed on this record, permitting questioning the state of mind of those plaintiffs, who were three, four, five hundred feet away, concerning the Vietnam War, and invasion of privacy of their thoughts . . . I say this must not stand, sir. . . .

"I implore you, sir, to reserve decision and consider it with great deliberation and care, and I urge Your Honor not to impose or permit to be imposed upon us the tremendous expense of an appeal, which there surely will be. I ask you to set aside this verdict."

The plaintiffs left the courtroom for the Hollenden House, where a victory celebration had been planned. Sarah Scheuer reached the door at the same time as Burt Fulton, who stood aside to let her pass. The lawyer's face was expressionless. Mrs. Scheuer couldn't contain her feelings.

"I want you to know," Mrs. Scheuer said, "I do believe there is a God in heaven. One day when something like this happens to one of your children, maybe then you will understand how we feel."

Fulton told her she was a bad sport.

Accosted by reporters in the lobby of the Hollenden House, where defense counsel and some of their clients had also planned a get-together, Fulton commented that the trial had been "a tough business. It's not a fun thing." He congratulated Del Corso on having refused the plaintiffs' offer to drop the charges against him if he testified as an expert.

Charlie Brown was more effusive. He told the press, "Gentlemen, you have now heard the last words on Kent State.

"They are very fine and credible Americans," he said of the guardsmen. "I was proud to represent them."

Sergeant McManus, who for five years had felt persecuted, heard the verdicts on his car radio that evening. He was so overcome that he had to pull off the road. "I cried," he told a reporter. "I realized I'm thirty years old and these last five years have been extremely hectic. It's a tragedy, but you have to enforce the will of the people. We did that. We protected lives. . . . The people of the state have been fantastic."

Herschler and his wife also cried when they heard the news on television. "Maybe we will live a little freer and looser for some time now," he told reporters. "This is what we prayed for."

Robert Canterbury said the verdict would not change anyone's mind about what had happened in 1970. He expressed sympathy for the plaintiffs. "I talked to one or more during the trial," he said, "and I know what the problems are. I certainly feel a sense of compassion for them."

Del Corso was jubilant. Remembering what he had told the federal grand jury, I was stunned to hear him tell reporters on the courthouse steps that the decision "was a great support for law enforcement."

Robert White, blinking in the late afternoon sun on the courthouse steps, remarked that he was "pleased and relieved, but I cannot say that I am happy, It is not possible to be happy."

Governor Rhodes was circumspect. Comments, he remarked, were premature until the results of the appeal were in.

The plaintiffs expressed bitterness and disappointment. Arthur Krause announced that the trial had proved that the Constitution had been destroyed. Dean Kahler said that he was "in depths of darkness. We've been denied, and we won't quit now. Justice is human, and what is human is that which may err."

Elaine Holstein remarked that the verdict "gives license to the government to shoot anyone who doesn't agree with them."

"I spent two days there at the trial," Mrs. Grace said in Syracuse, "and I saw Judge Young constantly put down the lawyers for our side. It got so bad I couldn't stand it anymore so I came back home. . . . We're supposed to be civilized, but we're just the same as Portugal."

Joe Lewis said the trial was a mockery of justice.

Doug Wrentmore, profoundly depressed, took refuge in numerological calculations, noting that the last day of the trial and his birthday were August 27 and November 27; that two and seven made nine, the number of living victims; that the jury had voted against him nine to three, which, when multiplied, made 27.

John Adams said that the decision reinforced the dangerous tendency of U.S. law-enforcement agencies to depend on guns. We believe, he said, "the tragedy and the trial verdict have implications for every U.S. citizen because civil authorities now have a license to silence legal demonstrations."

Tom Grace and Alan Canfora predicted that the verdicts would strengthen the revolutionary movement in the United States.

I commented that the greatest tragedy of the verdict was that it disillusioned fine people with our government and laws.

During the five days of sweating out the verdict, I had argued with our young clients that the problems of our society could better be solved by their participation than by their desertion. I assured them that we would eventually be victorious, that we would surely win an appeal and face a better judge and a better jury.

The hardest blow of all was my realization that not one of them believed me.

The threatened juror, it turned out, was the armature winder, Richard Williams. According to a story in the *Daily Kent Stater,* he had been approached three times on Tuesday, August 19, by a two-hundred-pound six-footer about thirty-five years of age. As Williams waited for a bus outside the courthouse at about four in the afternoon, the man told him that his house would be blown up and his family killed. The man approached him again about an hour and a half later, while Williams was playing pool in a bar a block and a half from his home. Three hours later, as he was walking home, the man had grabbed him by the cheeks and thrown him against a building. It was then that Williams had called the federal marshals. (The implication was that Williams was told to vote for the plaintiffs, for he was quoted as fearing that the threats might have been carried out "the day the trial ended.")

Blanche Layman, the alternate who would have replaced Williams, revealed after the trial that she would have voted for the plaintiffs. At the very least, if Williams, as I had urged, had been replaced, there would not have existed the requisite nine votes for a verdict. (As far as I know, no other witness to the threats against Williams was ever found, nor was anyone apprehended in connection with them.)

The jurors have since been very secretive; to this day they will not talk about their decisions. All we know is that Mrs. Gaskella was quoted in newspapers as saying that the jurors first reached a decision on Governor Rhodes on Monday and then considered the other defendants, and that there were never more than five votes against any one defendant. We can assume that the five were Blazina, Gaskella, Heckman, and the two tearful ladies, Dotterer and Klancar.

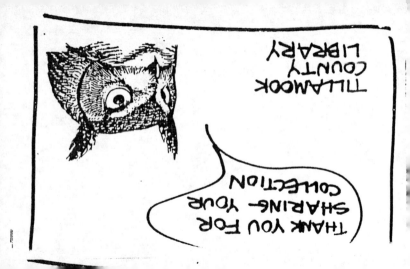

Juror Williams told a reporter that he found the Abell film and the Strubb tape persuasive against the plaintiffs.

Another newspaper account stated that the jurors had not understood the argument that the thirteen plaintiffs were to be considered as individuals, rather than as part of a crowd, and that they had voted in favor of all the guardsmen, even while seeing that their roles had differed, because they had interpreted the judge's groupings of the defendants in the instructions to mean that they had to find for or against them in groups.

Judge Young, of course, denied our motion to set aside the jury verdict. His uncle, former senator Stephen Young, called the trial a miscarriage of justice and said he regretted having sponsored his nephew for the federal bench. It was, he said, the "worst appointment" he had ever made. He stated that the judge had committed the "grossest sort of errors," and he criticized him for admitting evidence of the May 1–3 events, for calling Rhodes "Your Excellency," and for confusing the jury with his charge.

As a token of appreciation for my efforts, Jan Wrentmore gave me a small marble plaque, two inches by two inches in size. She said it had belonged to her husband and that he would have wanted me to have it as a keepsake. The inscription reads:

MEMBER

CENTURY CLUB

KENT STATE UNIVERSITY

OHIO

1910

I value it highly, as the only compensation I received in the case.

31

The Payoff

The thirteen plaintiffs turned the appeal over to the American Civil Liberties Union, which offered to advance funds for expenses and to provide the manpower. The ACLU assigned the task to Sanford J. Rosen, a thirty-seven-year-old San Francisco lawyer who had had a previous involvement with Kent State litigation. (In the spring of 1970 the ACLU had sent him to Kent from New York to look over the situation, and later he had worked on the case arising out of the illegal search of the Kent State dormitories and on the appeal of *Gilligan* v. *Morgan,* the case that had unsuccessfully challenged the practices of the Ohio National Guard.)

I believed during the trial that the judge had committed reversible error on at least four occasions: when he refused to prevent or limit the questioning of plantiffs' political beliefs; when he refused to let me question Captain Snyder on the guardsmen's setting up a defense of self-defense; when he refused to let me question General Del Corso as an expert or otherwise and to use his federal grand jury testimony to impeach him; and when he refused either to interrogate the threatened juror or to dismiss him, instead making the "blood on my hands" speech, which could only have heightened the jurors' fears and terrors.

In addition, I thought that a number of Judge Young's other rulings —or their cumulative effect—were highly prejudicial: his permitting repetitive testimony on the May 1–3 events, his refusal to ask the other jurors whether juror Watts had expressed his views to them, his cavalier rejection of the new federal rules of evidence, his concealment of evidence from the jury during the trial, and his refusal to let us drop the state claims.

Higher courts are reluctant to reverse jury verdicts; they will bend over backward to avoid second-guessing a jury's reading of the evidence. Impressed with this fact, Sanford Rosen, at his initial meeting with the clients, told them that the odds were a thousand to one against their winning the appeal.

I disputed him immediately. He had not lived through the long trial as I had. I told our clients that the 13,000-page record of the trial was loaded with solid grounds for reversal and that the Circuit Court of Appeals would not allow this judgment to stand. Judge Young, I reminded them, had often been reversed in the past. To tell already disheartened plaintiffs that they had practically no chance of winning—especially when it was inaccurate—was at the very least inconsiderate and bad for their morale.

Rosen, financed by the Methodist Church as well as the ACLU, submitted the brief to the Circuit Court of Appeals in Cincinnati in May 1976, accompanied by an eleven-volume appendix containing excerpts from the trial transcript, photographs, and documents. The appeal was based on the same grounds as our motion for a new trial.

The oral argument came more than a year later, on June 21, 1977. Rosen was still pessimistic about our chances of winning, but he thought now that the odds against him had shortened to one hundred to one, perhaps because the best possible panel of judges was on the case: Harry Phillips of Nashville, Tennessee; George Clifton Edwards, Jr., of Detroit, Michigan; and Pierce Lively of Lexington, Kentucky. Edwards, a former Detroit police chief, had expertise in the area of crowd control; Phillips, a former naval officer, could be expected to entertain high standards of military behavior; and Lively, a recent Nixon appointee, was regarded as fair-minded.

The mahogany-paneled courtroom in Cincinnati was packed that Tuesday morning. Most of the plaintiffs were present, the parents of the deceased students, the Graces, Jan Wrentmore, the Kahlers. John Adams was there. Sylvester Del Corso was on hand, along with Fulton and Brown, Blakemore, and Victor Goodman, a stocky Columbus lawyer who represented Governor Rhodes (Brooke Alloway had died).

Rosen was faced with the problem of making sense of his multifaceted appeal in the short space of twenty minutes. He began by focusing on four issues: whether the events of May 1–3 justified a ban on all Kent assemblies; whether substantial evidence existed that the guardsmen were in serious danger when they opened fire; Judge Young's treatment of the threatened juror; and the charge to the jury. Rosen was unable to make headway with the first two points because the jury's findings could be challenged only by showing that Judge Young's rulings had distorted the evidence—a matter too complex for the few minutes allotted. (Rosen could only refer the court to the brief.)

When Rosen reached the matter of the threatened juror and told how Judge Young, after refusing my request that he question the juror, had gone on to terrorize the entire panel, the three judges perked up their ears. They appeared to be surprised at Judge Young's speech, which they had read in the brief, and Judge Phillips commented that it was customary in such cases to question the entire jury.

The appeal had struck pay dirt. Appellate judges may be reluctant to reverse a jury verdict, but they would have to call a new trial if the jury's ability to decide a case solely on the evidence had been impaired.

When Fulton got up to speak, it was apparent that he knew that the hearing was not going well for the defense. "I certainly did not ask for sequestration [of the jury]," he said.

"That does not matter," Judge Phillips told him.

Fulton insisted that Judge Young had acted correctly, and he argued that there was no evidence that any juror had acted under duress.

"How could there be?" Judge Lively asked.

Judge Phillips began reading from the record, quoting Judge Young's speech to the jury: "I have been brought up in an old school that threats of the type that were made are not to be ignored and not to be taken lightly. There have been times when I have ignored such threats, and I have blood on my hands. . . ."

Fulton denied that the speech would have bothered him as a juror. "We are not talking about a criminal trial," he said, raising his voice. He argued that in a civil trial threats to jurors are not a serious matter. "We do not know how that juror voted or any other juror voted."

In substance, Brown stated that Judge Young had done a wonderful job and that since the identity of the threatened juror was unknown, it could have been an alternate who had not even voted.

On another issue, Victor Goodman tried to show that Rhodes had no responsibility for the Guard's training, regulations, and behavior. Judge Edwards, looking incredulous, asked whether troop regulations conveyed that it was the individual soldiers' decisions "whether their lives were in danger that authorized them to use force."

"I believe that this is a special decision for the men to make," Goodman agreed. He went on to cite the OPLAN: when all other means had failed, shooting was justified.

"Each and every individual soldier can determine whether or not he is in mortal peril?" Judge Edwards asked. "Is that what explains no order to fire?"

In his rebuttal Rosen countered Brown's assertion that the threatened juror could have been an alternate by showing that the judge had clearly indicated that the threat was made to a juror. He then repeated what I had said about the judge's instilling a sense of fear in the jury and noted my request that the juror be interrogated and removed if he had been swayed by the threats.

At a luncheon meeting afterward, Rosen told the plaintiffs they might now consider that they had one chance in ten of winning the appeal. He had been heartened by the judges' interest in the way Judge Young had handled the situation of the threatened juror.

The summer following the appellate hearing in Cincinnati was a difficult one for the plaintiffs. Even before the appeal was heard, the Kent State Board of Trustees announced a decision to extend the gymnasium over a portion of Blanket Hill, covering a part of the area in which the shootings had taken place.

The plaintiffs viewed the decision as a studied insult to the four dead students and an attempt to erase the memory of the traumatic event from the campus. Alan Canfora, some of his friends, and scores of sympathizers camped on the proposed construction site. Appeals were made to the university and various political bodies by the parents.

All appeals failed, and the civil disobedience effort reached a climax on July 12, when 194 persons were arrested and removed by bus. Among those arrested were the Reverend John Adams, Mr. and Mrs. Canfora, and the Scheuers, who even two years before would not have dreamed of sitting down in front of a bulldozer.

On September 12 the Circuit Court of Appeals unanimously ordered a new trial, singling out the mishandling of the threatened juror. Judge Lively, who wrote the decision, quoted my colloquy with Judge Young and stated:

> The defendants argue that the plaintiffs did not object to the district court's decision to permit the threatened juror to remain on the jury. An examination of the transcript makes it clear that counsel for the plaintiffs [Kelner] repeatedly requested that the threatened juror be excused . . . Furthermore, the trial judge repeatedly indicated that the juror would be excused and that there would be no point in questioning since he could not be permitted to participate in the deliberations . . .
>
> It was error for the trial court to determine . . . without any personal interrogation that a juror who had been threatened and assaulted and told that his home would be blown up could continue to serve unaffected . . . Further, if it appeared that any other jurors had been subjected indirectly to improper influences by reason of the knowledge of the threatened juror's experience, the district court would be required to consider declaring a mistrial, lamentable as that would be . . . No litigant should

be required to accept the verdict of a jury which has been subjected to such an intrusion in the absence of a hearing and determination that no probability exists that the jury's deliberations or verdict would be affected . . .

Having ordered a new trial, the appellate court addressed itself marginally to a number of other issues. It stated that the claims under state law could have been dropped if the request had been made at the beginning of the trial, and it indicated its belief that some of the plaintiffs' complaints about the handling of the evidence would be taken care of by the new federal rules of evidence.

The appellate court also granted two defense motions: to dismiss the claims against former university president White and to dismiss the plaintiffs' claims for separate damages on the issue of illegal dispersal of the noon rally. In doing this the court severed from the case the important issue of whether the students' First Amendment rights to freedom of peaceful assembly had been violated.

All the lawyers for the plaintiffs disagreed with the court's reasoning on this issue; they believed it was based on misreadings of both the facts and the law. The court stated that the fact that disturbances had occurred on the three preceding days, ending only at 3 A.M. on May 4, justified banning the May 4 assembly, and it cited cases showing that such bans did not violate the First Amendment. But the court was wrong about the events of May 3. There had been no march downtown or destruction on Sunday night, as it said, and the late-night disturbances growing out of the Main Street sit-down were caused by the Guard, not by the students. With regard to the law, in all the cases cited the ban on assemblies had been by *school* officials.

Planning for the new trial began almost immediately. That summer I had written to the clients to give them my views on what we should do in the event we would be returning to the courtroom. I mentioned that some of the actions of those protesting the construction of a gymnasium on part of Blanket Hill, such as breaking down fences, would not sit well with potential Cleveland jurors, and I cautioned about the danger that certain outside radical groups might exploit the situation for their own ends. The main purpose of my letter, however, was to state that our trial setup had to be changed. I recommended that two experienced trial lawyers conduct the next trial, with the others assisting—but not participating in—the examinations.

I arrived at the next family meeting in Cleveland, on October 30, 1977, exultant at the prospect of a new contest, one that I was confident we could win. I felt like a boxer who, knocked out by a foul blow, has been given a rematch—and I had never lost a second trial. We would have beaten our opponents the first time in a fair fight, and now, with a new referee (judge), and armed with the knowledge of our own witnesses' and our opponents' strengths and weaknesses, we would be stronger. We could make General Del Corso give his opinions of the shootings and obtain Captain Snyder's testimony that he had planted the gun on Jeffrey Miller's body in order to establish a phony defense of self-defense.

Yet we needed to make sure we didn't have Judge Young presiding again over our destiny. I also thought we must try to move the case out of Ohio, so we wouldn't be faced with another jury comprised largely of persons who had voted for Governor Rhodes. These goals were worth a try; even if they weren't successful, our efforts would serve notice that we believed that Judge Young and any Ohio jury were likely to be prejudiced.

I soon found that my advice was not to be heeded. The ACLU would not provide the funds and the manpower for the second trial unless Rosen ran the show as lead counsel. The clients were given no alternative. I immediately perceived the danger of this course, for Rosen had never tried a case before a jury. Certainly my pride was involved—I had expected to continue as chief trial counsel and had earned the right to do so—but my main concern was for the clients and their cause.

Rosen revealed that he had made settlement overtures to the other side on behalf of the clients. That was a tactical mistake. Even if a settlement was what the weary clients wanted, for them to make the first approach was bound to be interpreted as a sign of weakness. It would only embolden the other side to offer a minimum amount. I tried to encourage them to steel themselves for another trial, telling them that we were now in a position to win. I recommended that we move to transfer the trial to a federal court in another state and to disqualify Judge Young, but Rosen said there was little chance of winning such motions.

My own client, Mrs. Holstein, told me she had no choice and would have to join the others behind Rosen. Arthur Krause said apologetically, "I'm tired, Joe. Sick and tired of fighting. What else can I do?"

I withdrew from the case.

I felt deeply for the shooting victims and their families. They were tired, driven people. In Arthur Krause's words, what else could they do? All were exhausted from the long struggle, unhappy, unencouraged by Rosen's often expressed lack of optimism, and fearful that without the ACLU they would lack the funds and the manpower for the second trial.

I predicted that the case would be settled and never go through another trial.

In April 1978 the case was assigned to Judge Young, and Rosen decided against asking either for recusal (removal) of Judge Young or for a change of venue. I think he was confident that, unlike me, he would be able to work comfortably with Judge Young.

I thought about Rosen's decision for several weeks, trying to decide what to do. On the one hand, I would appear to be butting in if I were to offer unsought advice. On the other hand, I knew it would be disastrous for the clients' fate to be once more in Judge Young's hands. After a great deal of soul-searching, I sent a long letter to John Adams, spelling out the reasons for recusing the judge and moving the trial out of Ohio. "Even if a motion to disqualify Judge Young and to change venue were denied," I concluded, "the public knowledge emanating from such motions might put Judge Young and all concerned on better behavior. The benefits flowing from such motions could be enormous."

Later I learned that at a family meeting on May 3, before Adams received my letter, the clients had forcefully reopened the issue and got Rosen to change his stance. He now said that he would not decide finally on recusal until he had a chance to measure the judge personally at a pre-trial meeting scheduled for June 1.

At that meeting Rosen sought to overcome the problems of the judge's rulings by getting him to grant several motions to permit the liberal use of photographs during testimony, the reading of documents in evidence when needed, the use of federal grand jury testimony for impeachment purposes and as evidence, and the qualifying of key witnesses such as Del Corso as experts. Rosen also asked the judge to prevent the questioning of plaintiffs on their political beliefs. Although someone without experience of Judge Young could plausibly think that this approach would be successful, I knew that no matter what rulings the judge might make in advance, his rulings during the trial could still frustrate the flow of evidence.

Rosen apparently liked what he saw of Judge Young at the June 1 meeting, for he made no further reference to recusal, and he continued with plans for a second pre-trial meeting on October 26. He also continued to make references to a possible settlement. These overtures finally resulted in a small settlement offer by the defense.

The unwillingness of the clients to accept this offer caused Judge Young to perform for them the service that their own counsel had refused. On September 15 the judge resigned from the case.

"I had hoped," he wrote to the lawyers for both sides, "that it would be possible to get the matter settled and thus avoid the necessity of any further proceedings, but apparently this is not to be.

"According to the press, the legislators have appropriated somewhat in excess of $380,000 for the retrial. I hope that it might be possible that if the plaintiffs were to make a firm offer to accept slightly less than that amount in full settlement, with each side to pay its own costs, the defendants could persuade the legislature to go along with it.

"I realize that settlement for so small a sum would not be very palatable to the plaintiffs, but something is better than nothing. I do not believe that the plaintiffs can ever win these cases, no matter how often they are tried or retried."

The fact that Judge Young thought the plaintiffs could never win was not news to me. A few days later, when the judge's statements were repeated in the press—prejudicially to the plaintiffs' case because his remarks would influence potential jurors and other judges—Rosen finally, on those grounds, requested that Chief Judge Battisti grant a change of venue and assign a non-Ohio trial judge.

Several weeks later it was announced that the new judge would be William K. Thomas and that the case would stay in Cleveland.

Judge Thomas was a definite improvement. He had been the first preference of the Ohio lawyers on our team in 1975, and he was reputed to be a careful, fair-minded, scholarly judge. That reputation was confirmed on October 13 and 14 when he granted most of the motions Rosen had proposed earlier to Judge Young.

The difference between Judge Thomas and Judge Young can perhaps best be illustrated by the attitude Judge Thomas showed when Rosen requested certain rulings on the handling of evidence. At one point Rosen asked, "Your Honor, if a photograph has once been introduced in evidence, may we be permitted to show it to the jury on other occasions, when the subject of the photograph is pertinent to the testimony? A photograph, for example, might impeach testimony."

Judge Thomas indicated surprise that such a question would even be asked. Rosen explained that at the previous trial we had not been allowed to do this, that Judge Young had said that "photographs speak for themselves," and that the jury was not permitted to see the photographs in evidence until the end of the trial. Judge Thomas indicated he had never heard of anything like that, and he ruled that the photographs could be shown to the jury during the trial.

Rosen and Judge Thomas had a similar colloquy regarding documents such as the Matson-Frisina letter. Also, the state causes of action were dropped.

The rulings put the plaintiffs in an increasingly strong position. Yet settlement talks continued.

Although some of the clients were fed up after more than eight years of litigation, part of a trial lawyer's job in such circumstances is to keep up their spirits. The plaintiffs were now loaded for bear. They would have an opportunity to present the evidence fairly to a jury, and they would have a fair judge. If anybody had wanted to settle under those circumstances, it should have been the defendants, who were facing millions of dollars in judgments against them.

Jury selection for the new trial began on December 4, 1978, in the same federal building in which the 1975 trial was held, but in a different, more appropriate courtroom with high vaulted ceilings, handsome marble and gilt pilasters, and two enormous chandeliers. The entire wall behind Judge Thomas was dominated by a painting in which the female spirit of law auspiciously points to "Thou Shalt Not Kill" in the decalog.

Judge Thomas was a medium-sized man of sixty-seven with a composed ruddy face. He had white hair, wore dark horn-rimmed glasses, and had the relentless, unblinking expression of an eagle. He showed a no-nonsense ability to run his court with tight control: antics or side remarks on the part of the lawyers, permitted at the first trial, would be off limits here.

After ten days, on Friday, December 15, a jury of nine men and three women had been sworn. The newspapers published rumors of a $675,000 settlement. After a delay of one day, during which settlement discussions proceeded in Columbus, the state capital, the trial resumed on December 19. On December 21 the trial was adjourned until January 3.

The settlement came on January 4, 1979. Any experienced trial lawyer would have hung his head in shame upon learning the details:

$350,000 for Dean Kahler, paralyzed, sentenced to live in a wheelchair.

$42,500 for Joseph Lewis, with several feet of intestine missing, constant stomach trouble, and a numb leg.

$37,500 for Tom Grace, part of his left foot gone and frequent discomfort.

$27,500 for Donald Scott MacKenzie, shot through the neck and lacking a small piece of jawbone.

$22,500 for John Cleary, minus three ribs and part of a lung, persistently short of breath.

$15,000 each for Alan Canfora, shot through the wrist; Jim Russell, shot in the thigh and forehead; Robbie Stamps, shot in the back; and Doug Wrentmore, shot below the knee.

And to the parents of each of the four dead students:

$15,000 for the life of beautiful, brilliant nineteen-year-old Allison Krause.

$15,000 for the life of studious, dedicated Sandra Scheuer.

$15,000 for the life of William Schroeder, Eagle Scout and ROTC member.

$15,000 for the life of Jeffrey Miller, who had driven a taxi all summer to pay for his education.

These awards amounted to $600,000. In addition $25,000 was allowed for expenses and $50,000 for lawyers' fees.* The grand total was $675,000.

The settlement included a statement signed by Governor Rhodes, former adjutant general Del Corso, and the twenty-six other present and former national guardsmen who remained as defendants.

> In retrospect, the tragedy of May 4, 1970, should not have occurred. The students may have believed that they were right in continuing their mass protest in response to the Cambodian invasion, even though this protest followed the posting and reading by the University of an order to ban rallies and an order to disperse. These orders have since been determined by the Sixth Circuit Court of Appeals to have been lawful.
>
> Some of the Guardsmen on Blanket Hill, fearful and anxious from prior events, may have believed in their own minds that their lives were in danger. Hindsight suggests that another method would have resolved the confrontation. Better ways must be found to deal with such confrontations.
>
> We devoutly wish that a means had been found to avoid the May 4 events culminating in the Guard shootings and the irreversible deaths and injuries. We deeply regret those events and are profoundly saddened by the deaths of four students and wounding of nine others which resulted. We hope that the agreement to end this litigation will help to assuage the tragic memories regarding that sad day.

The last word properly belongs to the victims who, following the settlement, issued this statement:

> *Because of the experience that we have had during the past eight and one-half years, there are other words we are compelled to speak. We have become convinced that the issue of excessive use of force—or the use of deadly force—by law enforcement agencies or those acting with the authority of law enforcement agencies, is a critical national issue to which the attention of the American people must be drawn . . . we believe the average American is little aware of the official violence which has been used across our land indiscriminately and unjustifiably. . . .*
>
> *Through our long legal and political struggle we have become convinced that the present federal law which protects citizens from the deprivation of*

---

*Judge Thomas, using the written retainer agreements between the lawyers and their various clients as a guide, apportioned the $50,000 as follows: $33,740 to Steven Sindell, $6,305 to Fred Mandel, $8,995 to Joseph and Robert Kelner, and $960 to David Engdahl. The $25,000 in costs was awarded to the United Methodist Church. As of this writing, the $8,995 Kelner check is in an escrow account, awaiting the outcome of appeals by Sindell and the ACLU, each asserting claims to the funds. At such time as the appeal is decided, our $8,995 plus my royalties from this book shall be contributed to a foundation to be created for the protection of First Amendment rights. (J.K.)

their civil rights by law enforcement agencies or those acting with their authority is weak and inadequate. . . . A citizen can be killed by those acting under color of law almost with impunity. The families of the victims of those shootings and killings have little recourse and then only through expensive and lengthy process.

We believe that citizens and law enforcement must, in the words of the signed settlement, find *better ways. . . . We plead for a federal law which will compel the consideration and use of those better ways.*

We are simply average citizens who have attempted to be loyal to our country and constructive and responsible in our actions, but we have not had an average experience. We have learned through a tragic event that loyalty to our nation and its principles sometimes requires resistence to our government and its policies—a lesson many young people, including the children of some of us, had learned earlier. That has been our struggle—for others this struggle goes on. We will try to support them.

For Allison, Sandra, Jeffrey, and William

For Peace and Justice

Mr. and Mrs. Arthur Krause
Mr. and Mrs. Louis Schroeder
Mr. and Mrs. Martin Scheuer
Mr. and Mrs. Arthur Holstein
Mr. Dean Kahler
Mr. Joseph Lewis
Mr. Alan Canfora
Mr. John R. Cleary
Mr. Donald Scott MacKenzie
Mr. Douglas Wrentmore
Mr. Thomas Grace
Mr. Thomas Russell
Mr. Robert Stamps

APPENDIXES

A. OHIO NATIONAL GUARD CALL-OUTS, 1963-1973

Period	Activity	Area	Troops
Mar. 63	Flood Duty	Central Ohio	166
Mar. 64	Flood Duty	Central Ohio	145
12–22 Apr. 65	Tornado	Toledo	491
4–5 July 65	Civil Disturbance	Russells Point	1,111
28 Apr. 66	Flood Duty	Toledo	29
3–4 July 66	Civil Disturbance	Geneva on Lake	50
13–14 July 66	Flood Duty	Sandusky	50
19–31 July 66	Civil Disturbance	Cleveland	2,215
1–7 Sept. 66	Civil Disturbance	Dayton	1,139
13–18 June 67	Civil Disturbance	Cincinnati	909
28–29 July 67	Civil Disturbance	Lorain	129
25–30 July 67	Civil Disturbance	Toledo	1,155
13–15 Nov. 67	Civil Disturbance	Xenia	921
8–15 Apr. 68	Civil Disturbance	Cincinnati	1,310
10 Apr. 68	Student Disturb.	Columbus, OSU	
8–11 Apr. 68	Civil Disturbance	Youngstown	1,314
23–29 Apr. 68	Tornado	Wheelersburg	177
20–22 May 68	Student Disturb.	Athens	666
24–29 May 68	Flood Duty	Southern Ohio	428
24–30 June 68	Prison Riot	Ohio Pen, Columbus	730
3 July 68	Prison Riot	London Prison	233
18–25 July 68	Civil Disturbance	Akron	1,254
24–28 July 68	Glenville Riots	Cleveland	2,285
	an additional 13,715 troops were in federal drill status on standby but were not committed		
18 July to 3 Aug. 68	Prison Riot	Ohio Pen, Columbus	508
14 Aug. 68	Train Wreck	Urbana	236
20 Aug. to 23 Sept. 68	Prison Riot	Ohio Pen, Columbus	1,625
13–15 Jan. 69	Pipe Line Break	Lima	321
30 Jan. 69	Flood Duty	Napoleon	65
20–21 Mar. 69	Forest Fire	Waverly	5
20–30 Apr. 69	Prison Riot	Ohio Pen, Columbus	371
29 Apr. to 1 May 69	Prison Riot	Mansfield Reform.	77
8–10 May 69	Tornado	Kettering-Dayton	215
5–11 July 69	Flood Duty	Northern Ohio	803
17–20 July 69	Civil Disturbance	Youngstown	168
21–24 July 69	Civil Disturbance	Columbus	1,208
9–11 Aug. 69	Tornado	Cincinnati	684
10–11 Dec. 69	Student Disturb.	Akron University	634

2–3 Apr. 70	Train Wreck	Athens	19
8–10 Apr. 70	Student Disturb.	Cleveland	952
16–17 Apr. 70	Student Disturb.	Oxford	561
18–19 Apr. 70	Student Disturb.	Sandusky	96
29 Apr. to 5 May 70	Truckers' Strike	Cincinnati-Cleve.	3,257
29 Apr. to 9 May 70	Student Disturb.	Columbus, OSU	2,861
2–7 May 70	Student Disturb.	Kent, Kent State	1,196
15–19 June 70	Student Disturb.	Athens, Ohio U	1,885
21–28 June 70	Student Disturb.	Columbus, OSU	4,036
6–10 Aug. 70	Civil Disturbance	Lima	643
26–27 June 71	Tornado	Marysville	142
14–18 Nov. 72	Flood Duty	Northern Ohio	599
9–10 Apr. 73	Flood Duty	Toledo	83
10–13 May 73	Tornado	Willard-Kenton	217
16–18 Oct. 73	Storm Damage	Lake Erie area	12
5–6 Dec. 73	Truckers' Block	Central Ohio	204

B. OPLAN 2, OHIO NATIONAL GUARD (REVISED MAY 16, 1969), PAGES F-2 AND F-3

ANNEX F (PRE-EMPLOYMENT BRIEFING) TO OPLAN 2 (AID TO CIVIL AUTHORITIES)

. . . in order that you may act wisely regardless of personal feelings or beliefs. Do not fraternize with civilians or discuss with them at any time the circumstances of the military action.

6.   RULES OF ENGAGEMENT: In any action that you are required to take, use only the minimum force necessary. When the Riot Act has been read within hearing, it is unlawful for any group of three or more people to remain unlawfully or riotously assembled and you may use necessary and proper means to disperse or apprehend them. Keeping groups from assembling prevents crowds which may become unruly and take mob action. Your use of force should be in the sequence listed below:

    a.   Issue a military request to disperse.

        (1) Insure that an avenue of dispersal is available.

        (2) Allow ample time for them to obey the order.

        (3) Remain in area for sufficient time to prevent re-assembly.

    b.   Riot formations—show of force. Instructions in 6.a.(1) (2) (3) above apply.

    c.   Simple physical force, if feasible.

    d.   Rifle butt and bayonet: If people do not respond to request, direction and order, and if simple physical force is not feasible, you have the rifle butt and bayonet which may be used in that order, using only such force as is necessary.

    e.   Chemicals. If people fail to respond to requests or orders, and riot formation and rifle butts or bayonets prove ineffective, chemicals (baseball grenades or jumping grenades) will be used on order when available. When large demands for chemicals are required a chemical squad will be dispatched to assist you upon request.

    f.   Weapons. When all other means have failed or chemicals are not readily available, you are armed with the rifle and have been issued life (sic) ammunition. The following rules apply in the use of firearms:

        (1) Rifles will be carried with a round in the chamber in the safe position. Exercise care and be safety minded at all times.

(2) Indiscriminate firing of weapons is forbidden. Only single aimed shot (sic) at confirmed targets will be employed. Potential targets are:

(a) Sniper—(Determined by his firing upon, or in the direction of friendly forces or civilians) will be fired upon when clearly observed and it is determined that an attempt to apprehend would be hazardous or other means of neutralization are impractical.

(b) Arsonist—(Determined by acts of fire-setting of *inhabited* building or structure) will be fired on if there is apparent necessity and all other means of preventing the crime are first exhausted. That is, the arsonist on being ordered to halt during an attempt to apprehend, and failure to obey such order, where there is no other reasonable alternative, to prevent the escape of a felon from the scene of his felony.

(c) Other. In any instance where human life is endangered by the forcible, violent actions of a rioter, or when rioters to whom the Riot Act has been read cannot be dispersed by any other reasonable means, then shooting is justified.

(3) Full automatic weapons such as machine guns will be employed in riot control operations for their psychological effect. Such weapons will *not* be carried with a round in the chamber, but will be in a safe or half load position.

(4) When chemicals are employed and/or weapons fired, the report form issued to you with your ammunition will be completed and immediately brought to the company headquarters or reported by radio or telephone to me.

C.   LOG, KENT STATE CRIMINAL LITIGATION (OHIO)

1970

May 15   At press conference, Portage County Prosecutor Ronald Kane displays weapons found during search of Kent State dormitories

May 18   Portage County Coroner Robert Sybert rules that the 4 KSU students were killed by .30 caliber military bullets

May 21   Coroner Sybert recommends grand jury probe to Prosecutor Kane to determine if the 4 deaths are to be classified "accidental or homicidal"

June 26   Federal government pledges full cooperation to Kane; Jerris Leonard, assistant U.S. attorney general, chief of civil rights division, meets for three hours with Kane; tells Kane there is no plan for a federal grand jury

July 12   Kane seeks $75,000 to $100,000 from Governor Rhodes for grand jury investigation of shootings

July 22   Kane gets 3,000-page report from Ohio Highway Patrol; meets 6 hours with Chester Hayth, head of OHP

Kane gets Justice Department analysis of FBI investigation; JD concluded that if there was no riot, ONG could be prosecuted under Ohio law and that 6 individual guardsmen may be criminally liable

July 23   10-page Justice Department summary of FBI investigation appears in *Akron Beacon Journal;* Kane accused of leak by JD

July 31   Kane writes Judge Karas requesting reconvening of Portage County grand jury

Aug. 2   Adjutant General Del Corso requests Ohio grand jury; Governor Rhodes reported weighing Kane request for $100,000; Kane has announced he will subpoena Governor Rhodes to testify

Aug. 3   Rhodes directs Ohio Attorney General Paul Brown to convene special grand jury to investigate "(1) Acts leading to or inducing illegal or criminal acts in any way associated with 'campus unrest' that took place" in Kent or at KSU on May 1–5, 1970, and "(2) such illegal and criminal acts themselves" and, in addition, "the legality of official response to such illegal or criminal acts and to the general temper and situation prevailing" at Kent and KSU

Aug. 4   Kane writes U.S. Attorney General John Mitchell, protesting special grand jury

Aug. 7   R. L. Balyeat named to head special grand jury

Aug. 11   Balyeat gets reports of OHP, Bureau of Criminal Identification, Arson Bureau, adjutant general ONG, 39 volumes of FBI investigation and Justice Department summary

Aug. 14   Brown states there will be prosecutions over shootings; says study of FBI and Justice Department reports leads him to believe *Akron Beacon Journal* not untruthful (in blaming Guard)

Sep. 14   Jurors, special grand jury, visit KSU

Oct. 8   Special grand jury makes conclusions

Oct. 15   Special grand jury files report, press conference

Oct. 16   Special grand jury indicts 1 professor and 24 students

Oct. 24   Rhodes names 3 special counsel to handle indictments, one of whom is Seabury Ford

Oct. 28   Suits filed in U.S. District Court to expunge report of special grand jury and quash indictments; also requesting 3-judge panel to rule on constitutionality of Ohio riot laws

Nov. 9   ACLU announces Ramsey Clark will help defend Craig Morgan, one of 24 indicted students

Balyeat admits special grand jury never saw Justice Department summary of FBI reports

Nov. 14   U.S. District Court (Judge Thomas) upholds constitutionality of Ohio riot law

Dec. 8   Governor-elect Gilligan meets with students; no comment on special grand jury, will study FBI reports, etc.

1971

Jan. 12   Kane accuses Rhodes and others of thwarting him

Jan. 28   U.S. District Court (Thomas) orders special grand jury report expunged; indictments to stand

Aug. 22   U.S. Court of Appeals, 6th circuit, lets indictments stand

Sep. 10   Injunction sought in U.S. District Court to halt prosecution of 25; denied

Nov. 22   Trials of 25 begin, Ravenna

Dec. 8   After 3 verdicts on first 5 defendants, other 20 cases dropped for lack of evidence

D.   LOG, KENT STATE CRIMINAL LITIGATION (FEDERAL)

1970

May 5   FBI opens investigation

May 6   Nixon confers with 6 KSU students, orders full report from Justice Department; Agnew: it's not premeditated, but it's murder

May 7   Agnew: ONG overreacted, second degree murder

May 15   Justice Department preliminary report to Nixon

May 19   Attorney General Mitchell speech in Mississippi (one day after Jackson State shootings) condemns violent demonstrations and unrestrained reactions

May 21   Mitchell names Jerris Leonard, chief of civil rights division, JD, to head stepped-up probe

May 24   Press Secretary Klein announces Nixon to appoint special commission to investigate campus unrest

June 9   Jerris Leonard says no evidence of sniper at KSU in FBI reports

June 13   Nixon establishes Commission on Campus Unrest to report in three months; *has power to subpeona witnesses, documents,* etc.

June 26   Federal government pledges full cooperation to Portage County Prosecutor Kane; Kane and Jerris Leonard meet 3 hours; Leonard tells Kane, no plan for federal grand jury

July 22   Kane gets JD analysis FBI report: if no riot, ONG can be prosecuted under Ohio law; also states 6 individual guardsmen may be criminally liable under Ohio law

July 23   Kane accused by JD of leaking JD summary of FBI report to *Akron Beacon Journal*

July 25   FBI issues statement, does not draw conclusions

July 29   Mitchell states "apparent violations of federal law" in KSU shootings; federal government will move to prosecute violators if Ohio authorities do not

Aug. 19   Scranton Commission opens 3 days of hearings at KSU despite pleas for delay because of special state grand jury; *because of special grand jury, no shooters are asked to testify at any time;* two ONG, Srp and Stevenson, got U.S. District Court to compel withdrawal of subpoenas from Scranton Commission

Sep. 24   Jerris Leonard promises federal action if Ohio doesn't handle properly

Sep. 26 Scranton Commission reports to Nixon (forwent full exercise of subpoena powers in order not to interfere with special grand jury or federal prosecution promised by Mitchell)

Arthur Krause gets letter from JD, will move if Ohio grand jury ineffective

Oct. 31 *N.Y. Times* prints excerpts from 35-page summary FBI report "some reason to believe self-defense claim fabricated"

Nov. 17 Carl Stern on NBC: Nixon administration reassessing position on KSU, difficult to prosecute guardsmen involved, administration giving great weight to Ohio special grand jury report

Jerris Leonard quoted in *Evening Star,* no JD decision yet on KSU

Nov. 18 Ehrlichman-Mitchell "eyes only" memo, cites Leonard in *Star* and reminds Mitchell that he has seen Nixon memo stating *Nixon does not want a federal grand jury* to investigate KSU

Nov. 21 JD states no decision yet on calling federal grand jury

Dec. 10 Letter, Nixon to Scranton, Mitchell reviewing Commission report

Dec. 11 Hoover: extenuating circumstances led ONG to fire

Dec. 18 Mitchell: no decision yet on federal grand jury

1971

March 19 Memo, Jerris Leonard to Robert Finch: expect decision on federal grand jury in few weeks

March 21 *Washington Post* reports government has virtually decided against federal grand jury

March 24 John Adams and other Washington ministers meet one hour with Jerris Leonard

April 6 Mitchell on David Frost television show: national guardsmen just kids; snipers at KSU

May 25 Congressman Moorhead (Pa) and 19 other representatives ask Mitchell to begin federal grand jury investigation

June 21 Hearings, Senate Judiciary Committee: Scranton calls for federal grand jury

June 25 Senator Kennedy asks Mitchell to convene federal grand jury

July 24 JD says Mitchell soon to announce decision on federal grand jury

July 30 Four senators question David Norman (who has replaced Leonard at civil rights division) on delay in convening federal grand jury

Norman reveals that in March 1971 Leonard had made recommendation against federal grand jury

Aug. 13 Mitchell states JD closing files on KSU

Aug. 26 Senator Kennedy tells National Press Club that his committee is going to investigate JD handling of KSU

Nov. 18 KSU students deliver 10,000-name petition for federal grand jury to Nixon

1972

Feb. 23 Kleindienst at Senate hearings confirms attorney general will not reopen KSU case

April 9 Letter to Nixon from 9 mothers requests hearing at JD

June 13 Attorney General Kleindienst at press conference: JD considers KSU closed

July 11 Nixon denies petition and parents; no federal grand jury

Oct. 12   *Schroeder* v. *Richardson,* mandamus action in U.S. District Court, to com-
            pel attorney general to call federal grand jury

1973

Jan. 15   Entire JD summary FBI report inserted in *Congressional Record*
May 10   White House meeting, Dean Kahler et al. and deputy asst atty general
            William O'Conner, who tells Kahler that JD has evidence sufficient to
            secure indictments of several national guardsmen under S 18 US 242;
            O'Conner confirms this on telephone but says ONG liable for mis-
            demeanors only (but 1968 amendment makes crime a felony if death
            results)
May 11   50,000-name petition submitted to JD
May 17   R. C. Odle tells Ervin Committee that Mitchell was running Nixon reelec-
            tion campaign in May 1971
May 25   Leonard Garment rejects 50,000-name petition, no federal grand jury
June 13   Letter, Attorney General Richardson to KSU president Olds, asst atty
            general J. S. Pottinger taking fresh look to determine whether to con-
            vene a federal grand jury
Aug. 3   Richardson says JD reopening KSU investigation; Pottinger says federal
            grand jury may be called to weigh criminal charges
Oct. 20   "Saturday night massacre": Cox fired, Richardson resigns
Nov. 15   Saxbe, former Ohio National Guard colonel, nominated attorney general
Dec. 11   JD civil rights chief Pottinger says case to federal grand jury next week
Dec. 12   Saxbe tells Senate Judiciary Committee he will excuse himself with regard
            to KSU matters
Dec. 18   Federal grand jury impanelled in Cleveland, Judge Battisti

1974

Jan. 7–11   Federal grand jury testimony, Cleveland
Feb. 3   Federal grand jury testimony, Cleveland
Feb. 19   JD experts visit KSU, reenact, fire M-1s
Feb. 25   Federal grand jury has called more than 50 ONG
Feb. 26   Del Corso testifies federal grand jury
March 5   Rhodes testifies federal grand jury
March 29   After 3 days federal grand jury indicts 1 present and 7 former ONG
April 4   8 ONG plead not guilty
Aug. 3   Trial deferred from Sep. 30 to Oct. 15
Oct. 2   Judge Battisti defers trial Oct. 15 to Oct. 21
Oct. 22   Jury selected; defendants: Shafer, Zoller, McGee, Pierce, Perkins, Morris,
            McManus, Smith
Oct. 29   Trial
Oct. 30   Jury to KSU
Oct. 31   John Filo testifies
Nov. 1   Scott MacKenzie testifies
Nov. 5   Election day; Rhodes elected governor for third term after four year hiatus
Nov. 8   Battisti acquits the 8 guardsmen

E.   LOG, KENT STATE CIVIL LITIGATION

1970

June 10   Krause complaints filed, U.S. District Court and Ohio Court of Common Pleas, *Krause* v. *Rhodes*

July 31   Student leader Craig Morgan files complaint, U.S. District Court, on illegal search of Kent State dormitories by Ohio Highway Patrol and KSU police, on days following shooting when university closed; defendants are Chester Hayth, commander OHP, Donald Manly, OHP, Ronald Kane, prosecutor, Portage County, Donald Schwartzmiller, KSU police. *Morgan* v. *Hayth*

Aug. 24   Miller complaint filed, U.S. District Court

Sep. 8   Scheuer complaint filed, U.S. District Court

Oct. 3   Student leader Craig Morgan files suit in U.S. District Court seeking injunction to keep Ohio National Guard off campus, *Morgan* v. *Rhodes*

Oct. 28   *Hammond* v. *Brown* and *Adamek* v. *Brown,* suits filed in U.S. District Court seeking expunging of report of special Ohio grand jury and dismissal of indictments of 24 students and one professor. Brown is Paul Brown, attorney general of Ohio

1971

Jan. 9   Six of the wounded students: Cleary, MacKenzie, Wrentmore, Grace, Russell, Canfora, plus parents of Schroeder file suit, U.S. District Court

Jan. 28   U.S. District Court orders special state grand jury report expunged but lets indictments stand (Judge Thomas), *Hammond* v. *Brown, Adamek* v. *Brown*

March 4   U.S. District Court, Judge Connell, dismisses *Morgan* v. *Rhodes*

May 31   Kahler and Lewis complaints filed, U.S. District Court

June 2   U.S. District Court, Judge Connell, dismisses *Krause* v. *Rhodes, Miller* v. *Rhodes, Scheuer* v. *Rhodes* (and the nine other cases, combined with *Krause* v. *Rhodes*)

Aug. 22   U.S. Court of Appeals, 6th circuit, lets stand indictments of 25 by special state grand jury

Sep. 30   Ohio's 8th District Court of Appeals, 2-1, rules against lower court decision denying that Krause can sue Ohio; case ordered back to lower court for trial on basis that state is responsible for tortious acts of its agents

1972

Feb. 15   U.S. Court of Appeals, 6th Circuit, remands *Morgan* v. *Rhodes* to U.S. District Court on question of "pattern of training" of Ohio National Guard

March 14   R. Stamps files negligence suit against Ohio

May 31   Trial, *Morgan* v. *Hayth*

June 2   U.S. District Court, Judge Thomas, rules dormitory searches were illegal, fines OHP $5,000

July 19   Ohio Supreme Court overturns 8th District Circuit; Ohio cannot be sued without consent of legislature

Nov. 17   U.S. Court of Appeals, 6th Circuit, declines, 2-1, to overturn dismissal of *Krause* v. *Rhodes*

Dec. 11   U.S. Supreme Court dismisses appeal *Krause* v. *Ohio*

1973

Jan. 3   U.S. Court of Appeals, 6th Circuit, declines en banc hearing on *Krause* v. *Rhodes*

June 21   U.S. Supreme Court rules adversely on appeal *Morgan* v. *Rhodes* (now *Gilligan* v. *Morgan*) but says training of National Guard is question for jury to decide

June 22   *Stamps* v. *Rhodes* filed, U.S. District Court; with this all 13 victims are in suit, with 12 combined in *Krause* v. *Rhodes* and *Scheuer* v. *Rhodes* still separate although considered jointly by courts

Dec. 4   U.S. Supreme Court, oral arguments, *Krause* v. *Rhodes*

1974

April 17   U.S. Supreme Court opinion in *Krause* v. *Rhodes* (called *Scheuer* v. *Rhodes* because *Scheuer* reached Court earlier, while *Krause* asking for en banc by 6th Circuit). Court rules that suit against governor and guardsmen is not a suit against Ohio and remands to District Court for trial

July 3   *Krause* v. *Rhodes* to docket, Judge Don Young

1975

May 19   *Krause* v. *Rhodes* trial begins, U.S. District Court, Cleveland

Aug. 27   Verdict, *Krause* v. *Rhodes,* 9–3 against plaintiffs

1977

June 21   Oral argument, U.S. Court of Appeals, 6th Circuit, appeal of *Krause* v. *Rhodes*

Sep. 12   Opinion, U.S. Court of Appeals, 6th Circuit, orders new trial

1978

Sep. 15   Judge Young resigns from case over refusal of plaintiffs to accept settlement

Dec. 5   New trial begins, U.S. District Court, Cleveland, Judge Thomas

1979

Jan. 4   *Krause* v. *Rhodes* settled for $675,000 and statement by defendants

Source Notes

![black bar]

Following is a key to the abbreviations used throughout the Source Notes.

ABJ   *Akron Beacon Journal*
AR   *American Report*
CPD   *Cleveland Plain Dealer*
DKS   *Daily Kent Stater*
DX   *Defense Exhibit*
NR   *National Review*
NY   *The New Yorker*
NYT   *New York Times*
PX   Plaintiffs' Exhibit
R   The Reporter
SC   The Report of the President's Commission on Campus Unrest (Scranton Commission)
TM   *Time* Magazine
TS   Transcript, *Krause* et al. v. *Rhodes* et al., May 19–August 27, 1975

page

Prologue

8   Guard Wrong at Kent, CPD, Sept. 29, 1975

1. I Get Involved

16   "unnecessary, unwarranted . . ." SC, page 289
16   Pulitzer-prize winning supplement, *ABJ,* May 24, 1970
17   later expunged, *Hammond* v. *Brown; Adamek* v. *Brown*
17   President Nixon secretly ordered . . . memo, Ehrlichman to Leonard, Nov. 18, 1970
17   Battisti dismissed . . . *U.S.* v. *Shafer*

2. The Shooting Victims

24   66 civilians had been killed . . . *NY,* Oct. 3, 1970, article on National Guard by R. Adler

5. Picking the Jury

6. Blueprints for a Trial

8. Friday and Saturday Nights

9. It Speaks for Itself

10. The Man Who Shot Joseph Lewis, Jr.

11. The Steel Helmet

12. Witch Hunt

135   We called him because . . . *AR,* Special Supplement, Nov. 12, 1971, p. 7-S
135   On the witness stand . . . TS 7714
139   Here is the sort of testimony . . .
       Flesher, TS 5791
       B. Morris, TS 2630–2634
       Perkins, TS 1787
       Shafer, TS 1350
       Maj. Jones, TS 5058
139   "When we reached the practice area . . ." TS 3240
139   "I had been pelted . . ." TS 4445–4446
139   Lt. Howard Fallon said, TS 6554
140   "To the south . . ." J. Michener, *Kent State* (New York: Fawcett World, 1975), p. 356

17. The Adjutant General

142   Judge Young . . . has been making conflicting remarks, TS 1756, TS 2054
142   "Starting on the first of July . . ." TS 2008
142   He had joined, TS 7961
142   The Ohio National Guard was nationalized . . . *CPD,* Feb. 7, 1971; Oct. 8, 1970
143   On April 4, 1968 . . . TS 7960
143   He also circularized . . . Ohio ACLU press release, March 30, 1970; May 18, 1970;
       Oct. 27, 1970; Nov. 5, 1970
143   of the 31 callouts . . . Ed Grant and Mike Hall, *I Was There* (Lima, Ohio: CSS
       Publishing Co.), pp. 137–8
143   Del Corso went with . . . TS 3143–3153, 4546
144   Sunday morning . . . TS 8905
144   Del Corso left Kent . . . TS 8930
144   "The individual in the military . . ." TS 8002
144   "Based upon your years . . ." TS 8065–8076
145   Judge Young stopped me . . . TS 8065–8075
145   Judge Young wouldn't budge . . . TS 8074
146   under the new rules . . . Rule 801, Section D
146   Judge Young replied . . . TS 8079
146   Mandel then reminded . . . TS 8078–8080
146   "I don't think that every trivial . . ." TS 8082
148   I was no more successful . . . TS 8201–8292

18. The Matson-Frisina Letter

149   "During the last two days . . ." DX IG
150   Major Jones testified . . . TS 4953
150   After revealing that . . . TS 7388
151   "no control over the university . . ." TS 8492
151   "I certainly am . . ." TS 8492
151   "Judge," I added, "the paper is already . . ." TS 7394–7406
152   Robert Matson looked . . . TS 8491
152   Although he was the highest ranking official . . . TS 8457
152   "I believe that we left . . ." TS 8497
153   this was denied by both Colonel Fassinger and Sergeant Haas, TS 4575, TS 4693
153   seen two students get hit . . . TS 8546–8547
153   There had been considerable . . . TS 4744
153   Chaplain Simons stated . . . TS 7711–7717
153   Canterbury's intention . . . TS 7743
153   On the stand . . . TS 8350
153   told campus policeman Harold Rice . . . TS 8352
153   Although he claimed not to have read the letter . . . TS 8316

154   Canterbury's version . . . TS 8317–8318
154   "After informing us of . . ." TS 8324
154   Canterbury's own . . . TS 8203
154   When former university president . . . TS 8748
155   "I don't recall . . ." TS 8752
155   When on Sunday morning he returned . . . TS 8726–8730
155   tell him that the university . . . TS 8735
155   From the time of his return . . . TS 8754, 11557
155   Under Mandel's questioning . . . TS 8740–8760
155   Blakemore tried to introduce . . . TS 11560
156   "a wonderful thing . . ." TS 11553

19. What Price Power

157   James Allen Rhodes was born . . . *NYT,* July 2, 1968. "The Wonderful World of Gov.
       Rhodes," A. S. Zaidan, *R,* Oct. 6, 1966, p. 44; "Austerity in Ohio," R. Giles, *R*, Nov.
       7, 1963; *TM,* Oct. 12, 1962; "Ohio and Gov. Rhodes," Wm. F. Rickenbacker, *NR,* Jan.
       28, 1964
158   At about ten that Sunday . . . TS 8880
159   He had acted overtly . . . Oral opinion, Judge Thomas on motion, summary
       judgment, def. Rhodes and Del Corso, Oct. 10, 1978
160   "Subject to the absolute . . ." *State* v. *Coit* 8 Ohio Dec. 62, 63 (c.p. 1897)
162   Judge Young watched . . . TS 8786
163   I was not permitted . . . TS 8827–8834
163   "In the truckers strike . . ." TS 8832
164   "Mr. Kelner," Judge Young said, "as I have told you . . ." TS 8834–8835
164   As the tape was played . . . TS 8880
165   "About like this . . ." TS 8884
165   "Sir," I asked, "were there any . . ." TS 8885
166   "Now, sir, are you aware . . ." TS 8888–8890
166   "I had information from the intelligence . . ." TS 8889–8892
166   I reminded the Governor that he had been heard . . . TS 8904
167   "I referred to the crowds . . ." TS 8905
167   I asked him if he had heard . . . TS 8917–8918
167   Judge Young called us to the bench . . . TS 8919
168   Delaney left the Guard . . . TS 8941
168   Several weeks after . . . "The Guardmen's View of Tragedy at Kent State," W.
       B. Furlong, *NYT Magazine,* June 21, 1970
168   Under Sindell's questioning . . . TS 8944
168   Governor Rhodes called a private meeting . . . TS 8945–8946
168   "The Governor," Delaney said . . . TS 8948
169   "He said that the National Guard in . . ." TS 8948, 9013
169   In his cross-examination . . . . TS 8977
169   Alloway, the Governor's lawyer, asked . . . TS 9006
170   "In regard to the question . . ." TS 9013
170   At the end of the afternoon . . . TS 8996
170   Judge Young said . . . TS 8998

20. Absolute Proof in Sight and Sound

172   testimony of a campus policeman . . . TS 7985–7592
173   The film is not very clear . . . TS 9031
174   "substantial evidence . . ." J. Michener, p. 371
175   *The evidence of the film* . . . TS 9543–9551
175   Christopher Abell . . . TS 9031
175   Johnson stated that . . . TS 9515

21. A Seminar on Crowd Control

187   "It is my opinion . . ." TS 9968
188   Ahern explained that policemen . . . TS 9984
188   "In my opinion, moving against that . . ." TS 9989
189   "So that just a statement of fact . . ." TS 9999
189   "Because fire should only be . . ." TS 10002
190   "Because the use of rocks, bottles . . ." TS 10005
190   "I think going up the hill . . ." TS 10005
191   "I would say that it would be improper . . ." TS 10008
191   Fulton began his cross-examination . . . TS 10024
191   In this, of course, he was ignoring . . . TS 10039
191   Fulton then tried to show that . . . TS 10026
191   "Tell us about the outside groups . . ." TS 10054

22. "All the Rights and Privileges of Students"

196   Fulton and Brown seemed particularly worried . . . TS 9883
197   "You should understand that all four of the deceased . . ." TS 10015
197   Fulton also requested . . . TS 10157–10190
197   but Judge Young responded . . . TS 10177
197   The Judge gave us overnight . . . TS 10167
197   Fulton's request for . . . TS 10172–10173, 10196
197   Judge Young left the decision . . . TS 10200
198   A few days later . . . TS 10474

23. The Man in the Gold Coat

201   Sutliff, who was . . . TS 10204
202   "There was two fellows . . ." TS 10220
202   "The whole street was covered . . ." TS 10222
202   "They were coming down Main Street . . ." TS 10228
202   "And, like I say . . ." TS 10229
203   the Kent Fire Chief had notified . . . TS 10293
203   only a minute and a half . . . TS 10313
203   no call came until between . . . TS 10295
203   Helming testified that he was beaten . . . TS 10297
203   Helming testified that he spent 22 minutes . . . TS 10307
203   He didn't know that . . . TS 10322
204   "Who knows?" Galen replied. "What was most interesting about . . ." *ABJ*, Nov.
       25–27, 1971; *Ohio* v. *Rupe;* KSU Police Log
206   David Amsel, a Kent . . . TS 10342
206   White-haired Roy Thompson . . . TS 10358
206   On Friday night, when . . . TS 10363–10364
206   Thompson was the person who was heard . . . TS 10360
206   his men had been called there many times . . . TS 10369–10371
207   According to Thompson, the Kent City police . . . TS 10371
207   Now, for good measure . . . TS 10393
207   When I asked Thompson to find, TS 10395
207   "Did you say," I asked Thompson, TS 10398
207   He then changed his story, TS 10399
208   Thompson's testimony on the Monday morning, TS 10371
208   the decision to break up assemblies on campus . . . TS 10401
208   He told Charlie Brown, who examined him, that he had been working . . . TS
       10477–10479
208   his intention had been to write . . . TS 10545
208   had seen students passing out rocks . . . TS 10487
208   had mobilized 91 men . . . TS 10562

208   Manly said the main subjects discussed . . . TS 10640
209   When it came to specifying . . . TS 10646
209   General Canterbury's prerogative . . . TS 10636
209   Under cross-examination, Manly . . . TS 10648
209   "I believe you indicated earlier . . ." TS 10680
209   Satrom was in a hotel in Aurora . . . J. Michener, p. 123
210   McElroy telephoned General Del Corso . . . TS 10783–10784
210   Saturday passed without incident . . . TS 10783–10784
211   private engineering practice . . . TS 10688
211   graduated from the school in 1957 . . . TS 10930
211   Williams had not expected . . . TS 10936
211   Early Saturday morning he and . . . SC report, pp. 244–245
212   Williams told the Scranton Commission, SC report, p. 245
212   Its own contingency plans . . . TS 10949
212   As it turned out, the Guard . . . TS 10946
212   Fulton brought out . . . TS 10949
212   Therefore I asked him . . . TS 10956
212   Early in the year our staff had found . . . PE 47030, 47041, 37019
213   Fulton did not ask Mrs. Bishop . . . TS 10831
213   Prior to the firing . . . TS 10836
214   But the photographs taken before and during . . . PE 47030, 47041, 37019
214   I established that . . . TS 10856
215   Mrs. Bishop then claimed that she was . . . TS 10861
215   "Did you walk or run?" TS 10862–10864
215   Fulton objected that I was mis-stating the facts. TS 10886
215   "That's right," Judge Young agreed . . . TS 10886
215   Mrs. Bishop admitted that . . . TS 10893–10894

24. The Judge Makes a Suggestion

216   That Tuesday night . . . TS 10976
216   I added that we were "deeply concerned . . ." TS 10978
217   The judge remarked that . . . TS 10982
217   Fulton and Brown said they preferred not to . . . TS 10983
217   "I am awfully troubled . . ." TS 10986
218   "Well, under the circumstance . . ." TS 10987
218   "So I am going to have to excuse you . . ." TS 10988
218   Fulton tried to persuade him to release . . . TS 10989
218   The judge told us that the matter . . . TS 10996
219   Hinton, untrained and nearly blind . . . TS 11060
219   Repp's only shot . . . TS 11066
219   Repp had had at least . . . TS 11086
219   This testimony supported the defense contention . . .
        Fallon, TS 6560
        Martin, TS 6804
        Jones, TS 5187
        Zoller, TS 6278
220   claimed to have heard . . . TS 11169
220   "16 inch Thompson Contender," TS 11170
220   Brambeck, a gun collector . . . TS 11156
220   on a roadway . . . TS 11160
220   300 to 500 students . . . TS 11169
220   Arthur Lewis Reedy . . . TS 11282
220   Henry Dumbrowski . . . TS 11309
220   It turned out that he had investigated . . . TS 11360
220   found four to six tunnels in the hill . . . TS 11366
221   "When I started roving patrol . . ." TS 11253
221   However, under cross-examination . . . TS 11385

221 Tucker was confined to describing . . . TS 11428
221 First Lieutenant Dwight Cline . . . TS 11464
221 He said that rounds fired by Troop G . . . TS 11497
222 Dix was publisher of . . . TS 11529
222 Dix, Clayton Horn . . . *DKS,* Jan. 9, 1970
222 Dix testified, TS 11533

25. Rebuttal

225 We then moved to discontinue . . . TS 11607
225 Dr. Helpern explained . . . TS 11657–11661
226 His presentation was handicapped . . . TS 11639
226 He confined us to questions . . . TS 11821
226 the judge told me I should have . . . TS 11827
226 Consequently, the jury could hear, TS 11793–11795, 11805, 11859

26. "Blood on My Hands"

228 Wednesday morning, TS 11885
228 "I find that at least . . ." TS 11887
229 "The thing I am concerned with . . ." TS 11893
229 I told him I was against that . . . TS 11909
230 Brown and Fulton argued for . . . TS 11910
230 "I say this is going to infect this jury . . ." TS 11911
230 I was all alone . . . TS 11915
230 He promised to replace the threatened juror, TS 11917
230 "Sorry we have been so late . . ." TS 11931
230 "There have been times . . ." TS 11932
231 He cautioned the jurors about . . . TS 11937
231 "As to one of your members . . ." TS 11935
231 The jurors' mood . . . TS 11940
232 "Once we are sequestered . . ." TS 11942
232 Mrs. Blanche Layman . . . TS 11944

27. Flattery Gets Me Nowhere

235 Engdahl moved the discontinuance . . . TS 11999
235 "The charge is not only fair . . ." TS 12029

28. The Final Say (and) 29. "Fine American Human Beings"

Summation, plaintiffs and Summation, defendants, TS 12185–12428

30. "The Gratitude of All the People"

250 I am electing not to excuse that juror," TS 12519
250 The judge said he knew nothing more . . . TS 12520
253 The jurors found three mistakes . . . TS 12533, 12551
256 I rose. "I don't speak in anger . . ." TS 12579–12580
256 Accosted by reporters . . . *CPD,* Aug. 28, 1975
258 The threatened juror, it turned out . . . *DKS,* Oct. 2, 1975, p. 10

31. The Payoff

263 On September 12, the Circuit Court of Appeals unanimously . . . No. 76–1095
USCA, 6th Circuit

266   and Rosen decided against asking . . . 1r Rosen to Kent State families, April 20, 1978

266   I sent a long letter . . . 1r. Kelner to Adams, May 16, 1978

266   At that meeting . . . Plaintiffs' pre-trial memorandum, May 22, 1978

266   "I had hoped . . ." 1r. Judge Don Young to All Counsel in Kent State Cases, Sept. 15, 1978

267   requested that chief judge Battisti . . . 1r. Rosen to Battisti, Sept. 19, 1978

267   he granted most of the motions . . . 1r Rosen to Kent State families, Oct. 19, 1978

268   newspapers published rumors . . . *CPD,* Dec. 19, 1978, A-10; Dec. 19, 1978, A-18

269   Judge Thomas, using the written . . . Order of Judge Thomas, March 15, 1979

Index